School Resources, the Achievement Gap, and the Law

This book offers a novel and up-to-date exploration of the common belief that increasing conventional school resources will increase academic achievement and help close gaps between various advantaged and disadvantaged students. Taking the scholarship around this question, such as James S. Coleman's 1965 report on the Equality of Educational Opportunity, as a starting point, it brings in an extensive range of contemporary data sources and statistical analysis to offer an updated, robust, and considered review of the issue. Moving beyond these empirical questions, it also explores how these empirical findings have been utilized in "education adequacy" litigation, discussing the evolving law of adequacy cases, while explaining the challenges of introducing complex data and analyses within a litigation framework. Judges typically have little experience with the complexity of modern education data and the analyses required to draw sound inferences. It will thus be of interest to scholars, researchers, and faculty and jurists with expertise or interest in education policy, the economics and sociology of education, and public policy.

David J. Armor is a professor emeritus of public policy in the School of Public Policy and Government at George Mason University, USA.

John R. Munich is a partner at Stinson LLP, where he chairs the firm's Business and Commercial Litigation division and leads the Education Funding Litigation practice group.

Aron Malatinszky is a PhD student in the Department of Economics at Boston University, USA.

Routledge Research in Education Policy and Politics

The Routledge Research in Education Policy and Politics series aims to enhance our understanding of key challenges and facilitate on-going academic debate within the influential and growing field of Education Policy and Politics.

Books in the series include:

The Path to Successful Community School Policy Adoption
A Comparative Analysis of District-Level Policy Reform Processes
Emily Lubin Woods

Working in a Survival School
Exploring Policy Tensions, Marketisation and Performativities
Lee Del Col and Garth Stahl

Taming Chance in Education
Control, Prediction and Comparison
Daniel Pettersson and Andreas Nordin

Perspectives on the Place of Creativity in Education, Policy and Practice
Limitations and Open Spaces
Kevin Gormley

Gaslighting School Educational Policy in a Post-Truth World
Systems, Schools and Society
Grant Rodwell

School Resources, the Achievement Gap, and the Law
Reconsidering School Finance, Policies, and Resources in US Education Policy
David J. Armor, John R. Munich, and Aron Malatinszky

For more information about this series, please visit: www.routledge.com/Routledge-Research-in-Education-Policy-and-Politics/book-series/RREPP

School Resources, the Achievement Gap, and the Law
Reconsidering School Finance, Policies, and Resources in US Education Policy

David J. Armor, John R. Munich, and Aron Malatinszky

NEW YORK AND LONDON

First published 2024
by Routledge
605 Third Avenue, New York, NY 10158

and by Routledge
4 Park Square, Milton Park, Abingdon, Oxon, OX14 4RN

Routledge is an imprint of the Taylor & Francis Group, an informa business

© 2024 David J. Armor, John R. Munich, and Aron Malatinszky

The right of David J. Armor, John R. Munich, and Aron Malatinszky to be identified as authors of this work has been asserted in accordance with sections 77 and 78 of the Copyright, Designs and Patents Act 1988.

All rights reserved. No part of this book may be reprinted or reproduced or utilised in any form or by any electronic, mechanical, or other means, now known or hereafter invented, including photocopying and recording, or in any information storage or retrieval system, without permission in writing from the publishers.

Trademark notice: Product or corporate names may be trademarks or registered trademarks, and are used only for identification and explanation without intent to infringe.

ISBN: 978-1-032-49874-4 (hbk)
ISBN: 978-1-032-50575-6 (pbk)
ISBN: 978-1-003-39911-7 (ebk)

DOI: 10.4324/9781003399117

Typeset in Times New Roman
by Apex CoVantage, LLC

Contents

List of Figures	vii
List of Tables	x
List of Contributors	xi
Foreword by ERIC A. HANUSHEK	xiii

1 **Shock and Awe in Education: The 1966 Coleman Report and the 2020 COVID-19 Crisis**   1
DAVID J. ARMOR

2 **The State of School Resource Research**   9
DAVID J. ARMOR AND AQUILLA M. OSSIAN

3 **The State of Education Adequacy Law**   30
JOHN R. MUNICH

4 **Study Approach, Data, and Methods**   42
DAVID J. ARMOR AND ARON MALATINSZKY

5 **School Resource Impacts Using US National Assessments (NAEP)**   55
DAVID J. ARMOR

6 **The Case of New York State: Achievement and Adequacy**   63
DAVID J. ARMOR AND JOHN R. MUNICH

7 **The Case of New Mexico**   78
DAVID J. ARMOR AND JOHN R. MUNICH

8 **The Case of South Dakota**   89
DAVID J. ARMOR AND JOHN R. MUNICH

9 School Resource Effects in South Carolina   99
BRYAN MICHAEL FORES AND DAVID J. ARMOR

10 School Resource Effects in North Carolina   111
ANNA GRACE GARREN AND DAVID J. ARMOR

11 School Resource Effects Using International Assessments (PISA)   121
SONIA SOUSA AND E.J. PARK

12 The Impact of School Composition   132
ARON MALATINSZKY AND DAVID J. ARMOR

13 What Works If Conventional Resources Do Not?   141
DAVID J. ARMOR AND ANNA GRACE GARREN

14 Summary and Conclusions   151
DAVID J. ARMOR

Index   *157*

Figures

1.1	NAEP Eighth-Grade Math Scores by Race/Ethnicity (Long-Term Trends)	2
1.2	Per Pupil Expenditures and NAEP Eighth-Grade Math Scores	3
2.1	Per Pupil Expenditures and NAEP Math Scores	13
2.2	Academic Achievement Gains per $1,000 in Per Capita Expenditures for Four Years	15
2.3	School Spending Differences for Disadvantaged Versus Non-disadvantaged Students	17
2.4	Teacher Education Effects on Student Test Scores (Standardized Effect Sizes)	20
2.5	Teacher Experience Effects on Student Test Scores (Standardized Effect Sizes)	20
2.6	Teacher Certification Effects on Student Test Scores (Standardized Effect Sizes)	21
2.7	Effect of Principal Behaviors on Student Achievement	23
2.8	SIG Program's Impact on Math Scores (No Effect Is Statistically Significant)	25
2.9	Effects of School Reorganization by School Demographics	26
2.10	Effects of School Reorganization by Intervention Features	26
4.1	Hypothetical Results for Between Versus Within School Analysis of Test Scores	45
4.2	Hypothetical Correlations Between Test Scores and Student and School Characteristics	46
4.3	Hypothetical Standardized Effects for Student and School Characteristics	48
5.1	School Resource and Student Background Correlations with NAEP Eighth-Grade Math Scores, 2013	58
5.2	Standardized Effects of School Resources and Student Background on NAEP Eighth-Grade Math, 2013	59
5.3	School Resource Effects on Eighth-Grade Math Scores: Free Versus Paid Lunch Students	61

viii *Figures*

6.1	Variation of Test Scores Occurring Within Versus Between New York State Schools	69
6.2	School Resource and Student Background Correlations for New York State Grades 3–5 Math Scores	69
6.3	Standardized Effects for School Resources and Student Background for New York State Grades 3–5 Math, 2012	71
6.4	Adjusted Spending and Eighth-Grade Math Achievement in New York State	73
6.5	NAEP Eighth-Grade Math Scores for Black Students: United States Versus New Jersey	74
6.6	Impact on Student Lifetime Incomes by Class Size and Teacher Effectiveness	75
7.1	Variation in Test Scores Occurring Within Versus Between New Mexico Schools, 2014	81
7.2	Correlations and Significant Regression Coefficients for New Mexico Grades 3–5 Math Scores	82
7.3	Correlations and Significant Regression Coefficients for New Mexico Grades 3–5 Reading Scores	83
7.4	Math Scores Adjusted for Student Background vs. Per Pupil Expenditures for 15 Largest New Mexico Districts	87
7.5	Relationship Between Spending and Math Achievement, All Districts	87
8.1	South Dakota Math Achievement Gains from Grades 3 to 8 by Poverty Status	92
8.2	Explaining the Achievement Gap Between White and Native American Students	94
8.3	School Resource and Student Background Correlations with Math Scores; Middle Panel Shows School Resource Effects After Adjusting for Student Background (Grades 3–8, 2003 to 2007)	95
8.4	Per Pupil Expenditures and Achievement for Focus Districts Adjusted for Student Background (Grades 3–8 for All Years)	97
9.1	Variation in Test Scores Occurring Within and Between South Carolina Schools and Districts, 2005	104
9.2	School Resource and Student Background Correlations for South Carolina Math Scores, 2003–2006	106
9.3	Standardized Effects for Longitudinal Regression, South Carolina Grades 3–8 Math, 2003–2006	107
9.4	Standardized Effects for Student Fixed Effect Regression, South Carolina Grades 3–8 Math, 2003–2006	108
10.1	Variation in Test Scores Occurring Within Versus Between North Carolina Schools and Districts, 2005	114

10.2	School Resource and Student Background Correlations for North Carolina Math Scores, 2003–2006	115
10.3	Standardized Effects for Longitudinal Regression, North Carolina Math Scores, 2003–2005	117
10.4	Standardized Effects for Student Fixed Effects Regression, North Carolina Grades 3–8 Math, 2003–2005	118
11.1	School Resource and Student Background Correlations for 2012 PISA USA, Age 15	126
11.2	Standardized Effects for School Resource and Student Background, 2012 PISA USA, Age 15	128
12.1	Math Scores for Low-Income Students by Race and School SES, Arkansas	135
12.2	The Distribution of Within-Student Ranges for Low-Income Status	138
13.1	Average Effect Size on Achievement for Alternative Interventions	143
13.2	Tutoring Effect Sizes Before/After Adjusting for Validity	144
13.3	Student Background and School Resource Correlations with Math Scores, 2008–2015	148
13.4	Standardized Effects of School Resource on Math Scores, 2008–2015	149
14.1	NAEP Eighth-Grade Math Scores by Race/Ethnicity and Per Capita Expenditures for New York State	155

Tables

5.1	Descriptive Statistics for 2013 NAEP Eighth-Grade Math Sample	57
6.1	Student and School Characteristics for New York Grades 3–8, 2012	66
6.2	Estimated Effect of Increasing School Resources	71
7.1	New Mexico Average Student and School Characteristics	79
7.2	Estimated Effects of School/Student Characteristics on Grades 3–5 SBA Math Scores, 2010–2014	84
7.3	Estimated Effects of School/Student Characteristics on Grades 3–5 SBA Reading Scores, 2010–2014	85
8.1	Basic Statistics for South Dakota Data (Grades 3–8, 2003 to 2007)	92
9.1	Summary Statistics for South Carolina data, Grades 3–8, 2003–2006	103
9.2	Effect of Increasing School Resources on Math Scores in South Carolina	109
10.1	Summary Statistics for North Carolina data, Grades 3–8, 2003–2005	113
11.1	Descriptive Statistics for 2012 PISA 15-Year-Old Students, US Sample	124
13.1	Number of Studies, Weighted Average ES, Confidence Intervals, I^2, and τ^2	142
13.2	Summary of Houston Elementary Treatment Effects for Fryer Study	147
14.1	Summary of Estimated School Resource Effects (Standardized)	153

Contributors

David J. Armor is Professor Emeritus of Public Policy in the School of Policy and Government at George Mason University, Fairfax, Virginia, the United States. He is author of *Maximizing Intelligence, Forced Justice: School Desegregation and the Law* and of many other works in education and other social policies. He has served on the faculty at Harvard University and UCLA and was Senior Scientist at the Rand Corporation and an elected member of the Los Angeles Board of Education. He also served as Principal Deputy and Acting Assistant Secretary of Defense for Force Management and Personnel, and he has testified as an expert witness in numerous education adequacy and school desegregation cases.

Bryan Michael Fores is currently a Master's student in Public Policy at the Harvard Kennedy School of Government, where he is studying digital service delivery and applications of data science in policymaking. He began his career in the US Army as a Russian Cryptologic Linguist, and he later cultivated his analytical skills as an intelligence analyst supporting the US Navy. Concurrently, he pursued a BA in Government and International Politics at George Mason University, where he graduated summa cum laude in 2021. His undergraduate work featured a research assistantship under the guidance of Dr. David J. Armor, for which he received highest honors.

Anna Grace Garren is an undergraduate student at George Mason University, with a double majoring in Computational and Data Sciences and Public Administration. For Chapter 10, School Resource Effects in North Carolina, Anna analyzed the student data from North Carolina and reviewed the Leandro adequacy case. For Chapter 13, What Works if Conventional Resources Do Not, Anna reestimated the standardized effect of tutoring from the Dietrichson meta-analysis and reviewed Roland Fryer's studies on school interventions and resources. She is also a practitioner in education, working as a substitute teacher and robotics coach in the Fairfax County, Virginia, Public School System.

Aron Malatinszky is a PhD student in Economics at Boston University, United States. He holds a BA in Economics and Mathematics and an MA in Economics, both from Boston University. From 2020 to 2022, he was Pre-Doctoral Research Associate at J-PAL North America, a regional office of the Abdul Latif Jameel Poverty Action Lab at the Massachusetts Institute of Technology. His work with Dr. David J. Armor has been published in *Educational Evaluation and Policy Analysis* and the *British Journal of Sociology of Education*.

John R. Munich is a partner at Stinson LLP and Chair of the firm's Business and Commercial Litigation I Division. He is former Assistant United States Attorney for the District of Columbia and Missouri Deputy Attorney General. He has served as lead trial and appellate counsel on many of the most significant American education finance and school desegregation cases in the last 30 years, including *Missouri v. Jenkins, CFE v. State of New York, Berrien v. Benton Harbor School District, Davis v. State of South Dakota, Maisto v. State of New York,* and *CEE v. State of Missouri* (2007), among others. He is a frequent writer and speaker on education funding topics and author of "*Missouri v. Jenkins: A Remedy Without Objective Limitation,*" a chapter in *The Pursuit of Racial and Ethnic Equality in American Public Schools* (published by Michigan State University Press).

Aquilla M. Ossian serves as Project Manager for the US Department of Homeland Security, where she helps lead the Policy Branch. Aquilla obtained a Master of Public Policy degree from her Alma Mater, George Mason University, where she was Research Assistant for Dr. David J. Armor. After working with Armor on an independent research project focusing on the school and family effects on academic achievement, Aquilla redirected her postgraduate plans to pursue Public Policy with an emphasis on educational research. She assisted on Chapter 2, The State of School Resource Research, by way of criteria identification and identifying critical studies in the research literature review.

Sonia Sousa and E. J. Park received their PhDs in Public Policy from the George Mason University School of Policy and Government, where they also worked as Research Assistants. They are also co-authors of the 2912 paper, Effects of Family and School Factors on Cross-national Academic Achievement Using the 2009 and 2006 PISA Surveys, *Journal of Comparative Policy Analysis* 14(5): 1–20.

Foreword

Few issues are closer to the heart of parents than the education of their children. Parents want their children to succeed in school because of the well-founded belief that the outcomes of schooling are closely related to their future well-being. Beliefs in the power of schools to improve both economic and social outcomes of society unsurprisingly then enter directly into politics and fuel some of the most deeply held views about the roles of local, state, and federal government.

The public debates about schools cannot be attributed to doubts about the desirability of high-quality education. Everybody can agree on that. The debates instead revolve around more structural issues of how and how much we should fund our schools and what we should be doing to ensure that the funds going to schools in fact translate into the educational outcomes that we all support.

David J. Armor, John R. Munich, and Aron Malatinszky enter into those structural debates in Academic Achievement and School Resources. Their willingness to engage in this topic is not a surprise. Armor has over a half century of tussling with the evidence on school effectiveness and attempting to introduce it into the public debate. Munich has almost the same amount of time working through the evidence and politics in the courtroom. And Malatinszky, while a relative newcomer to the area, has gamely jumped into the world of evidence about education.

The substance of the book is also not a surprise. They address the policy issues surrounding schools by assembling the evidence. They can do this in a definitive way because they have been contributors to much of the discussion and debate through careful and thoughtful past presentations of the empirical evidence.

Their analysis is compelling, albeit it is hard to say that everybody has accepted their arguments and will agree with their presentation. And here lies one of the chief issues, an issue that they do not sidestep. Education policy, particularly as it evolves in the courtrooms of the nation, is not just a matter of evidence. Many people have a strong affinity for particular answers, and they view the evidence as being most useful if the evidence supports their preferences.

This bias toward the answer is perhaps clearest when the discussion gets to the evidence on school resources. A number of education practitioners and experts favors spending more money schools, and they are unwilling to listen to arguments that how those funds are used may be crucial to their impact on student outcomes. Thus, when the authors present evidence that not all uses of money—even those favored at certain times by decision-makers—are not equally effective, a number of people will simply reject the evidence. They should not.

The Armor team has produced a clear and well-documented discussion of the evidence on resources and school outcomes. There are ambiguities that are present, because this is a particularly difficult area in which to provide precise empirical results. The world of schools is complex, and the evidence must be extracted from incomplete data and confusing school experiences. But this book bravely lays out the evidence and shows how it accumulates overall findings that are directly related to policy—whether that policy is developed in the courts, in the state legislatures, or in the local school district.

An interesting aspect of the study is its willingness to discuss the ambiguities while providing the means to narrow the policy disputes. It is particularly useful to frame the discussion in terms of the multiple and continuing court cases having to do with school finance. Here is where the preferences for particular outcomes often clash with the evidence. Armor, Munich, and Malatinszky manage to remain largely detached from the less data-based world of the courtroom, although it is an obvious struggle for people who want to stick closely to the evidence.

The summary is clear: Education is important, and we should incorporate ideas of educational improvement into our policies. This book seeks to keep the policy discussions focused on the policies that are likely to lead to better outcomes for students. They stick closely to what can be seen from the actual operation of schools. By providing a broad and data-driven picture, they can hopefully win over decision-makers who have not always focused on the evidence.

Eric A. Hanushek
June 2023

1 Shock and Awe in Education

The 1966 Coleman Report and the 2020 COVID-19 Crisis

David J. Armor

The 2020 COVID-19 Crisis

As I began working on this treatise in 2017, the only event rising to "shock and awe" status in US education was the 1966 report written by James S. Coleman, "Equality of Educational Opportunity," which shook the policy world, declaring that school resources were less important than family background in determining educational achievement.

That all changed on October 24, 2022, with the release of the Spring 2022 results from the National Assessment of Educational Progress (NAEP), also known as the Nation's Report Card. The assessment had not taken place since Spring 2019, due to the massive shutdown of in-class instruction starting in early 2020. The unprecedented academic losses shocked the nation. Just eight months later, on June 21, 2023, results from the NAEP's Long-Term Trend study were released. This assessment is designed specifically to track trends or changes in NAEP scores over time. The Long-Term Trend study showed that the learning losses were even worse, and for some groups the results were devastating. In eighth-grade math, which experienced the worst losses, the COVID-19 shutdown wiped out 30 years of educational progress in just two short years. That is, the 2022 scores are roughly where they were in the year 1990!

The NAEP Long-Term Trend results for eighth-grade math for the past 45 years are shown in Figure 1.1, separately for each major race and ethnic group. In addition to the large overall loss of 10 points between 2019 and 2022, the chart shows several other striking trends that have heavy implications for discussions in later chapters of this book. While the COVID-19 shutdown losses are the most dramatic, they are not the only important ones.

First, black eighth-grade students have been losing ground in eighth-grade math since their high point in 2012, approximately when the No Child Left Behind (NCLB) Act expired, terminating certain accountability requirements making testing and reporting mandatory (many states continued doing so, however). Black students declined a dramatic 8 points between 2012 and 2020. Altogether, black students have lost a remarkable 21 points since 2012, and the

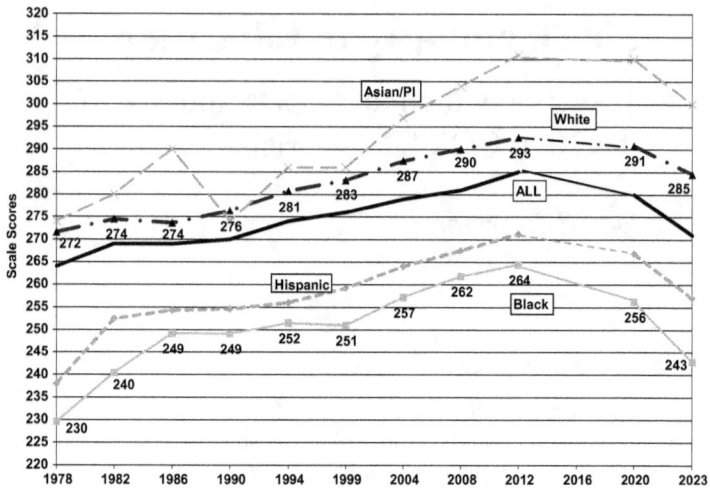

Figure 1.1 NAEP Eighth-Grade Math Scores by Race/Ethnicity (Long-Term Trends).

black–white eighth-grade math achievement gap has widened from 29 points in 2012 to 42 points, exactly where it was in 1978!

Second, while Asian students suffered the same losses from the COVID-19 shutdown as the other groups (about 10 points), they did not experience losses post-2012 after NCLB Act was terminated. This may demonstrate that Asian students and their families do not require the same sort of school policies as other groups to maintain achievement growth.

Finally, given these significant changes in test scores, what do they reveal about one of the key questions discussed in this study, the role of money? A very initial look at the relationship between inflation-adjusted expenditures and achievement is shown in Figure 1.2, focusing on eighth-grade math achievement, which suffered the most adverse effects of the COVID-19 shutdown.

Although both achievement and spending rose together between the late 1990s until the major recession of 2008–2009, there are two major time periods when a relationship is lacking: 1990 to about 1997, when achievement was rising significantly but expenditures were basically flat; and, more emphatically, when achievement was dropping (significantly) from 2013 to 2022 but per pupil expenditures increased by about $2,000 per pupil.

Of course, this simple relationship is not a rigorous causal analysis, but it is suggestive, and it is consistent with the thrust of the original Coleman Report, to which we now turn.

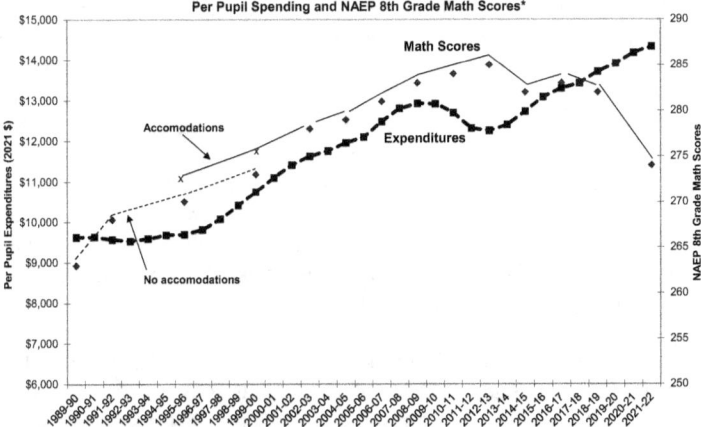

*In 1996 and 2000, testing was administered with and without accomodations; from 2005 onward, testing was with accomodations only

Figure 1.2 Per Pupil Expenditures and NAEP Eighth-Grade Math Scores.

The Coleman Report

More than 50 years ago, the passage of the Civil Rights Act of 1964 was one of the most remarkable pieces of civil rights legislation in US history. Given the history of segregated schools in America, a key provision in this massive bill called for a nationwide survey on "the equality of educational opportunity" for students from all backgrounds, with a special emphasis on understanding and improving the factors that affect the educational attainments of minority children.

The survey (EEOS for short) was the first of its kind. Of course, many smaller-scale studies evaluated the educational progress of minority students, but their scope was generally limited to specialized populations within school districts or states. Very little national data had been generated on the academic achievement of all students—including all minority groups. Even less national data were available on the many factors, both from the school and from a student's family, that were known to have an impact on the academic progress and success of minority children.

The study director was James S. Coleman, a professor of sociology at Johns Hopkins University. He and his colleagues designed a study that was staggering and unprecedented in its scope, even by today's standards. The national sample encompassed more than 570,000 students at Grades 1, 3, 6, 9, and 12, as well as nearly 70,000 teachers and 4,000 principals in 3,500 school districts. Standardized achievement tests to assess skills in mathematics, reading, and science were administered to all students, and self-administered questionnaires were completed by students in Grades 6 to 12 as well as by their teachers and principals. Teachers administered the questionnaires for earlier grades.

As a member of the research team, I can vouch for the expectations of Dr. Coleman and his colleagues.[1] The team expected the data to yield two major findings, according to the conventional wisdom of the day. First, they expected data to show that minority students had access to dramatically fewer school resources than white students, such as specialized facilities, teacher education and experience, teacher and principal salaries, small class sizes, and the like. Second, the data would also show that school resources are strongly related to academic achievement. Therefore, lower minority achievement—the "achievement gap" between black and white students—could be explained by the lack of critical school resources. Such findings could lead to policy changes that would equalize resources between white and minority children, thereby eliminating or at least reducing the achievement gap.

The actual findings of the "Coleman Report," as it was called, upended conventional wisdom and astonished the policy world.[2] The first shocking finding was that the resource differences in schools attended by black and white children were not as large as expected, once regional differences were taken into account. National differences arose in part because the South had fewer school resources than the North and because the South enrolled a majority of US black students. Examining school resources within regions, however, the Coleman Report found that resource differences between black and white students were much smaller than expected, in some cases even favoring the black children.

The second major finding of the Coleman Report was even more surprising to most educators and policymakers: school resources did not have major impacts on a child's academic achievement, once that child's family background—particularly socioeconomic status (SES)—was taken into account. A student's SES had much stronger influences on academic outcomes than school resources and policies, including most teacher characteristics such as educational background, credentials, and experience. Thus, the report concludes:

> [S]chools are remarkably similar in the way they relate to the achievement of their pupils when the socioeconomic background of the students is taken into account. It is known that socioeconomic factors bear a strong relation to academic achievement. When these factors are statistically controlled, however, it appears that differences between schools account for only a small fraction of differences in pupil achievement.[3]

Needless to say, the controversy sparked by these dramatic conclusions was immediate and intense. Education experts challenged Coleman's school measures, economists questioned his methodology, and journalists despaired at the complexity of this 700+ page report. A seminar was immediately formed at Harvard, chaired by two eminent scholars, which would re-examine the methodology, the data, and the conclusions[4]. Despite these efforts to clarify and critique the Coleman Report, the debate over what we will call the "Coleman thesis" has continued up to the present time.

The arguments over the Coleman findings have not been merely academic, limited to education policy and research circles. They have evolved into court battles, in the so-called Education Adequacy lawsuits. Basically, adequacy lawsuits occur when a group of public school districts sue their state governments over inadequate funding. Most state constitutions include a public education clause that requires the state to provide "adequate" education to all students between certain ages (usually 5 to 16 or so).

Education Adequacy lawsuits argue that the state government has violated the state constitution by not providing sufficient resources to bring all groups of students (particularly those below the poverty line) to roughly the same levels of proficiency. These cases are brought in state court systems, and if the plaintiffs prevail, they ask the court to order the state legislature to provide more funds to plaintiff school districts—usually districts with high proportions of low-income students. These lawsuits have been brought in 30 states or so, and in many cases, state governments have been ordered by a state supreme court to increase payments to plaintiff districts or to all school districts with high poverty rates.

Once they are sued, state governments usually assemble a defense that includes experts testifying whether, and by how much, additional school resources (especially funding) will raise student achievement, particularly for disadvantaged students. The senior authors of this book, David J. Armor and John R. Munich, have worked on a number of these cases, Armor as a social science expert and Munich as an attorney for the defendant, which is usually the state government. The kinds of social science and education issues raised in these cases are similar to those examined in the Coleman Report. In effect, some of the expert studies for these cases become mini replications of the original Coleman Report, only at a state level instead of the national level.

This study revisits the Coleman findings once again using a variety of data sources. In fact, a major difference between this study and the Coleman Report is that there is no reliance on a single source of data or a single methodological approach. This study examines the relationship between school resources and academic achievement using a dozen or more recent data sources, and it applies more than one methodology to each set of data. Some of the data come from educational adequacy lawsuits, including cases from New York State, Washington State, South Dakota, South Carolina, and New Mexico, where the data were used in court to show the relationship between funding and other school resources and achievement test scores. Other data in this report includes US national achievement data generated by the NAEP and international achievement data generated by the Program for International Student Assessment (PISA) studies.

There have been many advances in the study of academic achievement since the Coleman study, and this study draws upon a variety of newer statistical methods and techniques that offer more robust assessments of the impact of school resources on achievement. While some of the analyses use simple correlation and graphical techniques to show the relationship between school resources and achievement, other analyses are based on more sophisticated time series and panel designs using statewide longitudinal achievement data. Basically, the robustness of the Coleman thesis is tested using methodologies that are more sophisticated than those used for the Coleman Report, and they are applied to data that are much more recent and originate from multiple sources.

In addition to the empirical and statistical analyses, the study also discusses many of the legal issues in state adequacy cases, including how the empirical studies are used (or not used) in the court findings and decisions. These legal studies provide an evaluation of legal policy implications of this social science research evidence and its impact on court decisions.

Before turning to the main substance of this book, a general description of the content of each chapter is offered. Chapter 2 reviews some of the more recent and more comprehensive research studies regarding the impact of various types of school resources on academic achievement, including funding. This chapter also defines what "school resources" means and how that is distinguished from a somewhat broader concept of "school programs."

Chapter 3 is an overview of the case law from the adequacy lawsuits with emphasis on the lawsuits that have contributed data to this book. Particular emphasis is given to the way in which each court decision utilizes or fails to utilize the social science data as introduced by expert witnesses.

Next, Chapter 4 describes the research approach and specific statistical methods used in the various chapters that introduce and rely upon empirical data for conclusions. Most of the research data used in these cases do not fit the "gold standard" for explanatory studies, that is, they are not derived from "randomized controlled trials" or randomized controlled trial (RCT) research designs. The best alternative, in the absence of RCT designs, are those approaches that offer the most "plausible" causal interpretations of the relationships between school resources and achievement. Finally, this chapter will grapple with a key policy question, which is how to evaluate the size of effects in terms of their importance for policy decisions.

The first major empirical analysis of the relationship between resources and achievement is presented in Chapter 5. It is an analysis of data from the NAEP, the major national achievement testing program. While these data are cross-sectional, that is, just one point in time, their advantages are (1) large and representative samples of students in every state and (2) having a comprehensive number of both school resources and student background measures. This chapter also serves to introduce the several quantitative methods that will be used for the analyses of the state-level data in subsequent chapters.

The next five chapters (Chapters 6 to 10) present the case studies that constitute the most important information to be presented in this book. It presents and discusses the expert studies used in the hearing on the relationship between resources and achievement, and it also lays out the major legal questions presented in the adequacy lawsuits. An important issue discussed in these chapters is how, and to what extent, the courts relied upon the social science data as presented by expert witnesses, and to what extent the expert studies affected decisions made by the courts, both primary and appellate.

To this point, all of the discussion about school resources and achievement has relied upon national- and state-level data for the United States. Chapter 11 uses international achievement data gathered by the Organization for Economic Co-operation and Development in its major assessment, the PISA, to examine the relationship between school resources and academic achievement for large, developed countries with fully modern education systems on par with the United States. In addition to the United States, these countries are Japan, South Korea, United Kingdom, Germany, France, Italy, Spain, Canada, and Australia.

Returning to US data, Chapter 12 examines the relationship between achievement and another type of school resource, which is the economic and racial composition of schools. Unlike the other resources discussed here, composition is a special type of resource that reflects the amount of racial or economic integration or diversity that is present in a specific school or classroom. Social scientists have studied the effects of racial or economic school integration extensively ever since the Supreme Court declared state-sanctioned racial segregation unconstitutional in 1954 and, in 1971, approved extensive mandatory busing plans to achieve racial balance in all or most schools.

Despite the more extensive achievement data and the more sophisticated statistical techniques used in this book, our findings about the effects of school resources on achievement are not that dissimilar to Coleman's. This is quite remarkable, considering the limitations of Coleman's data and statistical methods at the time.

Lest this be too discouraging a conclusion, we devote Chapter 13 to some of school strategies or programs that might prove more promising in raising achievement than simply adding more school resources. While many of these programs and policies are still experimental—that is, not implemented on a large scale in multiple school districts—these special techniques might provide a more promising pathway for reducing achievement disparities among various groups of children.

Finally, Chapter 14 offers a summary and discussion of the findings of this book, and how these new findings compare to earlier findings, including those from the original Coleman Report. Although we are interested in the broad issue of the relationship between school resources and achievement, a concern of special importance is the vexing policy problem of achievement gaps and how to close them.

Notes

1 Author Armor had a small role designing certain survey instruments and analyzing data in the original study.
2 Coleman, J.S. et al. (1966). *Equality of Educational Opportunity*, Washington, DC, U.S. Government Printing Office.
3 *Ibid.*, pp. 21–22.
4 Mosteller, F. and Moynihan, D.P., eds. (1972). *On the Equality of Educational Opportunity*, New York, Random House.

2 The State of School Resource Research

David J. Armor and Aquilla M. Ossian

Introduction

The research literature on the impact of school resources on academic achievement is immense. The goal of this chapter is not to review this entire literature, which by itself would consume an entire book or more. Rather, our goal is to review the more recent and more important studies that evaluate the effects of school resources on academic achievement. We will elaborate on the meaning of "more recent" and "more important" studies.

"More recent" studies means that the study should have been published by at least 2005, or roughly within the past 15 years or so. The reasons have to do with data availability, data quality, and technical advancements in statistical analysis and computation. Data availability and quality improved greatly following implementation of the No Child Left Behind (NCLB) Act in 2002. The Act required every state to establish academic standards and to conduct annual assessment for multiple grades, using standardized achievement tests. The assessments had to be published (e.g., made available to schools and parents) and had to distinguish students by demographic characteristics such as gender, race and ethnicity, and poverty status. Although a few states were already doing this, it took several years for this policy to become widespread and for the creation of statewide test results for individual students. By 2010, most states had created these "longitudinal" databases (i.e., student test scores tracked over time), and some of these databases were utilized in the case studies reported in Chapters 6 through 9 of this volume.

These statewide databases are very large, as are some of the relevant national databases such as the National Assessment of Educational Progress (NAEP) data used in Chapter 5. Some important statistical techniques demand substantial computer power (with respect to both size of memory and processing speed), and this power was not available until the past ten years or so. More discussion on the statistical methods used in this book is found in Chapter 4.

"Most important," here, invokes several requirements. First, studies must assess academic achievement using recognized and widely used standardized

DOI: 10.4324/9781003399117-2

achievement tests. This includes standardized tests used by national and state education agencies to measure academic attainment and to assess academic proficiency, such as the tests used for the NAEP. Many state education agencies use tests similar to NAEP, and both reading and math skills are usually assessed. Studies that use specialized tests (as opposed to standardized tests), particularly those aimed at testing for specialized content of a particular course of study, have potential reliability and validity issues.

Second, the studies must have adequate controls on student background characteristics or they must employ experimental, randomized (RCT) designs. This requirement arises because it is well known that certain student demographic and economic characteristics have strong effects on academic outcomes. If student background factors are not taken into account, the relationship between school resources and test scores may be biased and unreliable (see Chapter 4). Even randomized experiments usually assess student background in case the randomized assignment is compromised by differential attrition of students from the treatment and control groups.

Third, if the study is not an RCT design (and most are not), it must utilize quasi-experimental designs or at least longitudinal designs that incorporate student background characteristics. The type of analytic methods applied is not limited to any particular model. For example, cross-sectional designs are included as long as they are also longitudinal designs—which can assess changes in achievement over time. As discussed in more detail in Chapter 4, pooled cross-sectional longitudinal designs can allow "plausible" causal inferences, provided there are adequate controls for student background, even though results need to be verified by more rigorous designs.

Finally, an emphasis is placed on meta-analyses which review a large number of studies and apply selection criteria such as those listed earlier. Meta-analyses have become quite common in recent years, and the better ones also apply selective criteria such as those described earlier. There are some exceptions to this general rule, particularly for studies that, for whatever reason, received a lot of attention in the education research field, such as the Tennessee Star experiment on class size or the famous debate between Hanushek and Hedges on the effect of expenditures on academic achievement. Generally, however, greater reliance is placed on more recent studies using more extensive data and more sophisticated meta-analytic research designs.

Exceptions are also made in the case of important national studies like the NAEP, which in some respects resembles the original Coleman study. While the NAEP studies are quite useful for suggesting relationships between school resources and achievement (see Chapter 5), its cross-sectional design means that causal inferences are more tentative than with longitudinal data. The longitudinal data now being collected by most states about the impact of school resources allow the application of more rigorous methodologies described in Chapter 4.

Approach

To simplify the review, studies on school resource effects are grouped into several categories, some of which are rather arbitrary to reflect the different types of research that has been carried out in this field. Some categories reflect a particular type of resource (e.g., actual expenditures or a teacher characteristic), while others denote more comprehensive interventions such as school reorganizations.

School Expenditures

In examining the impact of school resources on academic achievement, perhaps the most direct and most important question is, "[D]oes increasing school spending raise achievement levels?" Indeed, this question was the primary focus of a well-known book on the topic, *Does Money Matter?* Published by the prestigious think-tank, Brookings Institution, in Washington, DC.[1] The book focused on a debate between economist Eric A. Hanushek, a critic of the thesis, and Larry Hedges, who supported the thesis. The findings in this book will be discussed later in this section.

Although the Brookings book has important historical interest in framing the debate over school resources and achievement, since that time there has been a great expansion of school data resources and many more studies of the relationship between school spending and academic outcomes. What might have been true in the mid-1990s may or may not be supported when scrutinized using the vastly greater stores of data on education resources and outcomes.

This section will review research and existing data on the relationships between public K–12 monetary school expenditures and classroom size on academic achievement. School expenditures will be expressed on a per capita basis in order to control for the size of a school district.[2] Although expenditures are conceptually distinct from class size, the reason for placing these two resources in the same section is that, unlike most other school resources, there is a direct one-to-one relationship between the two. That is, in order to reduce class sizes—a popular recommendation among school reformers—a school district has to hire more teachers. Since teacher salaries comprise a very high fraction of total school expenditures (particularly what are called "operational" expenditures as compared to "capital" expenditures), often on the order of 80 percent, class size and expenditures are inextricably intertwined. This relationship also suggests that teacher salaries might be a resource to be considered in this chapter, but since salary depends heavily on the teacher characteristics of education and experience, the impact of teacher salaries is considered in the "Teacher Characteristics" section along with other teacher attributes.

When examining the effect of school expenditures on academic achievement, given the great variations in the sizes of school districts, it is standard procedure to define it as "per capita expenditures," to obtain a measure that is independent of the size of a school district. One obtains this quantity by dividing total expenditures (usually for a whole school district) by the student enrollment at a particular point in time, usually in the fall after students start school. Alternatively, since some students are absent on a given day, some school districts calculate "expenditures per ADA" by using average daily attendance as the denominator.

National Data

Before turning to the research literature on this question, there are data sources that allow us to examine this relationship at the national level. The National Center for Education Statistics (NCES) sponsors a periodic NAEP, which tests the academic achievement of students at Grades 4, 8, and 12 in order to help evaluate the performance of our public K–12 school systems. In addition, NCES maintains other databases with information about the characteristics of and resources available to all public schools in the nation. With these data sources, the relationship between academic achievement and public school expenditures can be examined.[3]

A 2023 paper by Armor explored the relationship between expenditures and NAEP mathematics achievement scores for Grades 4 and 8.[4] Figure 2.1 shows what appears to be a positive relationship between money and achievement, in that math scores rise as expenditures increase for a 30-year period. Then NAEP scores suddenly started dropping in 2015. A major study by education economist C. Kirabo Jackson and others in 2020 argued that the drop was caused by a reduction in school expenditures arising from the serious recession of 2008–2009, which had some financial impacts lingering until 2010–2011.[5]

A closer look reveals that the relationship between expenditures and achievement is more complex. Between 1990 and 1996, both fourth- and eighth-grade math scores rise by 9 points but expenditures are nearly flat. For the next 15 years, scores rise by another 11 points, while real expenditures (corrected for inflation) rise from about $10,000 to $13,000 per pupil. Then, starting in 2011, expenditures fall sharply for about three years until they start rising again, reaching their 2011 level in 2016. Between 2009 and 2013, when expenditures were falling, math scores continued rising by 2 points for both grade levels. Finally, when expenditures started rising again in 2014, math scores started declining. Scores continue to decline despite the fact that expenditures returned to their pre-recession levels and continued to rise until 2022 and beyond. Thus, after 2010, there is no clear relationship between expenditures and math test scores.

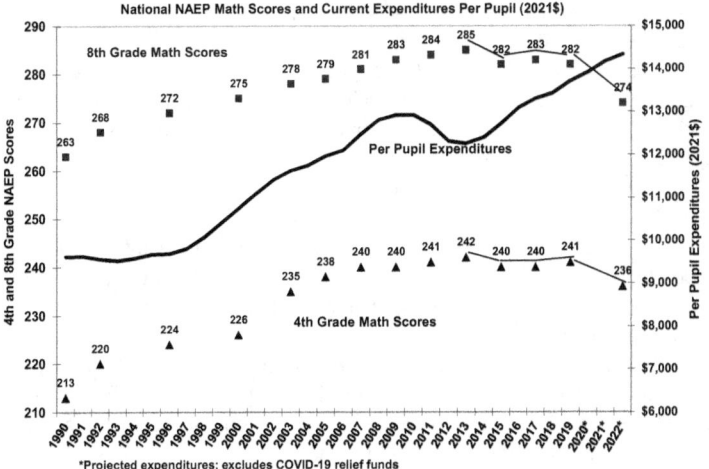

Figure 2.1 Per Pupil Expenditures and NAEP Math Scores.

Reading scores for fourth- and eighth-grade students follow a somewhat different pattern. Reading scores did increase between 1990 and 2015, but it was not a steady increase like math scores. Scores fluctuated during the late 1990s before settling into a fairly regular pattern for eighth graders, increasing from 262 to 268 between 2004 and 2013. Like math scores, reading scores declined steadily between 2013 and 2022, while school expenditures were increasing. Again, there is no clear relationship between expenditures and reading test scores after 2010.

According to the Armor paper, the decline of both reading and math scores after 2013 is more likely due to changing national laws about public school "accountability" requirements. In 2001, the US Congress passed the NCLB Act. This Act contained "accountability requirements," whereby every state receiving federal funds had to develop education standards for each grade level, standardized achievement tests, and publication of test results by race/ethnicity and poverty status. Moreover, the law required minimum "adequate yearly progress (AYP)" benchmarks to reduce test score disparities among racial, ethnic, and socioeconomic groups, with a goal of eliminating these gaps by the year 2014.

The AYP goals, while admirable, were perhaps unrealistic. Schools not meeting these goals were subject to increasing sanctions, including total school restructuring after four or five years. Real progress was made in raising achievement levels, but it also became clear that the goal of eliminating achievement gaps was not going to be realized by 2014. Achievement gaps did narrow but less than anticipated because non-disadvantaged students gained at nearly the same rates as disadvantaged students.

The impact of ending NCLB Act and AYP goals is seen more clearly in Figure 1.1, which shows eighth-grade math trends by race and ethnicity. Although Black and Hispanic students were improving before NCLB Act, the adoption of NCLB Act and AYP requirements in 2000 led to even greater gains for these two disadvantaged groups. The Hispanic and Black gaps with White students were actually closing between 2000 and 2013: during this time, both the Black–White and the Hispanic–White gaps decreased by 9 points—a non-trivial reduction of about one-fourth of the gap. As impressive as these gains were, they were less than the NCLB Act's objective of eliminating the gaps entirely by 2014.

Following adoption of the new Every Student Succeeds Act (ESSA) program, the AYP requirements were dropped. Perhaps because of these changes, eighth-grade math scores of both White and Hispanic students dropped by 2 points in 2015 while Black students dropped 3 points. After 2015, Black–White gap remained constant but the Hispanic–White gap grew from 22 to 24 points between 2013 and 2019. Adding the unprecedented losses due to the COVID-19 shutdown, in 2022 eighth-grade math scores were back to their levels in 2003—a staggering setback of 20 years of progress.

The important message of this analysis, for this chapter, is that school expenditures do not appear to be the primary driving force for improving academic achievement nor are they a major tool for closing achievement gaps between advantaged and disadvantaged groups of students. Accountability policies, on the other hand, may be quite effective for improving academic achievement as measured by standardized scores, although they did not reduce achievement gaps among various demographic groups.

The Research Literature on Expenditure Effects

The lack of a consistent relationship between national school expenditures and academic achievement does not settle the issue. Many experts consider that the data used in Figures 2.1 and 2.2 reflect a simple "correlation" analysis, and as such the meaning of the relationship is not settled because the data do not satisfy the requirements for proper "causal inference." Causation can only be proven or disproved, scientifically, by "randomized control trials" or RCT for short. Although the authors would qualify this argument in certain ways, for now this conclusion is accepted for "what the science tells us."

A true RCT design would require that students be randomly assigned to treatment versus control condition of higher spending versus lower spending, with everything else held constant except the spending itself. Moreover, because of the phenomenon of "expectancy effects," neither students nor teachers can be aware that they are in an experiment, because it is known that expected outcomes can influence results.[6]

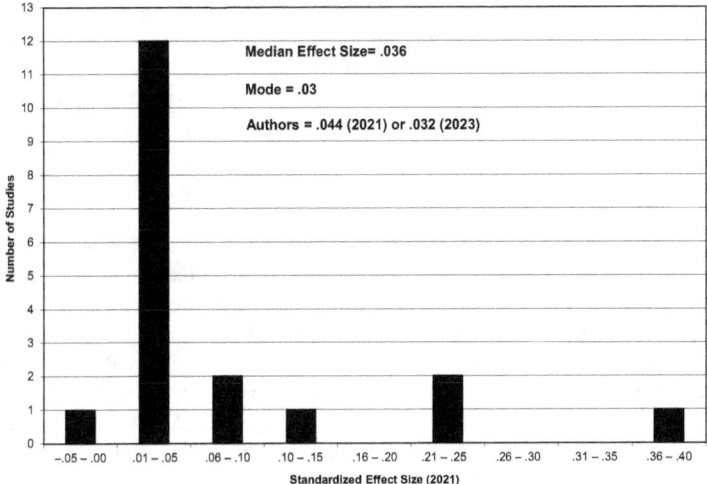

Figure 2.2 Academic Achievement Gains per $1,000 in Per Capita Expenditures for Four Years.

Strictly speaking, such an experimental design is not possible because at a minimum the same teacher would have to teach classes in the two conditions, higher and lower expenditures. At best, treatment and control groups would attempt to have teachers matched in all characteristics except for their salaries, and the teachers in the treatment condition would receive higher salaries than the teachers in the control condition. To our knowledge, there is no true RCT design that has tested the causal effect of school expenditures on achievement.

There are, however, a number of studies in the literature that have used quasi-experimental designs, such as regression discontinuity designs or instrumental variable designs. If these studies are executed carefully, they can come very close to meeting the requirements for RCT designs, and as such they can be interpreted as demonstrating "likely" or "plausible" causal effects. A meta-analysis by Jackson and Mackevicius (2021, 2023) identified over 20 studies meeting the criteria for causal inference.[7] Figure 2.2 shows a summary of this study's findings for the effects of an increase of $1,000 in per capita spending (for four years) on academic achievement.

An expert report by Dr. Jay P. Greene in another New York State adequacy case criticizes the Jackson and Mackevicius studies, not only for differing estimates for the effects of expenditures on achievement but also because each version of their meta analyses uses different criteria to include or exclude various studies, thereby creating uncertainty about the true effects of expenditures and their statistical significance.[8]

Given the highly skewed distribution of effect sizes, with more than half of the studies (15 of 23) yielding standardized effect sizes averaging .03, our conclusion is that substantial increases in per capita spending is likely to raise achievement by only a small amount. Even if increased expenditures could be applied only to schools with substantial proportions of disadvantaged students, the size of the effect is not large enough to substantially reduce the achievement gap between White and Black students, or between students in poverty compared to students not in poverty.

We will illustrate what these effect sizes actually mean by showing how much of the current Black–White learning gap of 32 points might be affected if a school district could raise school expenditures by various amounts. Given effect sizes for .03 per $1,000 increase for four years, let's say we could confine spending increases of $2,000 per student to predominantly Black middle schools for four years. This converts to an increase in Black scores of about 1.5 points. Since the current Black–White gap for eighth-grade math is 32 points, the gain due to these increased expenditures would mean a reduction of only about one-twentieth of the gap.

Spending Gaps by Race and Poverty

One frequently reads opinions that the achievement gap between Black and White or poor and non-poor students is caused by unequal school spending between schools that are predominantly Black or low income and schools that are predominantly White or higher income. The original Coleman Report found spending and other school resource differences between Black and White students at the national level, but those differences largely faded when spending was broken down by region and then compared between southern and non-southern states. The report found that public schools in the South spent considerably less than schools in the North and West, and since most Black students at that time lived in the South, this led to a national comparison favoring White students. Within regions, however, the spending was mostly equal.

A similar but more recent study, using a more sophisticated methodology, examined that same issue with current expenditures classified by various race, ethnic, and socioeconomic measures.[9] The results are displayed in Figure 2.3. In addition to the comparison of Black versus White, Hispanic versus White, and free lunch versus paid lunch, a poverty calculation was made from US Census data that assessed family poverty.

Just as Coleman et al. found in the mid-1960s, when differences in spending are examined at the national level for various types of student disadvantage, generally there is a large difference favoring the advantaged group. Figure 2.3 shows that, at the national level, per pupil spending for Black students averages $395 less than White students. However, when those same expenditures are assessed within each state and those Black–White differences are averaged, the

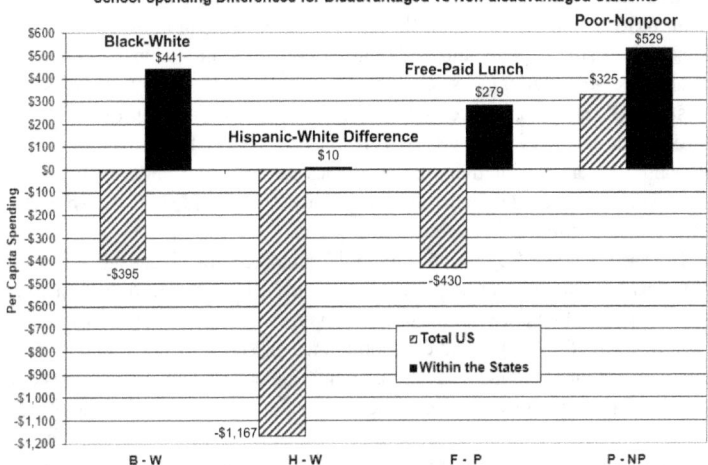

Figure 2.3 School Spending Differences for Disadvantaged Versus Non-disadvantaged Students.

relationship reverses and per pupil spending on Black students is $441 higher than that on White students. A similar reversal occurs for free versus paid lunch students. Within state, there is virtually no difference between spending for Hispanic and White students, but at the national level Hispanics attend school districts that spend nearly $1,200 per pupil less than White students. This finding indicates that Hispanic students tend to be concentrated in states (and school districts) with much lower-than-average school expenditures than the nation as a whole.

Class Size

Of the many types of school resources or reforms that have the potential to improve student achievement, perhaps the most ubiquitous has been reduction of class sizes. It has considerable appeal just from a "common sense" standpoint: it seems logical that smaller numbers of students in a classroom should make it easier for teachers to impart knowledge effectively, particularly to less capable students who struggle to master course content. Smaller numbers of students should, theoretically, make it easier for a teacher to spend some extra time with those students who need the most help.

The research on this school resource, however, reveals a much more complex and nuanced relationship between class size and achievement. At one time it was widely believed that reduced class size would increase student achievement, based primarily on a well-designed field experiment knows as the "Tennessee Star" study.[10] The study randomly assigned both students and teachers to larger versus smaller classes, which were set to be 22 students per class and 15 students per class, respectively. This represents a reduction of about one-third—although there were variations in these class sizes from school to school. Standardized effects for the smaller classes ranged from about .2 to .3 and, moreover, they were larger for minority and low-income students—precisely the groups most in need of achievement gains.

Because of the RCT design, the "gold standard" for establishing a causal relationship, many education policy experts at the time believed that class size reduction would be a key to closing achievement gaps. However, critiques of the study's methodology reduced confidence in some of the findings. Most notable was that of Hanushek (1999), who found both design and analysis deficiencies.[11] His conclusion was that there might have been a significant effect of class size reduction in kindergarten but not the other grades. He also argued that the effects of teacher quality are larger than class size effects and that improving teacher quality is more cost-effective than reducing class size, which is "one of the most costly reform policies actively discussed" (p. 159).

The widely disseminated results of the Tennessee program led California to adopt a massive, statewide policy to reduce class sizes in 1996. There were numerous evaluations of the effects of this class size reduction on academic achievement, and not all studies provide the same estimates of effects.[12] Generally, the more rigorous evaluations concluded that the reductions had very small or no effects.[13] Basically, all of the evaluations of the Californian program found that, because of the very large scale of the California initiative, many of the new teachers hired to reduce class sizes were less experienced and had lower rates of certification. Thus, the potential benefit of smaller classes was offset by teacher qualifications—which were lowest for schools with more minority and low-income students.

The results of the California class size reduction initiative dampened the enthusiasm for reducing class size as the primary method to improve student achievement. Accordingly, most attempts to improve school quality have returned to a focus on teacher characteristics, a subject to which we now turn.

Teacher Characteristics

The category of *teacher characteristics* is commonly thought to be the most important school resource for increasing student achievement. This is a logical conclusion, since teachers are the primary "agents" for transmitting knowledge and skills to students. While there is little doubt that teachers represent the most important school resources for student achievement, the research on school effectiveness has revealed an increasing complexity of assessing teacher quality and effectiveness.

At one time, educators and researchers assumed that such characteristics as teacher education, certification (licensing), and experience were the best indicators of teacher quality. As knowledge has accumulated, however, there is growing awareness that, while these objective "credentials" have some relevance for quality, there may be other teacher attributes and assessment methods that provide a more definitive assessment of quality. Some education experts now argue that teacher quality should be measured directly by using the learning outcomes of students taught by a particular teacher. This is sometimes called the "value added" model of teacher evaluation.

The review in this section will be confined to traditional measures of teacher quality with emphasis on the objective credentials of education, certification, and experience. Not only do these credentials have the most direct connection to expenditures, but they are also considered to have considerable impact on student learning. In addition, we will consider several other teacher-based measures such as subject-matter knowledge, teacher turnover, professional development, and teacher efficacy. Teacher quality scores based on the "value added" technique will be considered in Chapter 13. As with other school resources considered in this chapter, we rely heavily on meta-analyses of studies that evaluate teacher resources and particularly those completed after 2010 or so to ensure that the highest quality studies are included.

One of the most comprehensive and rigorous meta-analyses of teacher effects is also fairly recent (Coenen et al., 2018).[14] To be included in the meta-analysis, studies had to focus on student test scores as outcomes and needed to use more rigorous analytic methods. In this meta-analysis, panel or quasi-experimental data that controlled for student background was required. A total of 58 studies met these design criteria, 14 of which were unpublished reports, and the vast majority were published in 2004 or later. This meta-analysis evaluated teacher education, years of experience, certification, and teacher knowledge tests.

Figure 2.4 summarizes effect sizes for the 14 evaluations of teacher education. All but two of the effect sizes are very small, with standardized effect sizes less than or equal to .01. Even the largest effect, .04, is fairly weak, given the size of the achievement gap that adequacy cases are hoping to close. As explained in the discussion for the effects of school expenditures, adequacy cases are almost always focused on raising achievement for lower-income or lower-socioeconomic status students whose achievement lags behind higher-income students by nearly one standard deviation. Clearly, increasing teacher education requirements is not likely to raise student achievement by very much, even though teachers with master's or higher degrees usually receive higher pay that those with just a bachelor's degree.

Figure 2.5 summarizes effect sizes for 13 evaluations of teacher experience. Note, first, that these evaluations usually compare teachers with a certain number of years of experience to inexperienced teachers with two years of experience or less. While there is some difference between teachers

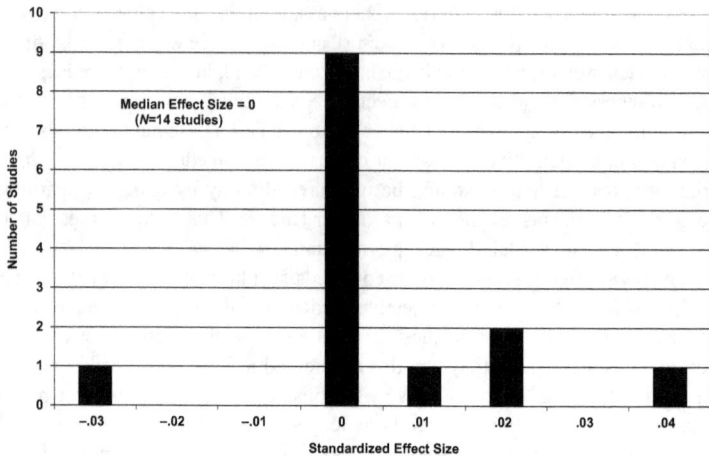

Figure 2.4 Teacher Education Effects on Student Test Scores (Standardized Effect Sizes).

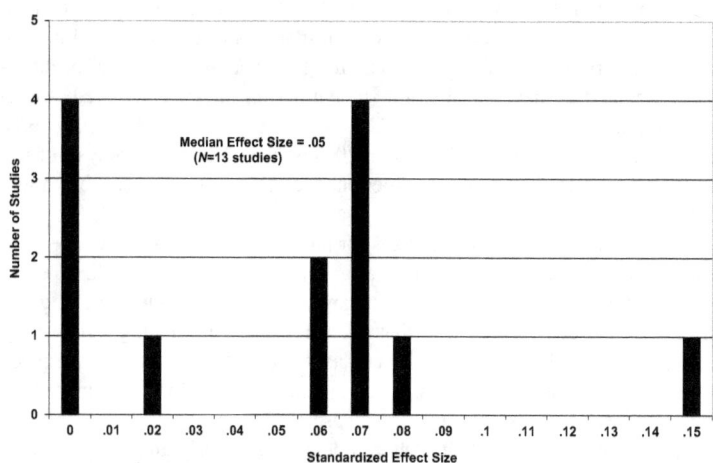

Figure 2.5 Teacher Experience Effects on Student Test Scores (Standardized Effect Sizes).

with ten years of experience versus five, those differences are smaller when compared with inexperienced teachers. This teacher attribute has considerably stronger impact on achievement than teacher education, with a majority of evaluations showing standardized effects greater than .05; one study even shows a standardized effect of .15. However, since there are four studies showing no effects of experience, the median expected effect size here is .05—somewhat larger than the effect of an additional $1,000 per capita expenditures.

The effect of teacher certification on student achievement is shown in Figure 2.6. A total of 17 studies evaluated this characteristic, and the effect of certification shows more variation than either education or experience. One study shows a small negative effect, six studies show no effect, and three studies show an effect of .07. The largest effect is .12, but the overall median effect size is .05—the same average effect as teacher experience.

Finally, Coenen et al.'s evaluation included a small number of studies (seven) that evaluated the impact of teacher test scores in the subject matter taught by the teachers, which in most cases was math. Excluding one outlier effect of .20, the average effect size of the other six studies was .05, quite similar to the effect sizes of other teacher characteristics.[15] So subject-matter skill as measured by teacher test scores does not impact student achievement more than experience or certification.

There are three additional teacher characteristics that are not addressed in Coenen et al.'s meta-analysis, which can impact student achievement. These are teacher efficacy, teacher turnover, and teacher value-added assessments. The last of these, value-added assessments, will be taken up in Chapter 13, because it is a newer characteristic that potentially has much larger impacts on student achievement than the more conventional attributes considered in this section.

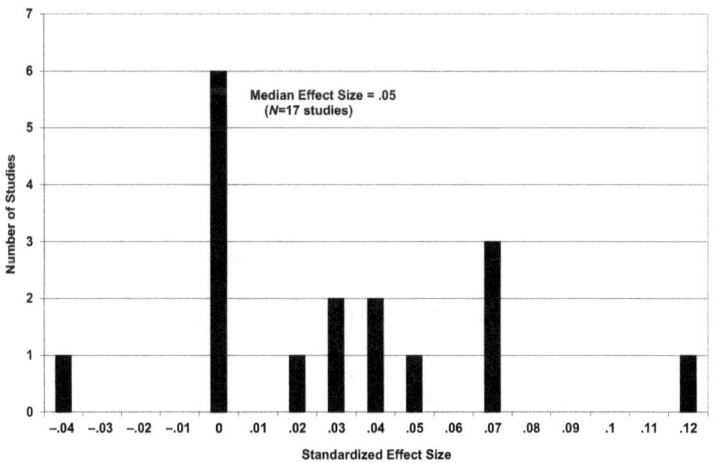

Figure 2.6 Teacher Certification Effects on Student Test Scores (Standardized Effect Sizes).

There is some evidence that teacher efficacy has an impact on academic achievement. Teacher efficacy is based on teachers' own ratings of their effectiveness in imparting knowledge to students, thereby boosting student achievement on various subject-matter tests. As such, this attribute has the same goal as a value-added assessment, but it is a self-rating method rather than one based on actual student test scores. According to a recent meta-analysis (Kim & Seo, 2018), there are 16 such studies (involving 4,130 teachers).[16] While the overall correlation between self-efficacy and student achievement is .10, there is a large variation depending on the efficacy scale used ranging from .01 to .12. The weighted average of these correlations is .05, and this is without any explicit controls for student background factors. Therefore, self-rated teacher efficacy scores are not a strong and consistent predictor of student achievement.

The final teacher attribute considered here is teacher turnover rate, that is, the percentage of teachers who leave a school in a given year. There are only a modest number of studies of this attribute, and we could not identify a comprehensive meta-analysis focusing on teacher turnover. Accordingly, we summarize the findings of two comprehensive studies of teacher turnover in two states: one in North Carolina by Sorensen and Ladd (2020)[17] and one in Texas by Hanushek et al. (2016).[18]

Basically, the North Carolina study found that schools with higher teacher turnover rates do have significantly lower student achievement scores, but also that these schools also have higher rates of inexperienced teachers, lower teacher certification rates, and more teachers teaching outside their fields of licensure. Thus, while teacher turnover has a negative relationship with student achievement, it most likely reflects the impact of less qualified and less experienced teachers. Likewise, the Texas study concluded that "we replicate existing findings of adverse selection out of schools and negative effects of turnover in lower-achievement schools." They find that these effects are fully explained by the loss of more experienced teachers.

Principal and Leadership Characteristics

Closely related to teacher characteristics are the characteristics of school administrators, of which the most important is the *principal* position. Although most of the time principals do not conduct classroom instruction, they do administer and guide the school's academic program and, perhaps most important, hire the teachers who implement that program at the classroom level. Thus, while principals do not directly impact student achievement via classroom instruction, they may have indirect impacts through their overall school management practices, including decisions to hire and/or dismiss classroom teachers.

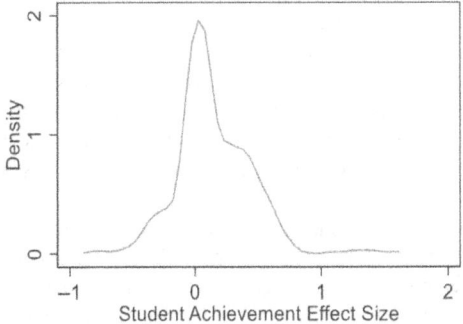

Figure 2.7 Effect of Principal Behaviors on Student Achievement.
Source: Liebowitz and Porter (2019), Figure S2.

The literature on principal effects is much smaller than that of teacher effects, but there is one fairly comprehensive meta-analysis by Liebowitz and Porter (2019).[19] This review found 346 cases in 31 studies that included student achievement as the outcome measure. The principal behaviors that had the strongest effects on student achievement were instructional management (selecting teachers, helping establish the instructional program, etc.) and "internal relations," although statistical significance was only established at the .10 level.

Figure 2.7 shows the distribution of effect sizes across the studies that included student achievement as an outcome. The modal effect size is near 0, and the median effect size is only about .10, so the magnitude of effect sizes for principals' leadership behaviors is not that different from the impact of certain teacher characteristics such as experience levels. While principals can make a difference on student achievement, the impact is not large enough to overcome the achievement gap between students from high- versus low-income families or the gap between Black and White students, which is nearly a full standard deviation (see Figure 1.1).

School Reorganization Studies

To this point, we have been examining the effects of school resources one at a time. After the NCLB law was operating for about eight years, it became clear that its primary goal of closing achievement grants was not being met. Accordingly, in 2009, as part of the American Recovery and Reinvestment Act, the Department of Education authorized a new program of school reform that was far more intrusive than the accountability provisions of NCLB.

The School Improvement Grant (SIG) program envisaged major school reorganizations that could "turn around" school programs in order to improve achievement scores of low-income and minority student populations. School reorganization covered a broad range of techniques and policies that aim to improve student achievement by making extensive changes in multiple aspects of school organization, including administrators, teachers, curriculum, and other policy areas. The SIG program authorized four levels of reorganization of increasing "intensity": transformation, turnaround, restart, or closure. Transformation involved replacing the principal and adopting rigorous teacher evaluation programs and other instructional reforms. Turnaround included the transformation components and added replacing at least 50 percent of teachers. Restart required converting the school to a charter school, and closure meant closing a low-performing school and sending its students to higher-achieving schools.

There have been a number of evaluations of these SIG program and similar reforms, but this review will focus on several studies that comprise the most important and comprehensive evaluations (or critiques). At the outset, we note that these studies do not agree on the impact that SIG and other school reorganization studies have had on academic achievement. Areas of agreement and disagreement will be noted as appropriate.

The first major study reviewed is based on the official evaluation of the SIG program sponsored by the Institute of Education Science. This effort was carried out as a joint project of Mathematica, Inc. and the American Institutes of Research, both respected research organizations.[20] In short, the authors concluded, "We found that SIG had no impact on any of the outcomes we examined, including math and reading test scores, high school graduation rates, and college enrollment rates."

We reproduce a figure from this SIG report to demonstrate the magnitude of the estimated effects. Figure 2.8 shows standardized effects of SIG reforms on math scores for each post-SIG year (the baseline school year for all evaluations was 2009–2010). The largest effect is shown for the restart method, but even here the average effect size is just .07, and it was shown only in the second year of implementation. It is noted, however, that there were only ten such cases. It is surprising that the effect of the turnaround method for math scores is only .05, given that this method replaces at least 50 percent of the teachers in each school.

The effects of SIG reforms were even weaker for reading scores. None of the reform measures has effects exceeding .05, and even this weak effect is attained only for the restart method involving just ten schools. It is especially noteworthy that these SIG interventions are holistic, involving major structural, personnel, and resource changes—and cost US taxpayers $3.5 billion. Since SIG interventions involve quite drastic and costly methods of school reform, it is unlikely that they can be sold to most state education agencies, given their weak effects on student achievement.

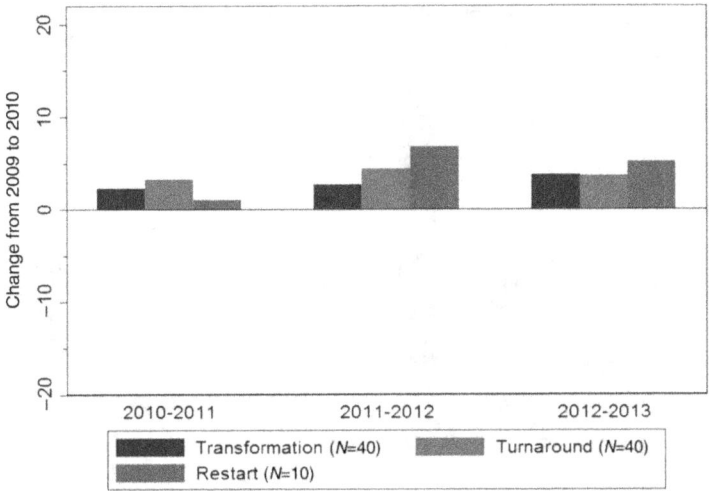

Figure 2.8 SIG Program's Impact on Math Scores (No Effect Is Statistically Significant).
Source: Dragoset, L. et al (2019), Figure 3.

It is noted that this official evaluation of the SIG program is not without criticism. In particular, the study was strongly criticized in a report by Alan Ginsburg and Marshall S. Smith, the latter a former Undersecretary of Education and noted education researcher at Stanford.[21] In particular, they believed the sample used by the Mathematica-ARI evaluation was too small and overrepresented inner-city schools and students from disadvantaged backgrounds—groups that might not benefit as much as more representative populations. In particular, they found significant SIG impacts from programs in Denver, Houston, Massachusetts, Ohio, and San Francisco.

In an effort to resolve the differing conclusions between the official SIG evaluation and critics of methods used by the official study, we turn to another more comprehensive and more recent study of turnaround and other high-impact reform policies. This evaluation, conducted by Schueler et al. (2022) (see also Schueler et al. [2020]), was a formal meta-analysis based on 141 effect estimates from 67 different studies of school turnaround interventions.[22] As such, it is the largest meta-analysis carried out on this important topic.

The Schueler et al. meta-analysis did find statistically significant effects for some turnaround interventions, but these effects are quite limited as to the specific techniques used in the turnaround as well as the demographic settings of the schools involved. A summary of the demographic settings and the techniques used are shown in Figures 2.9 and 2.10, respectively.

First, and most disappointing, Figure 2.9 shows that, according to this review, turnaround efforts have not been successful in either low-income

26 David J. Armor and Aquilla M. Ossian

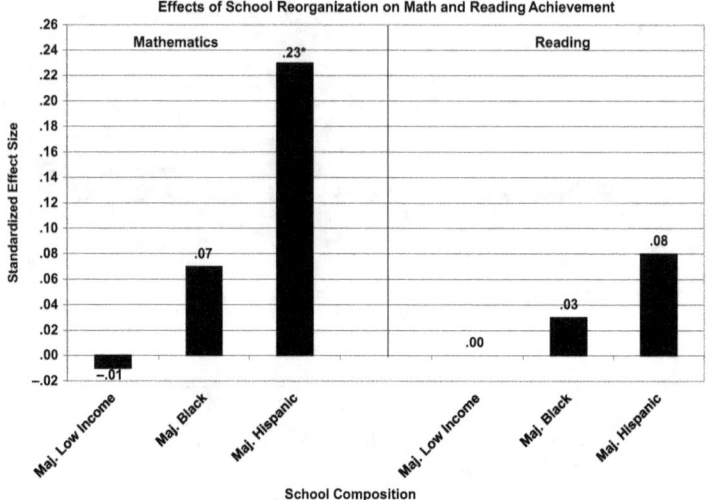

Figure 2.9 Effects of School Reorganization by School Demographics.
Note: + denotes $p \leq .10$; * $p \leq .05$.
Source: Adapted from Table 6 in Schueler et al. (2020).

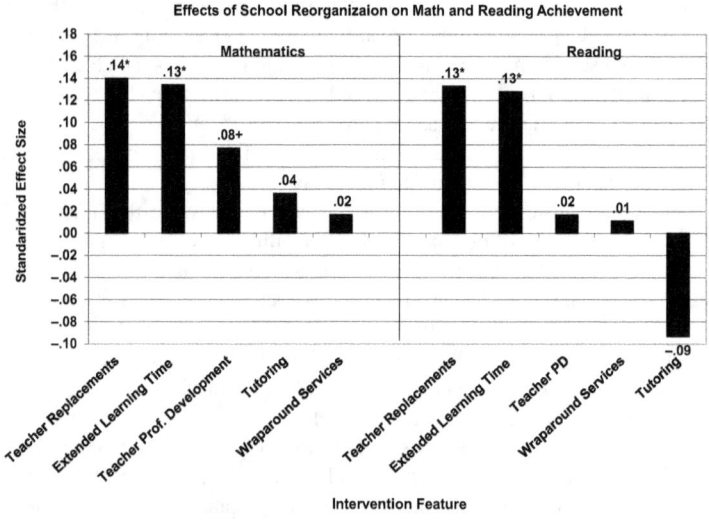

Figure 2.10 Effects of School Reorganization by Intervention Features.
Note: + denotes $p \leq .10$; * $p \leq .05$.
Source: Adapted from Table 10 in Schueler et al. (2020).

schools or majority Black schools, two of the conditions that have manifested serious achievement gaps with majority middle class and majority White schools. In contrast, turnaround efforts have been more successful in majority Hispanic districts, and these turnarounds have had substantial impacts on math achievement, with an average improvement of nearly one-fourth of a standardized effect. In these same Hispanic districts, the standardized effect for reading is much smaller at .08 (and not statistically significant).

Second, it is clear from results summarized in Figure 2.10 that only two specific techniques used in turnaround efforts generated significant improvement in achievement: replacing teachers (presumably with more capable teachers) and increasing learning time in the form of longer school days or longer school years. Each of these reforms have standardized effects on achievement test scores of about .13 or .14, although presumably—because of the findings shown in Figure 2.11—those techniques were only effective in majority Hispanic schools. It is encouraging that these two techniques appear to improve reading scores to the same degree.

While these results are very encouraging, we are left with several concerns. First, school turnaround methods, despite being fairly drastic interventions, do not appear to help improve the Black–White achievement gap—and the reasons are unclear. Second, the turnaround methods that actually have meaningful impact on achievement appear to depend on fairly drastic reforms, particularly replacing up to half of the teachers. Teacher replacement on this scale is likely to be met with opposition, especially in cities with strong teachers unions—the very places where achievement gaps may be most concerning.

Summary

It is quite remarkable, given the relatively limited data and simplistic methodology of the 1965 Coleman Report—compared to the sophisticated methodologies available today and the vastly greater sources of student and school data—that we do not see larger differences between the Coleman findings and those reviewed here.

The Coleman study had to rely on a one-time national survey of students, teachers, and schools, administered to just a fraction of the school population. The data and studies reviewed here involve millions of students in virtually every state in the union, and the statistical techniques are among the most sophisticated possible with today's technology. Yet the conclusions about the relative effects of school resources versus student background are not that different. In both studies, the impact of school resources of all kinds, including the funding which purchases these resources, are quite modest.

In the chapters that follow, we shall explore a series of case studies to investigate whether, and to what extent, we can find school resources that have a greater impact than the school resources identified in the major studies reviewed here.

Notes

1 Burtless, G., ed. (1996). *Does Money Matter?*, Washington, DC, Brookings Institution Press.
2 Per capita measures can be expenditures either per student or per average daily attendance (ADA).
3 There are other data sources that can be used for this purpose; for example, the SEDA project at Stanford.
4 Armor, D.J. (2023, January). *Interpreting the Covid Impact on Achievement*, Washington, DC, The Thomas B. Fordham Institute, https://fordhaminstitute.org/national/commentary/interpreting-covid-impact-achievement
5 Jackson, C.K., Wigger, C. and Xiong, H. (2020, Fall). The costs of cutting spending. *Education Next* 20(4): 64–71; Jackson, C.K., Wigger, C. and Xiong, H. (2021, May). Do school spending cuts matter? Evidence from the great recession. *American Economic Journal: Economic Policy* 13(2): 304–335.
6 Rosenthal, R. and Jacobson, L. (1992). *Pygmalion in the Classroom*, Norwalk, CT, Crown House Publishers.
7 Jackson, C.K. and Mackevicius, C. (2021). *The Distribution of School Spending Impacts*, NBER Working Paper 28517, Cambridge, MA, National Bureau of Economic Research, https://doi.org/10.3386/w28517; Jackson, C.K. and Mackevicius, C. (2023). *What Impacts Can We Expect from School Spending Policy? Evidence from Evaluations in the U.S.*, Evanston, IL, Northwestern University.
8 Lindsey, M.B. and Jay, P. Greene. (2023). New Yorkers for Students' Educational Rights et al. v. *The State of New York: Expert Report of Jay P. Greene*, PhD, The Heritage Foundation, Washington, DC.
9 Shores, K.A., Hojung, L. and Elinor, W. (2021). *The Distribution of School Resources in The United States*, Providence, RI, Annenberg Institute, Brown University.
10 Finn, J.D. and Achilles, C.M. (1990). Answers and questions about class size: A statewide experiment. *American Educational Research Journal* 27(3): 557–577.
11 Hanushek, E. (1999). Some findings from an independent investigation of the Tennessee STAR experiment and from other investigations of class size effects. *Educational Evaluation and Policy Analysis* 21(2): 143–165.
12 Bohrnstedt, G.W. and Stecher, B.M., eds. (2002). *What We Have Learned About Class Size Reduction in California: Capstone Report*, Palo Alto, CA, American Institutes for Research.
13 Jepsen, C. and Rivkin, S. (2009). Class size reduction and student achievement the potential tradeoff between teacher quality and class size. *Journal of Human Resources* 44(1): 223–250.
14 Coenen, J., Cornelisz, I., Groot, W., van den Brink, H.M. and Klaveren, C.V. (2018). Teacher characteristics and their effects on student test scores: A systematic review. *Journal of Economic Surveys* 32(3): 848–877.
15 The outlier was .20 for predicting that students would be taking a vocation track based on age 12 test score.
16 Kim, K.R. and Seo, E.H. (2018). The relationship between teacher efficacy and students' academic achievement: A meta-analysis. *Social Behavior and Personality* 46(4): 529–540.
17 Sorensen, L.C. and Ladd, H.F. (2020). The hidden costs of teacher turnover. *AERA Open* 6(1): 1–24.
18 Hanushek, E.A., Rivkin, S.G. and Schiman, J.C. (2016). Dynamic effects of teacher turnover on the quality of instruction. *Economics of Education Review* 55: 132–148.
19 Liebowitz, D.D. and Porter, L. (2019). The effect of principal behaviors on student, teacher, and school outcomes: A systematic review and meta-analysis of the empirical literature. *Review of Educational Research* 89(5): 785–827.

20 Dragoset, L., Thomas, J., Herrmann, M., Deke, J., James-Burdumy, S. and Luca, D.L. (2019). The impact of school improvement grants on student outcomes: Findings from a national evaluation using a regression discontinuity design. *Journal of Research on Educational Effectiveness* 12(2): 215–250.
21 Ginsburg, A. and Smith, M.S. (2018). *Why Critics Were Wrong to Write Off the Federal School Improvement Grant Program*, FutureEd, Washington, DC, Georgetown University.
22 Schueler, B.E., Asher, C.A., Larned, K.E., Mehrotra, S. and Pollard, C. (2022). Improving low-performing schools: A meta-analysis of impact evaluation studies. *American Educational Research Journal* 59(5): 975–1010. An earlier version of this study was published as Schueler, B.E., Asher, C.A., Larned, K.E., Mehrotra, S. and Pollard, C. (2020). *Improving Low-Performing Schools: A Meta-Analysis of Impact Evaluation Studies: EdWorkingPaper*, Providence, RI, Annenberg Institute at Brown University, 20–274.

3 The State of Education Adequacy Law

John R. Munich

Background

In the United States, state and federal public policy and spending decisions are, by constitutional authority, generally delegated to the executive and legislative branches of government. But since the beginnings of the nation, advocates have resorted to using the courts as levers of public policy reform through the initiation of lawsuits seeking judicially ordered changes, especially when the litigants have not been able to have their preferred policy choices enacted through the legislative and executive branch avenues. As Alexis de Tocqueville remarked in his 1835 observations on the new American republic, "There is hardly any political question in the United States that sooner or later does not turn into a judicial question."[1] There is perhaps no greater verification of de Tocqueville's finding—particularly in the past several decades—than the many efforts education advocates have made to change the way public schools are funded through the vehicle of litigation, principally through the so-called school funding "adequacy" lawsuits, especially in the state courts.

The extent and breadth of these efforts are amply demonstrated in the fact that school-funding plaintiffs have litigated some version of an education adequacy lawsuit in at least 46 states.[2] In essence, these lawsuits allege that state funding for public K–12 education is not sufficient to meet typical state constitutional provisions requiring a "adequate," "sufficient" or "thorough" public education. The case often thought of as marking the beginning of the adequacy litigation movement, *Robinson v. Cahill*, 62 N.J. 473 (1973), was decided almost 50 years ago in New Jersey. Today, adequacy litigation can be thought of as the latest iteration of American school finance litigation, following series of the so-called equity lawsuits and desegregation cases that were prominent from the 1950s well into the 1990s.[3]

While a few school desegregation cases linger on today, they largely began to wane during the 1990s after a series of three Supreme Court decisions spurred federal trial courts to release school districts and states from judicial supervision over desegregation programs. By the mid-1980s and 1990s, many desegregation cases were well into their remedial phases, with courts overseeing sometimes far-reaching remedies intended to provide compensatory relief to formerly *de jure* segregated public schools. In a number of these cases, courts had ordered state and local governments to provide increased funding, sometimes in very substantial amounts, to those schools.[4] In two of the most striking examples, federal courts on opposite ends of the state of Missouri ordered the state to pay a combined $3 billion over a number of years to remedy the effects of what they found to be past *de jure* discrimination in the state. *Liddell v. Board of Educ.*, 4:72-cv-00100 (E.D. Mo.) (Trial testimony of Dr. Christine Rossell) (1996), *Missouri v. Jenkins*, 515 U.S. 70 (1995).

State Court Equity Lawsuits

While federal court desegregation cases were focused on stopping and remedying unlawful racial segregation in violation of the Equal Protection clause of the Fourteenth Amendment to the federal Constitution, state court "equity" lawsuits—which might be considered as the "first wave" of American public school funding litigation—were aimed at remedying public funding differences across schools and districts in a given state. In these early equity lawsuits, plaintiffs argued that large disparities in public funding available to school districts across a state violated state and federal equal protection provisions and state constitutional provisions establishing the right to a free public education. In fact, in many states there were (and still are) substantial differences in per pupil spending across geographical areas, largely because most states' public school funding systems rely to varying degrees on local property taxes as part of their funding mechanisms; these locally raised funds are usually complimented by state-raised revenues generated by state income or other taxes.

One by-product of this type of system is that school districts with high property tax valuations—urban districts that contain highly assessed commercial property or more rural districts that encompass resort areas or large industrial complexes—can generate higher funding from their local real estate taxes and accordingly are able to spend more and to fund their schools at higher levels per pupil than other districts with comparatively lower assessed valuations per pupil. These kinds of obvious and easily proven disparities meant that plaintiffs who brought lawsuits based on an equity theory experienced great success based on a simple, easy-to-make argument—children from property-poor districts should not receive fewer educational resources than students who attended schools in districts with higher property wealth.

Success in these equity cases was not immediate, however. In one of the earliest efforts, filed in federal court and asserting a violation of the plaintiffs' federal constitution rights, *Rodriguez v. San Antonio*, plaintiffs failed to convince the federal courts that funding schools through local property taxes was discriminatory and in violation of the equal protection clause of the Fourteenth Amendment. The US Supreme Court held in *Rodriguez* that the states had great discretion in governing local education matters, and found that because the Federal Constitution did not mention education in its text, education did not exist as a "fundamental right." Moreover, the Supreme Court also found that wealth classifications did not qualify as a "suspect class" under the Federal Constitution, and therefore, the Supreme Court examined the alleged classifications under a deferential, "rational basis" standard, examining only whether there was a rational basis for the Texas school funding system challenged in *Rodriguez*.

But, while equity plaintiffs failed to gain traction in the federal courts, they had greater success bringing their cases in state courts. One of the earliest examples was *Serrano v. Priest*, where the plaintiffs challenged California's system for funding schools through a combination of local property taxes and state revenues. Under the California system in place at the time, public schools were funded primarily from local property taxes, leading to great variances in per pupil spending across different school districts. Ultimately, this caused significant school funding disparities among the property-rich and property-poor districts. The trial court sided with the plaintiffs, and two years later, in *Serrano II*, the California Supreme Court affirmed the trial court's decision. The courts found that under the California Constitution, education was a fundamental interest and that classifications based on wealth in the distribution of education funds were subject to exacting scrutiny by the courts.

While some advocates seek to extinguish the reliance of state education funding systems on local, property tax-driven revenues, others maintain that to eliminate local school funding components would be a mistake. Local taxes on real estate are much more stable year to year than revenues derived from more volatile sources such as income and sales taxes. Property values are generally more stable, and therefore "even out" the highs and lows that may affect income and sales taxes in alternating economic cycles. Additionally, local property taxes (and the votes taken by the voters of a city/county/school district or their elected representatives) allow for greater local choice and accountability in public school funding. Finally, unlike sales taxes, for example, local property taxes are more difficult for residents to evade or dodge, again making their revenue streams more consistent and reliable.[5]

Many times, as a result of court-ordered remedies in equity lawsuits, states in the late 1970s and 1980s began to reform their funding systems, introducing equalizing components into their school funding mechanisms. Under these measures, relatively fewer state revenue dollars would flow to property-rich districts, while additional "equalizing" payments would be directed toward those districts that had lower local property valuations per pupil.[6] A very few states, including New Mexico for example, went even further and virtually eliminated or greatly reduced the local property tax component to their funding systems. The result of these various measures was to greatly reduce existing disparities per pupil school expenditures across districts in a number of states.

Following these successes in state courts and legislatures, the theories advanced by plaintiffs in school funding lawsuits evolved, and advocates began to refocus their arguments away from traditional "equity" claims to focus on "adequacy" allegations. In essence, the foundational debate turned away from whether all public school students should receive equal funding to the superseding question of whether all students were receiving an amount adequate to meet their particular needs, considering individual student factors such as poverty, student disabilities, and English language status, which are all widely regarded as negatively affecting student achievement outcomes. Rather than litigating the distribution of state school funding, school funding plaintiffs instead turned to focusing their claims on the overall adequacy of the amounts provided by state statutory school funding regimens.

Modern Adequacy Litigation

What are now known today as school funding adequacy lawsuits trace their origins to several seminal lawsuits filed in the 1970s. But these early efforts did not produce promising results for plaintiffs. One of the earliest lawsuits, asserting that alleged funding inadequacies violated plaintiffs' federal constitutional rights, was rejected by the US Supreme Court in *San Antonio Independent School District v. Rodriguez, supra*. The *Rodriguez* Court held that the education was not a "fundamental right" for purposes of the Fourteenth Amendment's Due Process and Equal Protection clauses, and therefore plaintiffs could not pursue their claims in federal court. This was a seminal moment for school funding advocates, as they were forced to recalibrate and consolidate their efforts to obtain court-ordered additional school funding in state courts using claims brought under state constitutions.[7]

The Foundations of Modern Adequacy Lawsuits

Some of the earliest attempts at bringing adequacy cases in state courts after the plaintiffs' loss in *Rodriguez* did not fare any better, as they encountered skeptical courts wary of wading into the political thicket surrounding how much money should be invested by their states annually for public education. A number of early adequacy cases failed in the face of separation of powers or political question rulings by state courts. For example, some courts employed the six-factor test set forth in *Baker v. Carr*, 369 U.S. 186, 209 (1962) to determine whether the issue of school funding adequacy is a political question beyond their scope of authority. Two of the *Carr* criteria would almost certainly weigh against a state court's taking jurisdiction of an adequacy case in virtually instances: whether there is a "textually demonstrable commitment" of the issue in the constitution to another political branch and whether "a lack of judicially discoverable and manageable standards" exists to resolve the case on its merits.

In one of the earliest examples applying this standard, the New York Court of Appeals held that it lacked jurisdiction to hear plaintiffs' adequacy claims in *Levittown U.S.F.D. v. Nyquist*, 57 N.Y.S.2d 27 (1982). The court concluded that "this . . . is the very essence of our governmental and political, policy," and it would therefore "normally be inappropriate for the courts to intrude upon such decision-making." *Id.* At 39. Courts in a number of other states, including Illinois, Indiana, and Rhode Island, similarly held that they lacked jurisdiction over school funding disputes, either on separation of powers or on political question grounds. For example, *Committee for Educational Rights v. Edgar*, 672 N.E.2d 1178 (1996) (Illinois Supreme Court held that it did not have "judicially manageable standards" by which to determine whether the State was providing the education required by the Illinois Constitution); *Oklahoma Education Association v. State*, 158 P.3d 1058, 1066 (2007) (Oklahoma Supreme Court held that lack of judicially ascertainable standards renders school funding challenge non-justiciable).

The Current Landscape of Adequacy Cases

Despite these setbacks, plaintiffs in other states have been able to overcome jurisdictional hurdles and have their adequacy claims tried on the merits, albeit not always with successful outcomes. One of the major successes for plaintiffs came in 1989, with the Kentucky Supreme Court's decision in *Rose v. Council for Better Education*, 790 S.W.2d 186 (1989). There, an association of 65 school districts filed suit against the governor and various other state leaders, alleging that the legislature had failed to uphold the "efficient system of common schools" standard required under the Kentucky Constitution. The trial court had found that an efficient school system must "provide sufficient physical facilities, teachers, support personnel, and instructional materials to enhance the educational process." The Supreme Court held that the legislature has the responsibility to ensure that the taxpayer money for school resources is used appropriately. The court also outlined seven competencies that a public education must provide every student to satisfy the education clause in the Kentucky Constitution: sufficient oral and written communication skills to enable the student to function in a complex and rapidly changing civilization; sufficient knowledge of economic, social, and political systems to enable the student to make informed choices; sufficient understanding of governmental processes to enable the student to understand the issues that affect his or her community, state, and nation; sufficient self-knowledge and knowledge of his or her mental and physical wellness; sufficient grounding in the arts to enable each student to appreciate his or her cultural and historical heritage; sufficient training or preparation for advanced training in either academic or vocational fields so as to enable each child to choose and pursue life work intelligently; and sufficient levels of academic or vocational skills to enable public school students to compete favorably with their counterparts in surrounding states, in academics or in the job market. 790 S.W.2d 186.

Rose was notable as an early success for plaintiffs for a couple of reasons. First, the result was a big win for plaintiffs in a politically conservative state, showing that adequacy cases could be won in any part of the United States that did not have in place adverse legal precedent barring jurisdiction of these cases. But more significantly, the Court's opinion set forth a list of criteria that could apply in any state. Those criteria focused not directly on financial criteria, but instead looked at student outcomes as the measure of adequacy. The upshot of this outcome-driven analysis meant that, if applied elsewhere, any state that did not have top-tier student outcomes could be in jeopardy of a ruling that its school system—no matter how well funded it was—failed to satisfy a state's adequacy standards.[8]

Over time, one of the most significant—and long-running—adequacy lawsuits took hold in New Jersey, where during the course of the case, plaintiffs' goals turned from equity to adequacy. *Abbott v. State of New Jersey*, 100 N.J. 269 (1985).[9] Plaintiffs based their claims on the New Jersey Constitution's requirement of a "thorough and efficient" education. They asserted that New Jersey's 31 poorest districts, known as the "Abbott districts," failed to meet this standard. Prevailing on these claims, plaintiffs succeeded in obtaining court orders that greatly increased revenue and spending for these districts. Those wins were amplified in 1998, when the Supreme Court found that student performance in the Abbott districts was depressed due to inadequate funding, ordering significantly greater funding for schools in those districts, resulting in per pupil funding amounts in the Abbott districts that were unheard of in most school districts.[10] These very high funding levels led to whole school reform programs in all the schools, half-day preschool programs for three- and four-year-olds, improved technology, alternative schools, school to work, and college transition programs, and a variety of supplemental programs, as well as extensive building and renovation of facilities.

Another example of a significant adequacy case took place in New York and concerned the New York City (NYC) school system, one of the nation's largest public school districts. *Campaign for Fiscal Equity (CFE) v. State of New York*, 769 N.Y.S.2d 106, 801 N.E.2d 326 (2003). The lawsuit centered on NYC's worst-performing community school districts and was led by a number of education advocacy organizations. The case ran for years with multiple trips through the New York trial and appellate courts.

The appellate courts in *CFE* held that the New York Constitution's requirement of "free common schools" imposed a duty upon the state to create and fund public schools, wherein each student has access to a "sound basic education" and "minimally adequate" facilities, teaching, and curriculum. The trial judge, in turn, interpreted the Court of Appeals' standard to require a showing whether NYC schools provided an education sufficient to graduate students who could become "engaged, capable voters" with the "intellectual tools to evaluate complex issues, such as campaign finance reform, tax policy and global warming." In turn, plaintiffs advanced several arguments and related evidence in court: NYC public school students performed poorly, as illustrated particularly by their scores on state academic tests and low graduation rates; NYC schools were overcrowded with large class sizes; NYC schools employed large numbers of unqualified teachers; and NYC schools overall lacked sufficient resources to provide a sound basic education.

Over the past two decades or so, state court adequacy lawsuits of one form or another have gone to trial in a number of states, including Kansas, Missouri, South Dakota, New York, Connecticut, New Mexico, Florida, Washington, and Montana, among others.[11] By their very nature, school adequacy trials are often lengthy and complex, involving testimony and data studies from social science, education, demography, and economic expert witnesses; testimony from dozens of witnesses; and the filing/admission of hundreds, if not thousands, of exhibits into evidence. The trials have often lasted for months and very often adequacy plaintiffs have been assisted at trial by large, sophisticated business law firms, sometimes working on a pro bono or reduced rate basis. Given that millions or billions of dollars are at issue in these cases, not to mention the standards of education that will govern a state's public school program, none of this should be surprising.[12]

Theories and Proof in Adequacy Litigation

One of the primary issues for decision in most adequacy lawsuits is the easy-to-articulate but difficult-to-study question of "does money matter?" This central issue implicates complex, politically loaded questions about the achievement gap that persists in every state between children from disadvantaged backgrounds and their peers from non-disadvantaged families.

Most courts require that a party seeking to prove "inadequacy" must prove that there is a causal relation between alleged educational inadequacies and the state's funding system. Typically, plaintiffs seek increased funding and assert that additional dollars should flow to provide additional services to at-risk students; they also may contend that a State's failure to appropriate more money is directly responsible for disappointing student performance, as measured in a variety of ways, that may exist in a state. State defendants, in contrast, may claim that public school appropriations are adequate but that local districts misuse or underuse the available dollars; they may also assert that additional money, without other fundamental, structural changes in public education cannot close an achievement gap caused by non-school factors such as poverty and its correlated socioeconomic factors. In essence, plaintiffs argue that "more money matters most," while defendants respond "how you spend the money matters most."[13]

Given this lineup of opposing claims, the expert testimony and other evidence in adequacy cases are most often directed to three main categories: (1) measures of school resources (inputs); (2) measures of student performance (outputs); and (3) the relationship between those two factors (causation). Plaintiffs will often attempt to demonstrate that a deficit of school resources is directly causing poor student performance, while state defendants seek to show that funding levels are adequate and, in any event, there is no direct causal relationship between increased funding and higher student achievement.[14] Questions about the measures and effects of inputs and outputs tend to focus on state and local data with correlated testimony provided by witnesses such as education department officials, school administrators, teachers, parents, students, and legislators. On the issue of causation, however, trial evidence is generally provided by expert witnesses who have studied the relationship, or lack thereof, between spending and student achievement.[15]

Across the 50 states, there exist varying models of school funding systems. But most states utilize a statutorily created school funding formula that directs the annual allocation of public school funding across a state's school districts. In many instances, the triggering event for an adequacy lawsuit is a state's reduction in or failure to increase the amount of money moving through its funding formula to the state's school districts. In general, plaintiffs in an adequacy suit seek to prove that there is an overall lack of sufficient school funding/resources, often focusing on districts that enroll a high percentage of at-risk children. Often, such evidence will focus on alleged shortages of hard resources, such as books, technology, and other learning materials; deficits in the capital facilities; and insufficient staff, including teachers, aides, counselors, and ancillary positions.

Adequacy plaintiffs may also seek to demonstrate that school funding and resource decisions (and their evidence of insufficiency) adversely affect the performance of at-risk students. States defending against an adequacy lawsuit will often highlight input evidence—highlighting the total funding districts receive from all sources—and evidence as to how efficiently school districts spend those funds. Defense witnesses may testify, for example, that the state funding formula steers additional funds to at-risk students (in some states, significantly more) and highlight additional targeted funding from state and federal sources. There may also be evidence that a state's districts do not prioritize learning over administrative and staffing costs, that schools fail to utilize all funding available to them (or have failed to pursue available state grant funding), and that the districts' existing resources are in fact adequate, based on a variety of measures and potential expert analyses.

In addition to the school resource evidence described earlier, each side in an adequacy trial might also seek to introduce evidence of newly enacted education initiatives and argue about their effectiveness. Examples of such initiatives include teacher evaluation systems incorporating a student growth component, implementation of a Common Core curriculum, specific reading/ math programs and systems driving increased accountability from the districts to the state. In a few instances, where adequacy litigation is threatened over a period of time, legislatures have even sought to preempt such a suit by enacting substantial amendments to the state funding formula. These types of radical changes can either make adequacy claims moot or, depending on the timing of the changes and the status of the adequacy lawsuit, interfere with plaintiffs' anticipated proof, requiring a rewrite of plaintiffs' planned evidence and expert analyses. Generally speaking, plaintiffs will argue that these kinds of legislative amendments are not enough or even harmful, while the states may argue they are effective or so new that they must be given sufficient time to work.

The other side of the adequacy equation—outcome evidence—is a little more straightforward but with an added wrinkle. Measures commonly examined include scores on state-mandated standardized tests, high school graduation rates, and college-going and college-persistence rates. But there is a difficulty in evaluating student achievement outcomes, in that there exist relatively few means of comparing students in one state to students in other states or the nation as a whole. States administer their own standardized tests with scoring and standards unique to a particular state, meaning cross-state comparisons are very difficult if not impossible.[16] The same is true even for graduation rates, with states using multiple, varying ways of calculating that outcome measure, meaning that state-to-state comparisons are often difficult.

Adequacy plaintiffs often point to "low" standardized test scores for students, or a subset of students, and argue that those scores are the resultant evidence of a state's underfunded school funding system. State defendants in high-performing states may point to that metric as conclusive evidence that the state's system is constitutionally "adequate." If a state is not one of those enjoying high student achievement, the state may offer alternate explanations for those scores, that is, student/family characteristics or ineffective/inefficient school administration. Similarly, a state may attempt to mitigate evidence of "low" achievement by showing that students within certain subgroups demonstrate growth, that is, closing the achievement gap that exists in every state between students from disadvantaged background and those from families with higher socioeconomic status.[17]

Perhaps the most controversial and hard-fought issue in modern adequacy litigation is the question of causation—whether the accumulated evidence establishes a causal relationship between school inputs and student output. This remains a question that has nettled the fields of social science research in education and the processes of human learning for decades. It is important because it goes directly to the questions of "adequacy" and into whether a party even has standing to bring an adequacy claim.[18] Social scientists have studied these issues relentlessly, and the academic journals are filled with the results of their work—some researchers finding that there is a scientifically valid relationship between the level of school resources and how student perform, while other researchers conclude that there is no such scientifically valid relationship.[19]

In the modern school funding trial, aided by computer software and hardware capabilities unimaginable as recently as a decade ago, evidence of quantitative social science research into these difficult causation questions often stands front and center. Often, national education and social science experts will present testimony on this central issue of causation. Often, these experts will offer competing statistical analyses, frequently utilizing great volumes of individual student longitudinal data provided by a state's Department of Education. The point of these studies is to determine whether a state's student achievement over time is attributable to variations across students and districts in school resources like class size, teacher experience, or per pupil spending, or alternatively, whether achievement differences in a state are attributable to non-school factors like a child's poverty, the educational attainment of the parents, and other socioeconomic factors outside of school.

The battle lines on these issues could not be more clearly defined or harder fought. The expert witnesses put forward by adequacy plaintiffs maintain that there is a demonstrable, proven causal between school resources and student achievement. Conversely, those researchers generally presented by state defendants assert that disparities in student outcomes are mostly explained by non-school factors. Regardless of the side they take, social science experts testifying in adequacy lawsuits examine several categories of research/data when studying the causation issue. As discussed, there is an ample body of research accumulated over the years on the question of the effect of school resources (and family factors) on student outcomes, tracing back at least to the 1966 study that became known as the "Coleman Report."[20] In that study, Mr. Coleman and his fellow researchers found that the effect of in-school resources pales in comparison to family/socioeconomic factors in their influence on student outcomes. Since then, researchers have hotly debated this issue, with a number of experts confirming and reaffirming the Coleman findings, while other researchers claim to find proof for a robust causal relationship between spending and achievement. The second form of expert analysis presented at adequacy trials consists of some form of state-specific student data—usually state-level standardized test scores, indicators of per pupil spending and other quantitative resource measures, and student demographic information—to analyze which factors are most closely correlated with student outcomes. The results of these state-level studies, particularly with today's often-robust state data files and modern software and hardware capabilities, provide some of the most revealing evidence about what, and to what extent, various factors influence student achievement.

In the chapters that follow, there are several case studies of adequacy litigation in a number of states, including New York, South Dakota, South Carolina, and New Mexico. These studies will review the major legal questions raised, introduce summaries of the expert studies that rely on statistical analyses of large-scale state education data, and summarize court decisions. In most cases, the courts have been more sympathetic to plaintiff complaints and generally skeptical of the sophisticated expert studies, at least of the state defendants.

Notes

1 de Tocqueville, A. (1835/1945). *Democracy in America*, eds. P. Bradley and A.A. Knopf, New York, NY, 280.
2 Funding adequacy cases have been decided on the merits in every state except Mississippi, Nevada, Utah, and Hawaii.
3 See Dunn, J. and West, M. (2009). *From Schoolhouse to Courthouse—The Judiciary's Role in American Education*, Brookings Institution, Wasington, DC, 96.
4 See, e.g., *Missouri v. Jenkins*, in which the trial court ordered state and local governments to provide over $1.3 billion in additional funding to pay for physical upgrades, additional educational programs, and magnet schools intended to draw non-minority children to public schools within the urban Kansas City, Missouri district. In 1995, the US Supreme Court held that the sweeping remedy imposed by the lower court in Kanas City exceeded the scope of the original violation and thus was beyond the power of the district court to impose. 515 U.S. 70 (1995).
5 See, e.g., Lieberman, M. (2022, November 28). *Property Taxes Fuel K-12 Budgets. How Well Does That Work*, Education Week, *discussing* Kenyon, D.A. et al. (2023, February). *Rethinking the Property Tax-School Funding Dilemma*, Lincoln Land Institute, found at www.lincolninst.edu/publications/policy-briefs/rethinking-property-tax-school-funding-dilemma
6 See *Serrano v. Priest*, 557 P.2d 929 (Calif. 1976) *supra*; *Robinson v. Cahill*, 360 A.2d 400 (N.J. 1976) (New Jersey Supreme Court invalidated the state's school funding system based on violations of the New Jersey State Constitution).
7 Every state constitution contains an article establishing the right to a free public education for all citizens. They do this through varying language, with some states adopting language from surrounding states, but generally employ language guaranteeing a "free and public education," a "thorough and efficient" or "uniform and efficient" education or other similar descriptors.
8 Indeed, courts in a number of subsequent school funding decisions in other states have made reference to what have come to be known as the "Rose standards" in determining questions of education adequacy.
9 As a measure of the duration of the New Jersey courts' supervision of the state education system, as of 2020, the New Jersey Supreme Court had issue 23 separate decisions in the *Abbott* case since 1985.
10 The 31 "Abbott districts" have been estimated to receive over 20 percent more dollars per pupil than the average New Jersey school district and spend well in excess of $20,000 per pupil per year. It has been estimated that the 31 districts receive over 50 percent of total New Jersey educational funding while educating about 20 percent of the state's public school pupils. Hanushek, E.A. and Lindseth, A.A. (2009). *Schoolhouses, Courthouses and Statehouses*, Princeton, NJ, Princeton University Press, 110.
11 Most adequacy challenges that prevail in the face of motions seeking early or summary dismissal end up going to trial, contrary to the arc of most civil lawsuits, the great majority of which are settled prior to trial. The reason is that it is very difficult to settle an adequacy lawsuit because, in effect, a state's statutory funding formulas

would need to be modified by the legislature, which is most often not a party to the case. Lining up executive and legislative approval of something as substantial as a school funding formula change takes extraordinary political effort and time. The lawyers who represent the state cannot just agree that schools will receive "X dollars" in additional public funding.
12 Typically, most states' two predominant budget categories are Medicaid and public K–12 education.
13 Hanushek and Lindseth, *supra*, at 54 ff.
14 In most of these disputes, plaintiffs will tend to look only at state-supplied dollars, often leaving aside federal education dollars flowing to public school districts. Additionally, plaintiffs may seek to show that there is an imbalance between state and local funding (i.e., dollars from local property taxes), arguing that a disproportionate part of overall public school funding derives from local revenue sources. See, e.g., *ConVal School Dist. v. State of New Hampshire*, 213-2019-CV-00069 (Super. Court Rockingham County), which is set to go to trial in April 2023.
15 See, e.g., Hanushek and Lindseth, *supra*, at 52–57.
16 One of the few examples is the National Assessment of Educational Progress (NAEP), which tests samples of students across a number of states at Grades 4, 8, and 12, mainly in mathematics and reading, but also including science and writing.
17 One of the ironies of this entire debate is that for years, education advocates urged states to introduce "high" academic standards for their students to encourage higher learning and performance. But when a state does set higher standards, then perforce the result will be a lower number of students who will meet those higher standards. Adequacy plaintiffs will then turn this result back on the state and allege that its school funding system is constitutionally inadequate.
18 Regarding "adequacy" if there is not a relationship between the level of school resources and student outcomes, it is hard to define, much less measure, the question of adequacy under state constitutional provisions. As to standing, a common principle is that if a court cannot provide relief for the alleged wrong asserted by the plaintiff, that plaintiff has no standing to sue. Obviously, if school resource levels are not positively related to student achievement outcomes, it is hard to conceive how a court might remedy "inadequacy," however that concept might be defined.
19 The idea that more spending might not produce increased student achievement certainly seems counterintuitive. One prominent researcher in the field, however, explains why that can be so, at least in the United States. As Dr. Eric A. Hanushek explains, the largest single expenditure in American schools is teacher compensation and benefits, constituting upwards of 75 percent of a public school district's expenditures. But his research (and that of others) shows that the level of an individual teacher's salary is principally driven by three factors—years of experience, certification, and whether the teacher has advanced degrees—that have never been shown to influence student test scores. So in effect, districts are making salary decisions about teachers based on factors that do not influence student outcomes. See, e.g., Hanushek, E.A. (2007). The single salary schedule and other issues of teacher pay. *Peabody Journal of Education* 82: 574–586.
20 Coleman, J.S. et al. 1966. *Equality of Educational Opportunity*, Washington, D.C., U.S. Government Printing Office.

4 Study Approach, Data, and Methods

David J. Armor and Aron Malatinszky

Introduction

Over the years since the Coleman Report, research methods in education policies have undergone radical changes in scope and rigor. The Coleman Report was based on what researchers call a "cross-sectional" study design, meaning the data are a "snapshot" of student and school characteristics at one point in time. This presents a problem for drawing firm conclusions about whether any student or school characteristic actually "causes" a change in test scores.

In scientific research, drawing a sound inference about causation, or at least likely causation, requires three types of information about the causal factor and an outcome such as student test scores: (1) test scores must change if exposed to the factor; (2) test scores do not change (or at least not as much) for cases not exposed to the factor, or exposed to less of the factor; and (3) other potential causes need to be ruled out. For these reasons, a controlled experiment is the preferred method for establishing causation in education, either via randomized controlled trials (RCTs) or quasi-experimental designs when randomization is not feasible. In assessing causality for student resources, cross-sectional data fail conditions (1) and (2), although they can meet (3) if enough student background characteristics are assessed.

While controlled experiments are considered the "gold standard" in evaluation research, they are not without flaws. Sometimes experiments create artificial conditions that alter the real world, and outcomes are influenced by the experiment itself and not the "treatment." This is particularly true in human experiments because of "expectancy" effects. A classic example is the famous Hawthorne Experiment, when human factor specialists manipulated factory conditions to increase production, but evaluators found that increased production was not due to workplace changes—such as better lighting or soothing music—but rather to the fact that the workers were being studied. The reality of expectancy effects explains why new drugs must be tested using "double"-blind random designs, where neither the physician nor the patient knows which drug is real and which is a placebo in the treatment and control groups.

It is very difficult, if not impossible, to eliminate potential expectancy effects when it comes to testing the impact of a specific school resource via an RCT design. Moreover, practicality dictates that RCT designs test at most one or two components of school policy (e.g., like class size and teacher experience), whereas school programs and resources consist of numerous distinct components. In addition to class size and teacher experience, other potentially important resources include teacher education, teacher subject-matter expertise, teacher salary, teacher effectiveness in raising test scores (sometimes called "value added"), age and quality of textbooks, availability of computers, total per capita spending, principal characteristics, and so forth.

For this reason, many evaluation studies rely on "administrative" data, to borrow a term economists use for data that is collected during the normal course of business. In the case of schools, the scope and detail of administrative data were greatly enhanced by the No Child Left Behind law adopted in 2002. This law required that states and school districts administer standardized achievement tests annually to students in Grades 3 to 8 plus Grade 11, and that the state must publish annual test results grouped by student demographic and economic characteristics such as gender, race, ethnicity, and free/reduced lunch status (a poverty indicator). Together with school files that contain teacher and staff characteristics as well as expenditure data, most states maintain databases that can be used to produce regular reports on student achievement progress and various school characteristics.

While administrative data lack the causal precision of experimental data, they have several advantages: (1) fidelity, meaning they reflect the actual outcomes and processes of school operations; (2) they reflect a large number of interacting school and student characteristics; and (3) in most cases, the data are collected over time. This third feature is critical in generating plausible inferences, because it can satisfy one of the critical components of causal inference, namely a change in student test scores. The question then becomes how these administrative data can be used to generate plausible inferences about the impact of school resources on student outcomes.

Note the terminology of "plausible" causal inferences. This phrasing recognizes the difficulty of establishing definitive proof in the social sciences of the complex process of determining the causes of student achievement (as measured by test scores). Generally speaking, this terminology reflects our belief that establishing a causal inference is rarely definitive in education research, and it is a matter of adopting methodologies that may offer a better likelihood of revealing the most likely or most *plausible* causes of student achievement.

The Approach

The key question addressed in this study is whether, and to what extent, school resources impact student achievement as measured by test scores. Since it is well established that a student's social and economic background has a major influence on test scores, this study accepts the thesis that certain student background characteristics cause achievement differences. Such student characteristics as race and ethnicity, English language proficiency, parental education, family income (including poverty status), and various other family characteristics are causally related to test scores.[1]

In addition, since the school research literature reviewed in Chapter 2 shows numerous studies confirming or suggesting causal status of many school resource variables, this study also assumes that most school resources are causally related to test score outcomes, at least to some degree, and the primary question is to estimate the magnitude of their effects once student and family background is taken into account. School resources include instructional effort such as class size, pupil–teacher ratios, or hours of instruction in particular subject matters; it also includes teacher quality indicators as education, experience, certification, subject-matter knowledge, and teacher effectiveness (in raising student test scores). It is also reasonable to assume that overall expenditures are a resource, allowing schools to spend more (or less) on various instructional resources and programs.

Two types of data are used in this study. The first type is national and international assessments, which are cross-sectional designs much like that used in the original Coleman Report. The national assessment is the National Assessment of Educational Progress (NAEP), which is overseen by the US Department of Education and contains the most comprehensive data on the academic performance of American students. The international assessment is Program for International Student Assessment (PISA), which is one of the more comprehensive sets of data on the academic performance of students in countries similar to the United States.

The second type consists of administrative data from a number of states: New York, New Mexico, Washington State, South Dakota, South Carolina, and North Carolina. Data for the first four states are available from major adequacy lawsuits, where data were prepared and analyzed for presentation by David J. Armor and other expert witnesses. All of these statewide datasets are longitudinal; that is, assessment takes place over multiple years. This feature enables assessment of test scores and other characteristics as they change over time.

The relationship between school resources, student background, and achievement test data will be assessed using three methods of increasing sophistication and complexity. The methods are (1) between- versus within-school variation in test scores, (2) correlation analysis, and (3) multiple regression analysis.

Between Versus Within Analysis

The between versus within analysis of test scores partitions the variation of test scores between schools and within schools. The between-school variation reflects the effects of all school programs and policies that differ from

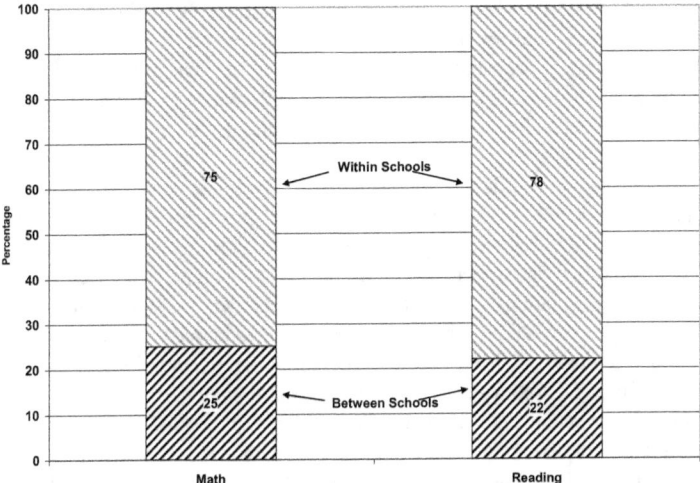

Figure 4.1 Hypothetical Results for Between Versus Within School Analysis of Test Scores.

one school to the next. The within-school variation reflects primarily individual student variation. As such, the within-school portion of the variation includes effects from all student and family demographic and socioeconomic characteristics, family differences in child-rearing practices (e.g., amount of preschool parental instruction), and any other family attributes known to affect test scores.

The advantage of this straightforward analysis is that individual variation can be estimated without having any explicit measures of student and family characteristics, and the same goes for potential school resource and program effects. As revealed in subsequent chapters, most student test score data show a pattern like Figure 4.1. Within-school variation tends to account for the dominant share of test score variations.

Therefore, even without specific measures of school resources, one observes the challenge of improving test scores by increasing school resources such as expenditures, teacher quality, class sizes, and so forth: school programs account for only a small portion of the variation in achievement test scores.

Correlation Analysis

The second method of analysis is also quite straightforward. It is based on simple correlations between test scores, on the one hand, and student and school characteristics, on the other. This statistic meets one of the requirements of causal analysis, in that it measures the extent to which changes in one characteristic are related to changes in another. Of course, in a cross-sectional analysis, changes are inferred by differences from one student to another, and depending on the characteristic, that may or may not be a reasonable assumption.

A correlation coefficient ranges from −1.0, indicating a perfect inverse relationship, to +1.0, which indicates a perfect positive relationship. A correlation of 0 between two characteristics means that there is no relationship between the two characteristics. Intermediate values represent weak, moderate, or strong relationships. In the case of social science studies of individual students, correlations smaller than ±.1 are considered weak, ±.1 to .2 are considered modest, ±.3 to .4 are considered moderate, and ±.5 to .7 are considered strong. Of course, the existence of a moderate correlation between a student and a school characteristic is not itself proof of causation, because one has to eliminate other possible causes of a difference in test scores.

For each set of data examined in this study, a correlation analysis will be shown similar to Figure 4.2. The correlations are divided into measures of student background and measures of school resources. Although the correlations in Figure 4.2 are hypothetical, the pattern of actual correlations for real data will be similar. Student background variables have many modest and moderate correlations (either positive or negative), while most school resource correlations are weak—almost always smaller than ±.1.

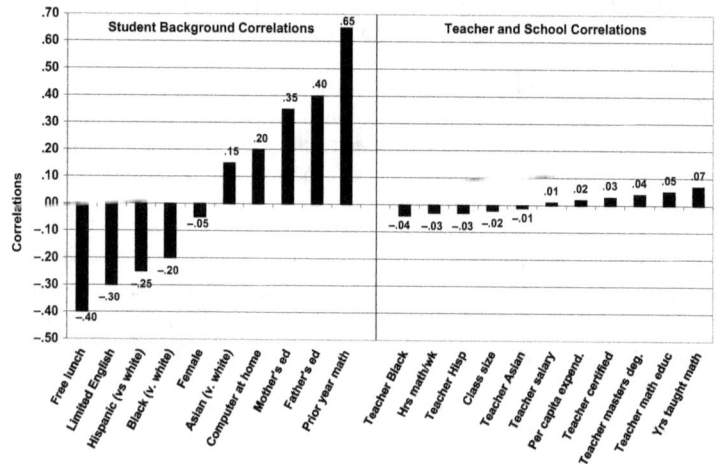

Figure 4.2 Hypothetical Correlations Between Test Scores and Student and School Characteristics.

Does a correlation of 0 indicate the absence of causation? While it is well known that correlation does not equal causation, it is also the case that causation requires correlation. If the attribute x causes an outcome y, then x and y must be correlated. The absence of correlation implies the absence of causation, at least for the total population of observations with measures of x and y. In the case of student test scores and school resources, the only way causation can exist for a correlation of 0 (or a very small correlation between .01 and .03) is if causation exists for a small subgroup of students, but not for all students.

There is another unlikely scenario where the correlation is a modest .2 for one large subgroup (say, students from lower-income families), but for higher-income students the correlation is −.2. In this case, the relationships within the two subgroups cancel each other out, making the correlation 0 in the total population. While such a situation is theoretically possible, it seems highly unlikely in the case of school resources. For example, if the resource was per capita expenditures, it would mean that more spending raised achievement modestly for students from less affluent families but lowered achievement for more affluent students.

In this study, if a correlation between a student or school characteristic and test scores is very small (smaller than ±.04), causality will be considered "improbable," but not impossible. Causality is even less probable if a multiple regression has been done to control the relationship for other potential causes.

Multiple Regression Analyses

Correlations offer important preliminary information for the impacts of various student and school characteristics on student achievement, but substantial improvement in causal inference can be made through the statistical technique of multiple regression analysis. This well-known statistical technique offers the ability to examine the potential effect of a given student or school characteristic while controlling for (or "removing") the effect of all other measured student and school characteristics. Indeed, given certain types of data, a particular type of regression analysis can even control for certain unmeasured characteristics.

This study will use several types of multiple regression methods depending on the type of data available for a particular case. For example, Chapters 4 and 10, the data for the US NAEP analysis and the international PISA analysis are cross-sectional, that is, both test scores and student and school characteristics are assessed at just one point in time. In contrast, all the statewide case studies in Chapters 6 to 9 uses data that are longitudinal, meaning that assessments are made on the same population of students as they progress over multiple grades and years. The availability of longitudinal data allows the use of more sophisticated regression models that provide more rigorous controls for student background data.

Four types of multiple regression techniques will be applied to these various sets of data. This section provides a general description of these methods at a level appropriate for the educated layman. A final technical section of this chapter offers the detailed mathematical models upon which these methods are based.

Cross-Sectional Data

Regression analysis applied to cross-sectional data is straightforward and is one of the most common techniques used in the social sciences. In education research, it can be used to estimate the effect of various school resources, controlling for the impact of all measured student background characteristics. If the most important student background characteristics have been assessed—which means those known to have major impact on test scores—then multiple regression gives a better approximation for the potential causal effect of each characteristic than the simple correlations shown in Figure 4.2.

A regression analysis can provide "standardized effect" estimates, which are widely used in education research. Figure 4.3 shows hypothetical standardized effects for the same variables shown in Figure 4.2. A standardized effect is like a correlation coefficient, except that it expresses the relationship between a given characteristic and test scores after the effects for all other characteristics have been removed. That is, it is the effect of that characteristic with "every other characteristic held constant," or *et paribus ceteris*, as economists say. Regression coefficients can be tested

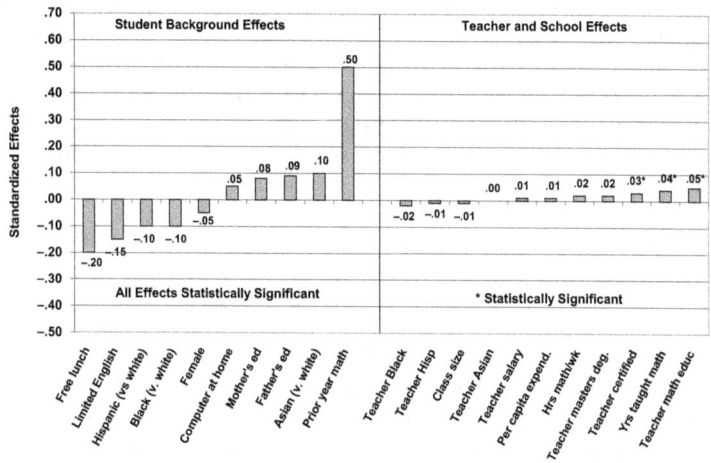

Figure 4.3 Hypothetical Standardized Effects for Student and School Characteristics.

for statistical significance, meaning the likelihood that a given coefficient occurs by chance.

For the teacher and school effect estimates, only those effects which are .03 or higher are statistically significant; the others are too low to be distinguishable from "chance." A school which increased the number of certified teachers, years taught math, and teachers with math majors or minors in college by one standard deviation would correspond to an increase in test scores of just .12 standard deviations, holding constant all student background characteristics.

Pooled Longitudinal Cross-Sectional Data

A pooled longitudinal cross-sectional regression can be applied to student and school measures that are assessed over multiple years and grades. The analysis is similar to a cross-sectional regression for one grade at one point in time, except that one can remove (control for) systematic fluctuations of test scores for particular grades or in particular school years. Otherwise, the analysis is identical to an ordinary cross-sectional design.

Value-Added Models for Longitudinal Data

For state datasets which contain test scores, student background, and school resource information over multiple grades and years, a more sophisticated regression model can control for change over time by including a student's prior year test scores as an independent variable. This allows one to assess the effect of teacher and school resources controlling for a student's test score before the student enters that teacher's class. Thus, a value-added regression increases the confidence about teacher's impact, because it assesses the value that that teacher (or other school characteristic) adds to the incoming students' existing achievement level.

Student Fixed Effect Models for Longitudinal Data

Student fixed effect models offer even greater precision to the estimation of school resource effects. A student fixed effect regression controls for all unchanging student characteristics (e.g., all characteristics of a student that occur before the start of schooling), whether they are measured or not. Since there are many student characteristics that are not measured in most state education data systems, such as basic cognitive ability, family characteristics like education and affluence, and early student learning, before the start of schooling, a student fixed effect model is the best way to control for all time-invariant student characteristics. An Appendix provides the mathematical models and technical descriptions for the multiple regression analyses used in this book.

Technical Appendix

Description of Regression Models Used

This section provides the mathematical models and technical descriptions for the multiple regression analyses used in this book.

To start, consider student achievement as a function of all educational inputs. To be concrete, for any student i in grade g at school s, let achievement Y in year t be a function of observable student characteristics X, school characteristics S, and other characteristics U:

$$Y_{igst} = f\left(X_{it},\ S_{gst},\ U_{igst}\right)$$

Functions like this are often referred to as education production functions; according to this function, any given combination of educational inputs, from school characteristics to idiosyncrasies impacting students' test-taking ability, results in a certain student outcome. What this function might truly look like is unknown; in principle, there are infinitely many functions that could describe a general relationship between inputs and achievement. Nonetheless, properties of the true education production function are of interest insofar as they reveal the extent to which educational inputs determine outcomes. By making explicit assumptions regarding the form of the education production function and how its inputs and outcomes can interact, one can use data to narrow down what the function most probably looks like.

All of the analyses in this study assume that the education production function is linear in its three inputs: observable student characteristics, observable school resources, and an error term containing the effect of all other observed and unobserved factors on achievement. This means that each observable explanatory variable affects student achievement through a multiplicative coefficient parameter; if a particular input has a coefficient of two, for example, then a one-unit increase in the input should increase the achievement by two units.

Moreover, each coefficient parameter amounts to the effect of its corresponding variable with all other variables held the same. The error term is a random variable with an unknown variance parameter; lower variance implies that one can predict outcomes using observable inputs with greater precision. Estimating a model amounts to finding the coefficient parameters and error term variance parameter that best capture the relationship observed in the data.

Each of the models described in this section relies on a different set of assumptions, some of which are stronger than others. The statistical inferences drawn from estimating a model are more credible when the assumptions the model requires are less restrictive and more likely to hold true.

Cross-Sectional Models

Given the cross-sectional data on students, the ordinary least squares approach to multiple regression analysis is the most basic and common procedure for estimating cross-sectional models. In the case of a single explanatory variable and a single outcome, one can visualize this method as drawing a "line of best fit" through coordinates in the plane corresponding to each data point. With multiple explanatory variables, this entails choosing coefficient parameters that minimize the sum of squared distances between the observed achievement of each student and the achievement produced by multiplying the student's inputs by their corresponding coefficients.

With cross-sectional data, educational inputs and outcomes may vary by individual, grade, and school but are observed in only one year; accordingly, year indices are omitted when representing the model in a regression equation. Following the notation of the general education production function, let X and S be vectors of observable student and school characteristics, respectively, and let u capture the effects of all remaining factors impacting outcomes so that

$$Y_{igs} = \alpha + X_i\beta + S_{gs}\gamma + u_{igs}$$

Here, β is a vector of coefficients corresponding to the linear effects of each student characteristic in X, and γ is a vector of coefficients corresponding to the linear effects of each school resource in S. Each of these vectors is a parameter of the linear model.

The key additional assumption behind this set of models is that the error term should have mean zero conditional on observable student characteristics and school resources; letting E be the expectation operator means that for all i, g, and s,

$$E\left(u_{igs} | X_i, S_{gs}\right) = 0$$

In plainer terms, given the characteristics and school resources observed for any given student, one can expect the effects of all other factors on achievement to cancel each other out.

In many cases, this assumption is easily violated, in which case one cannot expect estimated coefficients to be consistent with their true parameters. For instance, if an unobservable student characteristic in the error term, such as latent student ability, is positively correlated with a school resource, then one might expect the error term to take on different values conditional on the observed level of the school resource. This could occur if students are sorted into schools on the basis of unobserved characteristics that also impact outcomes. In this case, the multiple regression approach will overestimate the causal relationship between the school resource and student achievement; part of the estimated effect will in fact be due to an unobserved factor which happens to coincide with the school resource, resulting in a phenomenon of misattribution known as omitted variable bias.

Pooled Longitudinal Cross-Sectional Data

Though hardly a cure-all, it rarely hurts to have more data. Longitudinal data introduces multiple observations for each student, so that achievement, student characteristics, and school resources are measured at multiple points in time. When the variables are measured on a yearly basis, as in many educational administrative datasets, then the data are student-year observations for each variable. Some of these variables, such as student race, may be the same in each year for a given student. These variables are referred to as time-invariant. Other variables, such as achievement and school resources, may change over time, though by different amounts.

One way forward is to pool all of the longitudinal data on educational inputs and student achievement into one large dataset and borrow the multiple regression method from the cross-sectional case. To do so, each student-year is simply treated as a separate data point, and the same procedure for choosing parameters from the cross-sectional case is implemented, estimating

$$Y_{igst} = \alpha + X_{it}\beta + S_{gst}\gamma + u_{igst}$$

The additional data gathered over multiple years can make the resulting estimates more precise (in principle, a smaller set of parameter values could be consistent with the data when there are more data), but the gain in precision is for naught if the same restrictive assumptions from the cross-sectional case are violated and the results are inaccurate. Nonetheless, the pooled longitudinal model is a useful starting point for the next two models.

Value-Added Models for Longitudinal Data

Keeping in mind the plethora of circumstances and factors beyond observable student characteristics and school resources that could influence student achievement, the assumption that the error term is unrelated to the explanatory variables seems implausible. Longitudinal data give the researcher access to a student's academic history, which affords a valuable additional measure.

Consider a model where students' prior-year achievement is added as an explanatory variable with its own coefficient parameter. In a regression equation, this takes the form of

$$Y_{igst} = \alpha + \delta Y_{igs,t-1} + X_{it}\beta + S_{gst}\gamma + u_{igst}$$

The coefficients of the other explanatory variables now capture the effects of educational inputs on achievement, holding prior-year achievement fixed. These effects are added to the baseline outcome predicted by prior-year achievement, so models of this form are referred to as value-added models.

The key assumption behind value-added models is that the error term should have mean zero conditional on observable student characteristics, school resources, and prior-year achievement; for all i, g, s, and t,

$$E\left(u_{igst} | X_{it}, S_{gst}, Y_{igs,t-1}\right) = 0$$

Importantly, prior-year achievement is a function of prior-year educational inputs, including the prior-year error term, due to the education production function. Then the error term in a value-added model contains inputs beyond student characteristics and school resources that affect the achievement in the contemporaneous year but without the factors that affected achievement in the previous year. Accordingly, the identifying assumption can be less restrictive, as there are fewer components in the error term to worry about.

Fixed Effect Models for Longitudinal Data

Returning to the pooled longitudinal model, it is useful to separate the somewhat abstract and nebulous error term into tractable components. In particular, consider the same multiple regression model but with the error term expressed as the sum of multiple components:

$$u_{igst} = \eta_i + gr_g + sch_s + yr_t + \psi_{gs} + \sigma_{st} + \omega_{gt} + \zeta_{gst} + \varepsilon_{igst}$$

Intuitively, this framework merely classifies the elements of the error term into factors that are variable with respect to one set of units and fixed with respect to the others. For instance, η_i contains the effects of any educational input that is variable between students, but constant for each individual student, regardless of the school they attend or the grade level and year in which they are observed. In the expanded error term, η_i, gr_g, sch_s, and yr_t are student, grade, school and year fixed effects, respectively; ψ_{gs}, σ_{st}, and ω_{gt} capture two-way interactions for the latter three effects; ζ_{gst} captures their three-way interaction; and ε_{igst} represents the remaining idiosyncratic error.

Separating the error term into these components facilitates a simple reframing of the multiple regression model. Adding controls for the indices of the fixed effects and their interactions moves components from the error term to the set of independent variables. In particular, adding indicator variables for each student in a longitudinal dataset as well as for each value of the grade–year interaction is equivalent to estimating

$$Y_{igst} = \alpha + X_{it}\beta + S_{gst}\gamma + \eta_i + \omega_{gt} + u_{igst}$$

The result is a regression equation that is ready to be used in estimating the coefficient parameters of interest without any effects on the error term, which are fixed within students or within grade–year cells. Accordingly, the key assumption behind this "fixed effect" model is a less restrictive version of what was required for the pooled longitudinal model: the error term should have mean zero conditional on observable student characteristics, school resources, grade–year effects, and any student characteristics that are fixed with respect to time; for all i, g, s, and t,

$$E\left(u_{igst} | X_{it}, S_{gst}, \omega_{gs}, \eta_i \right) = 0$$

An equivalent way of stating this assumption is to say that given the characteristics, school resources, and grade-level timing observed for any given student as well as all time-invariant student factors (whether observed or unobserved), one can expect the effects of all other factors on achievement to cancel each other out.

Note

1 Race per se is not seen as a causal factor, but rather it is a surrogate for unmeasured family characteristics such as family structure, effectiveness of parental instruction before a child enters school, and other family characteristics.

5 School Resource Impacts Using US National Assessments (NAEP)

David J. Armor

Introduction

A rigorous assessment of school resource impacts in the United States was greatly enhanced by two major events in national education policy: the evolution of the National Assessment of Educational Progress (NAEP) starting in the 1980s, and the passage of the No Child Left Behind (NCLB) Act in 2002. Before 2002, state involvement in NAEP had been voluntary, although a majority of the states did participate. After NCLB, state participation was mandatory and the national samples became robust, generally over 150,000 students participating for each test administration.

Over the years, student, teacher, and school questionnaires evolved to gather increasingly detailed information on student background as well as school and teacher characteristics. The student questionnaires include a number of items that relate to a student's demographic characteristics and socioeconomic status (SES), factors that are well known to affect a student's academic performance, not only during the school years but also well before the start of school. It is firmly established that such family and home characteristics as poverty (indicated by free lunch status), parents' education levels, family structure, computers, and other household possessions (such as number of books and newspapers) contribute to a student's academic skills, apart from the effect of resources and teachers at school.[1] While race is not an SES factor per se, for certain disadvantaged groups (e.g., black, Hispanic, Native American), race may serve as a surrogate for unmeasured family background characteristics, such as wealth, income, and occupation, which are not assessed by NAEP.

Teacher and school questionnaires obtain important information about teacher and school characteristics, many of which are related to the quality of instruction. Importantly, the teacher's characteristics are those of the teacher who is teaching the math course each student is taking. Math teacher characteristics are education (including college math courses), tenure, experience, and types of certification; school characteristics include class size and hours for math courses students take per week. Although not a quality indicator per se,

DOI: 10.4324/9781003399117-5

teacher race/ethnicity is included to test the possibility that teachers might be more effective teaching students with similar race/ethnic backgrounds. Finally, the school questionnaire provides school poverty and racial/ethnic composition, which are considered potential resources, since school districts can have policies to promote racial/ethnic and SES integration.

Descriptive Statistics

Table 5.1 shows descriptive statistics for math achievement as well as the school resource and student background characteristics, which will be examined in this section. There are approximately 170,000 students with eighth-grade math scores, and the sample is approximately 50–50 male–female. Approximately 5 percent of the students are Limited English Proficient (LEP), while another 3 percent are former LEP students who had become proficient in English by the time of the NAEP study. A substantial number of students, about 40 percent, are on the free lunch program, which in 2013 is defined as below 120 percent of the poverty line, and another 5 percent are receiving reduced-price lunches, which is defined as between 120 and 185 percent of the poverty line.[2] Both mothers and fathers average about 13 years of education, meaning one year beyond high school graduation. Regarding family structure, about 60 percent of students report living with their original mother and father, while 18 percent are living with mother only and another 16 percent are living with their mother and stepfather.

Regarding school characteristics, about half of the math teachers report having tenure. While 90 percent are certified, 18 percent report an alternative certificate and 17 percent are nationally certified. More than half have an MA degree or higher, and about 70 percent have had math courses in their graduate training. They report an average of 11 years teaching math courses. Average math class size is 24 students, and students receive about five hours of math instruction per week.

How do these characteristics relate to math achievement? As explained in Chapter 3, all of the analyses in Chapter 4 will show at least two types of summary statistics for showing the relationship between a given student or school characteristic. The first are simple correlations between math scores and each student or school characteristic, and the second is a standardized effect for each characteristic, having statistically removed the effects of all other variables. In the case of this cross-sectional NAEP data, this involves a straightforward regression analysis.

Correlation Analysis

Figure 5.1 shows the simple correlations between a student's eighth-grade math scores and both student background and teacher and school resource characteristics. It is immediately noticeable that the correlations for student background

Table 5.1 Descriptive Statistics for 2013 NAEP Eighth-Grade Math Sample.

Variable	Number	Mean	SD	Minimum	Maximum
Math Score	170,073	285	35	148	404
Student Background					
Female	172,983	.49	.50	0	1
LEP	172,976	.05	.22	0	1
Former LEP	172,976	.03	.17	0	1
Free Lunch	172,330	.41	.49	0	1
Reduced lunch	172,330	.05	.22	0	1
Black (vs. White)	172,983	.12	.33	0	1
Hispanic	172,983	.28	.45	0	1
Asian	172,983	.04	.20	0	1
Native American	172,983	.02	.13	0	1
Multi-racial	172,983	.06	.24	0	1
Mother ed (years)	166,344	13.5	2.5	10	16
Father ed	165,996	13.0	2.6	10	16
Home fixtures	166,956	6.0	1.7	1	8
Computers	172,983	1.8	.5	0	2
Mom + dad (vs. foster)	172,983	.60	.49	0	1
Mom + stepdad	172,983	.13	.34	0	1
Dad + stepmom	172,983	.04	.21	0	1
Mom only	172,983	.18	.38	0	1
Foster home	172,983	.04	.21	0	1
School Resources					
Teacher black	153,660	.08	.28	0	1
Teacher Hispanic	152,153	.07	.26	0	1
Teacher Asian	153,660	.03	.18	0	1
Teacher Hawaiian	153,660	.00	.07	0	1
Teacher tenure	151,984	.51	.50	0	1
Teacher certified	153,142	.90	.30	0	1
Alt certificate	153,311	.18	.38	0	1
National certificate	152,160	.17	.38	0	1
Teacher MA+	152,953	.56	.50	0	1
Years taught math	152,953	11	7	1	23
Teacher math ed	152,236	.71	.45	0	1
Class size	148,723	24	5	13	28
Math hrs/week	152,942	4.9	1.4	2	8
School % Asian	172,933	4.9	8.6	0	100
School % Black	172,933	15.0	21.9	0	100
School % Hispanic	172,933	21.0	26.3	0	100
School % Native American	172,933	1.1	5.8	0	100
School % Filipino	172,933	.1	.5	0	13

characteristics are much stronger than the school and teacher correlations, by a factor of two or three. For example, the strongest inverse correlations for student characteristics are free lunch (nearly −.4), as well as LEP, Hispanic, and black (all around −.25), and having a Mom-only family. The strongest positive correlations are for home items index (+.44), mother's and father's education

58 David J. Armor

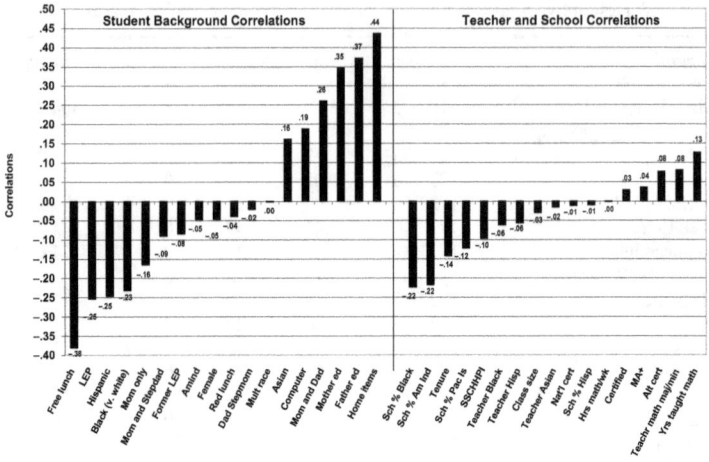

Figure 5.1 School Resource and Student Background Correlations with NAEP Eighth-Grade Math Scores, 2013.

(both around .35), and having one's original mother and father in the home versus a foster home (.26).[3]

The strongest correlations for teacher and school characteristics are the school racial/ethnic composition, with percentage of black and Hispanic having correlations of −.22 and school percentage of Asians having a correlation of +.13. These magnitudes are not surprising, given the corresponding correlations for race/ethnicity for the students. Regarding teacher quality indicators, the strongest correlations are +.08 for teachers with a master's degree or higher and also teachers with math education in college. The strongest meaningful inverse correlations occur for hours of math instruction per week (−.06) and alternative certificate (also −.06), although these are relatively weak correlations even before any controls for student background. The larger inverse correlations for black teachers (−.14) and Hispanic teachers (−.10) are not meaningful, at least not at this point, because these teachers are more likely to be in schools with larger proportions of black and Hispanic students, respectively, whose scores are lower than white and Asian students.

Standardized Effects

The standardized effects for these characteristic are shown in Figure 5.2. A standardized effect is similar to a correlation coefficient, except that it is the effect of the characteristic in question after removing the effect of all other characteristics listed in the Figure; that is, everything being equal for all other

School Resource Impacts Using US National Assessments (NAEP)

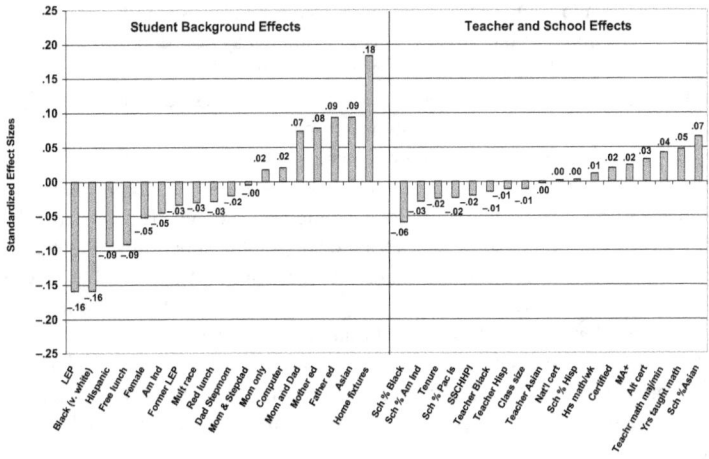

Figure 5.2 Standardized Effects of School Resources and Student Background on NAEP Eighth-Grade Math, 2013.

characteristics. The effects of primary interest here are the teacher and school characteristics.

All of the school and teacher effects are very small after controlling for student background. The strongest teacher effect is for years of teaching math, with an effect of .05. Since the standard deviation of teacher experience is seven years and the standard deviation of eighth-grade math scores is 35 (see Table 5.1), assuming this is a causal relationship, an effect of .05 means that—holding everything else constant—an increase of seven years in a teacher's experience in teaching math would lead to an increase of just 1.75 points in math scores (.05 × 35). Similarly, replacing a teacher without college math education with one that does would increase math scores by just 1.5 points (standardized effects less than .02 are not statistically significant). Considering that the 2013 math gap between poor (free lunch) and non-poor students is 27 points, and the black–white gap is 24 points, even substantial increases in these school resources would not close achievement gaps by much.

There are two school characteristics that are much stronger than the others and both are school racial composition. School percentage of blacks has the strongest inverse effect (−.06), although it is much lower than the raw correlation of −.22. Similarly, school percentage of Asians has the strongest positive effect (.07), although this is also much lower than the correlation of .13. Since the regression analysis controls for many student background characteristics, including race, the reduction of these effects is not surprising. The issue of school composition effects is taken up as a separate issue in Chapter 12. In short, the estimated effects of school composition may not be valid when based on cross-sectional data such as the NAEP data used here. Using special student fixed effect regression models, it is shown that these composition effects become much smaller, if not vanishing completely.

There are two major limitations when drawing conclusions from the results in Figure 5.2. First, these are results for the total sample, including students of all income levels and race/ethnic backgrounds. It is possible that the effects of school resources differ by demographic subgroups. Second, the data and analyses generating these effects are cross-sectional, and great caution must be exercised before assuming a cause-and-effect relationship. The second problem cannot be fixed with these data, because there is no way to control for a student's prior achievement history or other student background with cross-sectional data. The first problem can be dealt with by conducting the same analysis with subgroups of students, such as black or Hispanic students only.

Analysis of Subgroups

The standardized effects of school and teacher resources were calculated separately for black and Hispanic students. Disregarding school composition effects for the moment, the school and teacher effects for black students are very similar to effects for the total sample shown in Figure 5.2, with the stronger teacher effects on the order of .03 and .04. For Hispanic students, the school and teacher effects are slightly stronger, on the order of .04 and .05 for many. Notable effects are −.04 for class size and +.04 for teachers with college math and certified, .06 for years teaching math, and .07 for an alternate certificate (unclear meaning at this writing). Also notable is the −.05 for teachers with tenure.

Figure 5.3 shows a subgroup analysis for free versus paid lunch students, which in effect compares poverty-level students with higher low-income students.[4] Disregarding school composition characteristics (see Chapter 12), all resource effects are .05 or less. There are no important differences between low- and higher-income students in terms of those resources with the strongest effects. For poverty-level students, the strongest school resources are years teaching math (.05), alternative certificate versus no certificate (.05), and teachers with college math (.04). For higher-income students, the strongest resource effects are teachers with college math (.05), years teaching math (.04), and certified teacher versus no certificate (.04).

Basically, the results suggest that raising test scores for low-income students require the same resources as for higher-income students. Moreover, because these effects are quite small, increasing these resources by reasonable amounts

School Resource Impacts Using US National Assessments (NAEP) 61

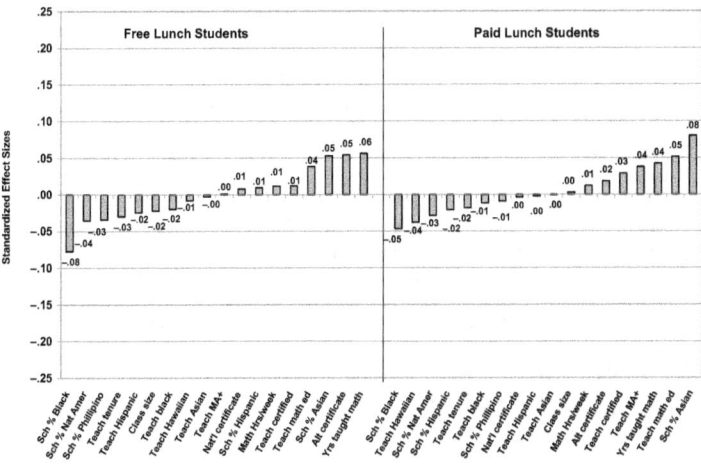

Figure 5.3 School Resource Effects on Eighth-Grade Math Scores: Free Versus Paid Lunch Students.

for disadvantaged students would only add a few points to their test scores, thereby still leaving a large achievement gap.

We need to emphasize that all of the results presented in this chapter for NAEP eighth-grade math scores are based on cross-sectional data and analyses, and as such they do not provide information on changes in test scores over time or multiple assessments of student and school characteristics over time. As explained in Chapter 4, in order to make the most plausible causal inferences using cross-sectional data (measures taken at only one point in time), we must be certain that the measured student background characteristics represent all causal factors that affect academic skills.

We are confident that, while the set of background factors measured here are important contributors to academic skills, they do not constitute a complete set of causal factors. For example, they do not include many family and parenting characteristics known to have strong impacts on cognitive skills of young children through such mechanisms as cognitive stimulation and emotional support during the formative preschool years.[5] If true RCT experiments or quasi-experimental designs are not possible, then student fixed effect models—which require a minimum of three repeated measures of all student and resource characteristics—or at least repeated measure (value-added) designs are required to make more plausible causal inferences. Some of these more rigorous techniques are applied to the case study data assessed in Chapters 6 to 10.

Notes

1 See, for example, Coleman, J.S. et al. (1966). *Equality of Educational Opportunity*, Washington, DC, U.S. Government Printing Office; Jencks, C. (1972). *Inequality*, New York, Basic Books; Armor, D.J. (2003). *Maximizing Intelligence*, New Brunswick, NJ, Transaction Publishers.
2 This is considerably higher than the national poverty rate in that year, mainly because when a school exceeds a certain percentage of student qualifying for free lunch, the whole school goes on the free lunch program.
3 A strong correlation can either be negative (−), indicating an inverse relationship, or positive (+), indicating a synchronous relationship.
4 In 2013, the Free Lunch indicator was a still a reasonably valid indicator of poverty, although in later years it became less valid because the school lunch program was extended to all students in a school that exceeded a certain percentage of poverty students.
5 See Armor, D.J. (2003). *Maximizing Intelligence*, op cit.

6 The Case of New York State

Achievement and Adequacy

David J. Armor and John R. Munich

Introduction

Evaluating the adequacy of education in New York State depends heavily on the lawsuit, *Campaign for Fiscal Equity v. New York State* (hereafter *CFE*), which was brought on behalf of students attending New York City (NYC) schools.[1] In the original *CFE* decision, the court found that students in NYC were not adequately funded, in violation of the state constitutional requirement that the State "offer all children the opportunity of a sound basic education." The court went on to interpret this as meaning that the public schools must teach "the basic literacy, calculating, and verbal skills necessary to enable children to eventually function productively as civic participants capable of voting and serving on a jury" (86 NY2d at 316).

In order to find a violation of this requirement, plaintiffs "have to establish a causal link between the present funding system and any proven failure to provide a sound basic education to New York City school children" (86 NY2d at 318).

The court ruled that plaintiffs did, indeed, establish a causal link between school funding and outcomes for NYC by showing that increased funding provides better teachers, facilities, and "instrumentalities of learning"—for example, smaller class sizes—and these improvements in turn yield improved student learning.

The requirement to establish a "causal link" between school resources and student achievement is significant, because it raises a potential disconnect between judicial requirements and social science standards for establishing causal relationships. As discussed in Chapter 4, establishing a causal connection in social science research is fraught with challenges, particularly when it concerns conditions required to prove that a given condition causes a particular behavior. If a causal relationship exists, we would expect a demonstrable relationship between school inputs and student achievement, either overall or at least for major subgroups (e.g., disadvantaged students). More will be said about the issue of causation during the discussion of New York research findings.

DOI: 10.4324/9781003399117-6

As a result of these court decisions, the state legislature reformed its school funding program in 2007 by enacting the Foundation Aid Formula program, promising an additional $5.5 billion directed at needy school districts. Unfortunately, due to a budget crisis in the 2009–2010 school year—undoubtedly due to the major national financial crisis in 2008—the state reneged on its new program and used state school funds to help balance the state budget. That led to the next adequacy lawsuit for New York State.

The New York Adequacy Lawsuit, *Maisto v. State of New York*

The main New York State adequacy lawsuit was the so-called Small Cities case, which originally saw 11 school districts bring suit against the state alleging the state was underfunding the state's public schools (*Maisto et al. v. State of New York*).[2] By the time the case went to trial in January 2015, eight school districts were still in the case. They claimed that the state had violated its constitutional duty to provide a "sound basic education" by reducing funding driven to districts through the state's Foundation Aid Formula, the funding mechanism that had been negotiated among the legislature, the executive and education constituents and enacted in 2007 as a response to the prior *CFE* court's rulings.

While those parties had agreed upon a formula that was designed to drive more state dollars to the state's schools, the recession following the financial crisis of 2008–2010 reduced state revenues and caused the state to reduce disbursements to districts under the Foundation Aid Formula and to take other steps that reduced expected increases in public school funding. The *Maisto* plaintiffs alleged that the Foundation Aid Formula's reductions exacerbated already-existing inadequacies in their schools and sought restoration of the reduced amounts plus additional funding amounts over and above the Foundation Aid Formula's provisions.

Data and Methods for the Armor Expert Study and Opinions

The State of New York operates one of the largest systems of elementary and secondary education in the nation. In the 2011–2012 school year, it enrolled 2.6 million students in kindergarten through Grade 12 organized into nearly 700 separate school districts (counting NYC as a single district). Approximately 200,000 students are enrolled at each grade level, and this means that achievement test scores are available for approximately 1.2 million students in Grades 3 to 8 each year. About 460,000 of these elementary and middle school students are enrolled in NYC schools, while 740,000 are enrolled in all other New York school districts.

The Case of New York State 65

For several reasons, NYC is not included in the analyses reported here. First, its schools are administered and organized differently than most school districts in the state, with 32 separate community school districts for elementary and middle schools (Grades K to 8) and five high school districts at the borough level (Manhattan, Queens, etc.). Second, since its total enrollment comprises more than a third of public school enrollment in the state, it has a potential disproportionate impact on relationships between school inputs and educational outcomes. Finally, and most important, no information is available for per pupil expenditures for the 32 community school districts, which means NYC is missing the most important school resource for an adequacy lawsuit.

The data used for this chapter comes from various databases maintained by the New York State Education Department, including the Basic Educational Data System and the Student Information Repository System. Specifically, this report uses several categories of individual student, school, and school district data for the school years 2010, 2011, and 2012. Individual student data include math and English Language Arts (ELA) achievement test scores for Grades 3 through 8. They also included student background characteristics such as free/reduced-price lunch, race, ethnicity, and limited English proficiency. School resource characteristics include average class sizes; teacher turnover rate; average teacher salary; and several indicators of teacher quality, including experience, education, percentage of certified teachers, and percentage of classes taught by teachers without certification in the fields taught. School district characteristics include enrollment, total per capita expenditures, and per capita expenditures for general education students.

A statistical summary of these student and school characteristics is shown in Table 6.1 for all New York State students (excluding NYC) enrolled in Grades 3 through 8 during the 2011–2012 school year. "District Type" is a distinction made by the State Department of Education that helps identify districts in terms of their overall socioeconomic status (SES) and demographic characteristics and the resulting potential need for assistance of various types. Census data on poverty and type of community are used to make this classification. The first category is Large City, which indicates Buffalo, Rochester, Syracuse, and Yonkers. This group of urban districts has the highest rate of poverty (80 percent free lunch) and disadvantaged minority students (75 percent Black and Hispanic). The next two, High Need Urban/Suburban and High Need Rural, are smaller districts but with fairly high poverty rates (60 and 40 percent free lunch, respectively); the Urban/Suburban districts also have 60 percent disadvantaged minority but the Rural districts have relatively low rates (only 10 percent). Finally, the Low Need districts have very low rates of poverty and disadvantaged minority (6 and 10 percent, respectively).

Student academic achievement is assessed by means of standardized tests, with math scores ranging from about 470 to 800. The standard deviation is

Table 6.1 Student and School Characteristics for New York Grades 3–8, 2012*

Characteristic	Number	Mean	SD	Minimum	Maximum
DISTRICT TYPE					
Large City	738,466	6%	24%	0%	100%
High Need Urban/ Suburban	738,466	12%	33%	0%	100%
High Need Rural	738,466	9%	29%	0%	100%
Average Need	738,466	48%	50%	0%	100%
Low Need	738,466	24%	43%	0%	100%
STUDENT ACHIEVEMENT					
Math score average	742,271	686	31	470	800
Reading score average	739,345	668	22	430	795
STUDENT BACKGROUND					
Free/red lunch	742,271	37%	48%	0%	100%
Black	742,271	11%	32%	0%	100%
Hispanic	742,271	13%	33%	0%	100%
Asian	742,271	4%	21%	0%	100%
White	742,271	70%	46%	0%	100%
Limited English	742,271	4%	19%	0%	100%
Special ed	742,271	13%	34%	0%	100%
SCHOOL RESOURCE					
Teachers not certified	742,165	4%	18%	0%	100%
Less than 3 years' experience	742,165	2.5%	3%	0%	20%
Master's degree	742,165	36%	27%	0%	100%
Out of field	742,165	1%	1.5%	0%	10%
Teacher turnover	738,415	13%	7.4%	0%	40%
Average class size	729,049	21.8	3.1	4	40
Teacher salary ($)	528,259	$78,841	$22,013	$37,840	$131,239
Per pupil, Total ($)	740,703	$20,449	$4,035	$12,158	$123,726
Per pupil, General Ed ($)	740,703	$11,262	$2,292	$5,628	$39,392

*Excludes NYC

approximately 30 points, meaning that about two-thirds of the math scores fall between 650 and 715 points. The tests are standardized separately for each grade level, so each grade level has approximately the same average and range.

It is well known in social science research that academic achievement is strongly related to student background characteristics, and particularly socioeconomic characteristics such as poverty, parent education level, occupation status, and many other family characteristics. Unfortunately, most school district and state education agencies record only one of these characteristics, that being related to the federal free lunch program, which corresponds approximately to family poverty. For this reason, student racial and ethnic background is also used in the analysis of academic achievement in order to control more fully for student background. It is emphasized here that *student racial and ethnic indicators are used as surrogates for other unmeasured SES characteristics.*

The strong relationship between student background and achievement test scores in New York can be illustrated by a few examples. Free lunch students score 676 on the math test compared to 695 for paid lunch students (and 884 for reduced lunch students), a difference of 19 points. This is nearly two-thirds of a standard deviation, and it is one of the stronger relationships between student SES and achievement. The only stronger relationship is between limited English and non-limited English students, which is 30 points—a full standard deviation. The difference between Black and White students' math scores is 20 points, but if we consider only Black and White students who are also free lunch, the difference drops to only 9 points. Most of that difference can be explained by other unmeasured SES differences.

Finally, Table 6.1 shows the school resource characteristics available for study, including teacher characteristics, average class sizes, and per capita expenditures. Note that total expenditures are almost twice the expenditures for general education, because total includes capital expenditures for construction and renovation as well as special education expenditures, which are much higher than those for regular students. For these reasons, the focus here is general education expenditures. Although the number of teachers who are not certified, teach out of field, or are relatively inexperienced is quite low, these categories have the strongest relationship with student achievement.

Relationship Between New York Academic Achievement and School Resources

There are several ways to assess the relationship between school resources and academic achievement. The first and most straightforward way divide variation in student test scores into two components, one that lies *within* a given school and one that lies *between* schools. Variability of student test scores *between* schools reflect all of resource and program differences that cause one school to perform better than another, whether or not measures of those resources or programs are available. Generally speaking, test score variations *within* a school cannot be attributable to a specific school program or resources, and therefore those variations can be attributed to individual student differences—again, whether or not we have measures for whatever those individual differences might be. The advantage of this method is that one does not have to have measures for specific school and student characteristics; the disadvantage is that one does not have any information about what school characteristics might be contributing to differences in test scores.

A second straightforward method is to compute simple correlations showing the relationship between students' test scores and measures of student characteristics or school resource. Correlations range from −1 to +1, with 0 indicating no relationship; a +1 indicates a perfect positive relationship between two variables and −1 indicates a perfect negative relationship.

Although correlation is not equivalent to causation, at least a correlation with a school characteristic means that there is a potential causal impact. Moreover, if a given school resource is not correlated with achievement, at least the burden shifts back to the school district to justify why they believe that there is an impact.

Finally, a multiple regression analysis can show how specific school resources relate to student test scores, taking into account differences in student background characteristics. The regression analysis can establish, at least, a *prima facie* case that a given resource is important for student achievement, because important student characteristics have been factored into the analysis. It does not prove causation, but at least the burden shifts to those claiming there is a causal relationship between school resources and achievement.

Within Versus between School Variation

Figure 6.1 shows the percentage of variation in test scores that are due to differences from one school to another, which is the upper limit, so to speak, of the impact of specific school resources that differ from one school to another within a school district. This variation is only 15 percent for ELA scores at elementary and middle schools, and it is 17 percent for elementary math scores. The highest between-school variation is for middle school math, although even here only 20 percent of the total variation in middle school math scores lies between schools. The overwhelming majority of variation, over 80 percent, lies within schools, and this is most likely attributed to differences in individual student background characteristics.

Correlations Between Achievement, Student Background, and School Resources

The evidence shown in Figure 6.1 strongly suggests that individual student characteristics are the primary causes for variations in achievement test scores. This conclusion is reinforced by the correlation analysis shown in Figure 6.2. This analysis shows the simple correlations between Grades 3 to 5 math scores and each of the student, school, and school district characteristics listed in Table 6.1. The correlations are shown separately for each year.

The pattern and magnitude of the correlations are quite similar from one year to the next.

In the case of school resources, with two exceptions, all of the correlations are weaker than ±.1 in all three years. The two exceptions are the percentage of teachers with master's degrees, which is .11 in all three years, and per pupil expenditures for general education students, which is .10 in 2011 and .12 in 2012. These are still very small correlations. A correlation of .10 means that the variation in expenditures explains only 1 percentage point of the variation in achievement.

The Case of New York State 69

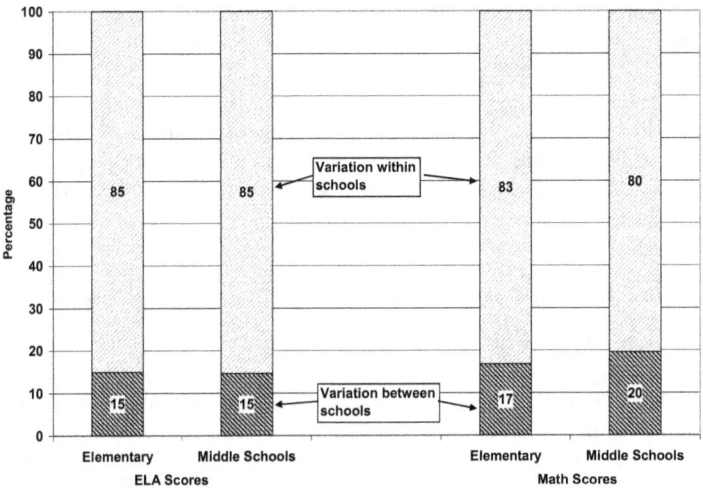

Figure 6.1 Variation of Test Scores Occurring Within Versus Between New York State Schools.

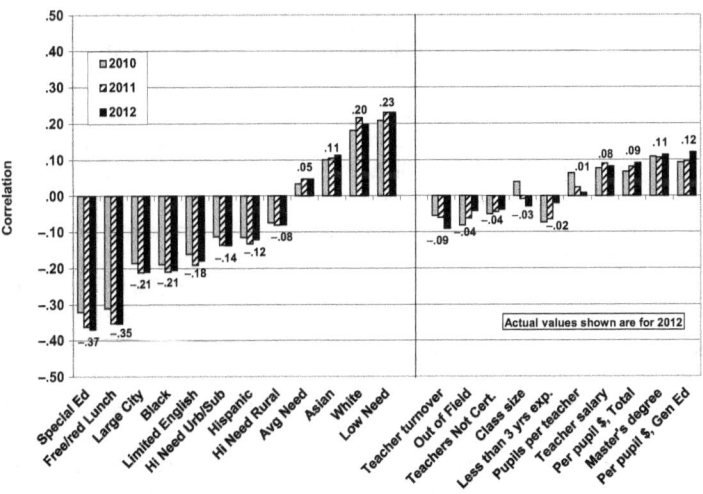

Figure 6.2 School Resource and Student Background Correlations for New York State Grades 3–5 Math Scores.

In contrast, the correlations between math scores and student background characteristics are much larger. The strongest correlation is for special education status (not an SES factor per se), which approaches −.4 in 2012. The strongest SES measure is free/reduced lunch, which is about −.35 in 2011 and 2012. Being Black and being from a large city have correlations of −.21, while being white is .20 and living in a Low Needs district is .23. With the exception of rural and average need districts, all of the remaining SES measures have correlations that are between ±.10 and ±.19.

Value-Added Regression Analysis[3]

While providing useful information about the relationship between school resources and student achievement, correlations provide only the simple relationship between achievement and a given student background characteristic. In order to provide an estimate of a school resource effect, one must execute a multiple regression analysis that provides an estimate of that resource's effect, taking into account (or holding constant) a student's background characteristics.

The regressions were run separately by grade level (elementary and middle schools) and within each grade level three models were estimated: one including class size and teacher salaries but excluding per capita expenditures, one including total per pupil expenditures but excluding class size and teacher salaries, and one like the former but excluding special ed students and replacing total expenditures with per pupil general education expenditures. Expenditures should not be included with class size and teacher salaries because of multicollinearity, since expenditures are largely a function of salaries and class size.

Figure 6.3 shows the multiple regression results for math scores. All of the district and student socioeconomic and demographic characteristics are statistically significant, despite controlling for students' prior year test scores. The SES characteristics with the strongest effects are free/reduced lunch (−.09), large district (−.08), and Black (−.05). Not surprisingly, prior year math scores have the strongest effect at .59. It is emphasized that because of the very large number of observations, both students and schools, even small relationships can be statistically significant. So in addition to evaluating whether a school resource has a statistically significant effect on test scores, the size of the effect must also be examined.

Teacher turnover, average class size, per pupil expenditures,[4] and teacher salary are the only school resource characteristics that are statistically significant in the expected direction, with standardized effect sizes of −.02, −.01, +.02, and +.03, respectively. These effect sizes, even though they are statistically significant, are very small and therefore their potential effects on elementary math scores are quite small.

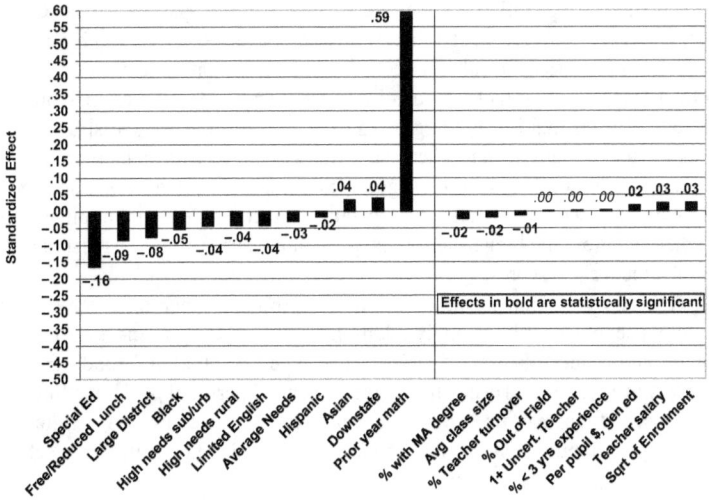

Figure 6.3 Standardized Effects for School Resources and Student Background for New York State Grades 3–5 Math, 2012.

Table 6.2 Estimated Effect of Increasing School Resources.

	Math Score	Resource
	Change	Change*
School Resource		
Class size	.54	−2.5 students
Teacher salary	.35	$9,000
Teacher turnover	.36	−.07
Per pupil $	.56	$2,500
Total change	1.8	

Note: *Approximately one standard deviation.

Table 6.2 shows the estimated impact on elementary math scores if the four school resources with statistically significant effects were increased/decreased by approximately one standard deviation. That is, if per pupil expenditures were increased by $2,500 and those increased funds reduced class size by 2.5 students, raised teacher salaries by $9,000, and reduced teacher turnover by 7 percentage points, math scores would increase by only 2 points. The results for reading are even lower—just a 1-point increase in elementary reading scores.

Another interpretation can be offered for the teacher salary effect. Given the difference between upstate and downstate salaries, an alternative model was tested that assumed salary effects could differ within these regions. In this model teacher salary had no statistically significant effect on math scores in upstate districts, but it had a larger positive effect for downstate districts, such that a $10,000 increase in teacher salary was associated with an increase of one point in math scores. This result suggests that teacher salary may be a surrogate for income or wealth, such that higher-salary districts reflect communities with higher incomes, and higher family income—not teacher salary—is responsible for the higher test scores.

A note of caution is also offered concerning teacher turnover effects. While a school board can apply additional funds directly to increase teacher salary and reduce class sizes, it is unclear whether additional funding alone will reduce turnover. Turnover involves teachers' personal decisions to leave a school, which may be for a variety of reasons, including travel time and housing availability. Many of these factors are outside the control of a school board.

Expert Study of Dr. Eric A. Hanushek

The following discussion of the New York adequacy case was adapted from an expert report submitted by Dr. Eric A. Hanushek. Dr. Hanushek has a long record of recognized scholarly work on the relationship between school resources and student achievement. In 2021, he was awarded the Yidan Prize in Education—the equivalent of a Nobel Prize for research in education.

An enormous amount of scientific analysis has focused on how spending and resources of schools relate to student outcomes. As a result, many education policy experts now believe that spending on schools is not systematically related to student outcomes. For example, over 15 years ago the National Research Council was asked to address issues of productivity within the system of funding schools. Its summary statement at that time was "money can and must be made to matter more than in the past if the nation is to reach its ambitious goal of improving achievement for all students."[5]

The New York state legislature currently provides funding for schools that exceed those in every state except the District of Columbia. New York State spending in 2011 was $19,708 per pupil (in 2013 dollars, adjusted for inflation), while the national average was $11,153—making New York spending 77 percent higher than the rest of the nation. Moreover, this spending was 46 percent higher than spending in 2000. New Jersey and Wyoming, two states with extensive court intervention in school spending, remain below New York in spending.

How is New York benefiting from its very high spending levels? Not very well. New York students consistently performed below the national average in

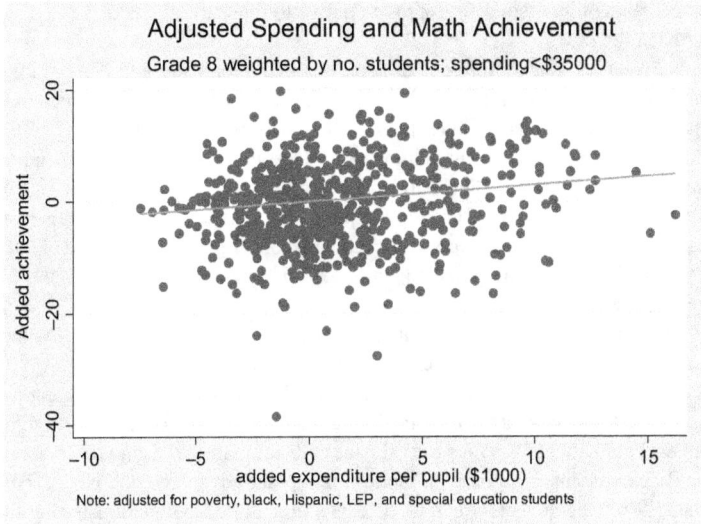

Figure 6.4 Adjusted Spending and Eighth-Grade Math Achievement in New York State.

2013, and in fact New York performed below the levels of more than 30 states with lower spending levels.

There is a small positive relationship between spending and achievement in some grades and subjects, but Hanushek's analyses show that the effect of added spending is always very small. While some of the relationships are statistically significant, the magnitude of the impact of different spending levels is always small. For example, Figure 6.4 plots the estimated impact of per pupil expenditures on math achievement in Grade 8, and it shows a slight upward-sloping line. While statistically significant, adding $5,000 per capita would yield only 1 or 2 points in eighth-grade math scores. Moreover, such gains could easily be obtained for little or no added spending through retargeting existing spending toward things that are known to matter, such as teachers with higher value added scores.

While New Jersey has always been a high-spending state, over recent decades its spending per pupil has increased dramatically compared to increases experienced by the United States as a whole. In 1990, New Jersey's inflation-adjusted current expenditures per pupil was just under $15,000. By 2010, it had risen to just over $19,000 before dropping slightly to $18,500 in 2011 due to the 2008 recession (all figures in 2013 dollars). Given these dramatic increases in spending in New Jersey, and if plaintiffs' assertions are correct, we should expect student test scores to improve relative to those of other states. This has not been the case.

New Jersey is a useful comparison. It is geographically and demographically close to New York State. It has experienced very large spending increases because of court orders. Nevertheless, it has very little to show for the added spending in terms of student achievement. Despite these very large spending increases, New Jersey's Black students actually progressed at the same rate as other states on the NAEP fourth-grade math test. This lack of expected performance gains for Black students also occurs for fourth-grade reading and eighth-grade reading. (Lack of gains is also observed for all students, nationally, for these grades and tests.)

The only slightly different pattern is found for eighth-grade math where New Jersey students (both Black and all students) perform better than the rest of the nation although the gains are fairly small relative to the overall spending increases; the results are shown in Figure 6.5. New Jersey Black eighth-grade students gain about 32 points over this period, compared to a gain of 25 points for Black students nationally. Despite this 7-point advantage, the New Jersey Black–White achievement gap in 2013 is still about 25 points, illustrating the challenge of closing this important education gap despite much higher spending on K–12 education.

If spending is not the answer to raising achievement, what is? Recent analysis of student outcomes emphasizes the pivotal role of effective teachers. The existing evidence on the impact of teachers suggests that improving the teaching force would have enormous impacts on students' outcomes and additionally on the state and national economy. This research, generally called value-added analysis, uses sophisticated statistical analysis to identify the variations in teacher impact on achievement test scores.[6] Similarly, there are good

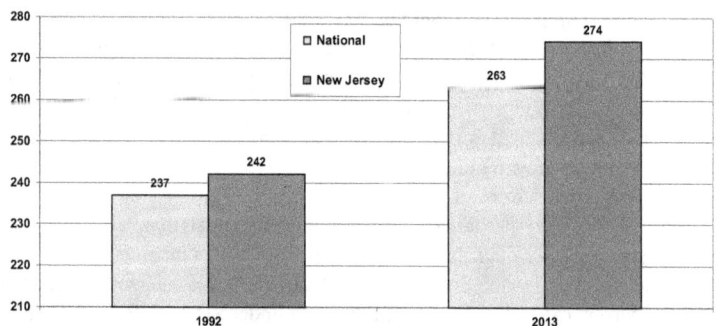

Figure 6.5 NAEP Eighth-Grade Math Scores for Black Students: United States Versus New Jersey.

estimates of the impact of achievement differences on the lifetime earnings of individuals.[7]

Figure 6.6 provides estimates of the present value of future student incomes according to where the teacher falls in the distribution of teacher effectiveness. The chart highlights the fact that the full impact of a teacher depends on two things: the effectiveness of the teacher and the number of students that he or she directly affects (i.e., the number of students in the class). A good teacher with 15 students in his or her class will have less overall impact than the same teacher with 20 students simply because with a larger class he or she is able to expand the learning of a greater number of students. Thus, the horizontal axis in the chart is class size. The vertical axis shows the present value of added incomes compared to an average teacher (the 0 point on the vertical axis).

Compared to an average teacher, in terms of individual incomes a 75th-percentile teacher annually can produce over $400,000 added lifetime income for a class of 30. This is the annual impact of a 75th-percentile teacher, and it would be repeated as long as the teacher continued to teach. On the other hand, a 10th-percentile teacher annually subtracts some $800,000 in present value (seen as the bottom line in Figure 6.6). In other words, retaining ineffective teachers is very costly to students.

It is difficult to overstate the importance of these findings about teacher effectiveness. School districts in general do not align salaries with teacher effectiveness. A highly effective teacher is generally just as likely to have a low salary as a high salary. The existing evidence suggests that teacher salaries are almost completely unrelated to effectiveness. Said differently, raising the salaries of all teachers according to existing salary schedules would raise the

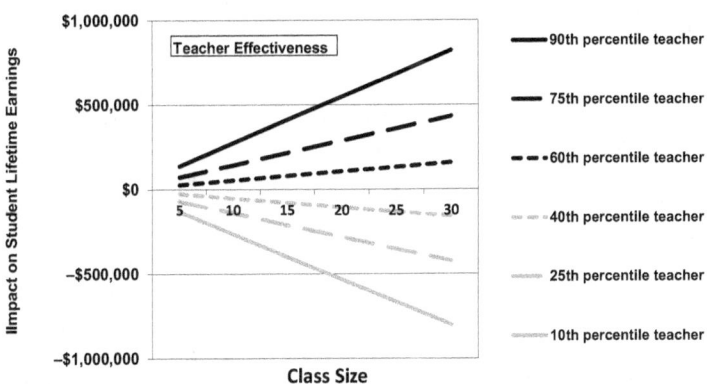

Figure 6.6 Impact on Student Lifetime Incomes by Class Size and Teacher Effectiveness.

salaries of both effective and ineffective teachers but would be unlikely to affect student achievement.

The New York Court Decisions

After hearing about two months of extensive evidence and testimony from the parties, the trial court—despite lamenting the "inadequate" performance of many of the children in the plaintiff districts—nevertheless ruled against the districts' claims against the state. The court held that the circumstances of the case were dissimilar from those surrounding the *CFE* case and concluded that "an examination similar to the analysis outlined in *CFE* regarding inputs, outputs, and causal linkage [was] not required."[8]

Instead, the court focused on the actions of the state following the final *CFE* decision and measured those against the facts and circumstances of the case. The court concluded that "the State ha[d] already taken steps to address the concerns raised in the *CFE* case and fundamentally changed the structure and methodology of education funding in the State of New York and ha[d] also increased the funding levels." The court also concluded that prior legislatures cannot bind future legislatures and therefore the 2007 enactment of the Foundation Aid Formula did not bar subsequent legislatures from adjusting the appropriations to the Foundation Aid Formula to respond to a worsening fiscal condition in state government. Because even after the cuts to the Foundation Aid Formula, the total increase in state school funding was still above the $2.5 billion increase that the Court of Appeals in *CFE III* found reasonable, the plaintiffs could not prevail on their claims that the state's failure to fully fund the Foundation Aid Formula was unconstitutional.

On appeal, the New York Appellate Division court reversed the trial court's decision and remanded the case to the trial court for additional fact-finding concerning the adequacy of the education inputs in each of the plaintiff districts and the issue of causation.[9]

On remand, the trial court did exactly that, filing a 113-page opinion addressing the issues the Appellate Division had specified. Assessing the overall level of resources in the eight plaintiff districts, the court found that each had access to a level of funding and inputs that met the standards set out in the Court of Appeals' *CFE I* decision in 1995. Because it did not find a lack of resources, the trial court did not address the question of causation.

Plaintiffs again appealed the trial court's dismissal of their claims to the appellate court, and once again, the appellate court reversed the trial court's second decision. Taking the unusual step of conducting a *de novo* review of the extensive evidence presented to the trial court, the appellate court went so far as to disagree with the trial court's findings that the plaintiffs' expert witnesses were not credible. The appellate court undertook its own analysis of the factual record on the resources in each of the plaintiff districts—relying extensively on the opinions of plaintiffs' experts who the trial court had found not credible—and concluded that the funding and resources available to the plaintiff districts were insufficient to provide a sound basic education to the districts' students. In conclusory terms, the appellate court also concluded that the inadequacies it found in the plaintiff districts were caused by the state's funding system.[10]

Notes

1 *Campaign for Fiscal Equity v. State of New York*, 86 (N.Y.2d 307, 655 N.E.2d 661, 631 N.Y.S.2d 565).
2 *Maisto et al. v. State of New York*, 56 Misc.3d 295 (NY Sup. Ct. 2016).
3 Value-added is a term indicating that a student's prior-year test score is included as a student background indicator.
4 The coefficient for per pupil expenditures was obtained in a separate regression, given that expenditures are determined largely by teacher salary and class size.
5 Ladd, H.F. and Janet, S.H. (1999). *Making Money Matter: Financing America's Schools*, Washington, DC, National Academy Press, 1.
6 Hanushek, E.A. (1971, May). Teacher characteristics and gains in student achievement: Estimation using micro data. *American Economic Review* 60(2): 280–288; Armor, D.J. Patricia, C.-O., Millicent, C., Niceima, K., Lorraine, M., Anthony, P., Edward, P. and Gail, Z. (1976). *Analysis of the School Preferred Reading Program in Selected Los Angeles Minority Schools*, Santa Monica, CA, Rand Corp; Aaronson, D., Lisa, B. and William, S. (2007, January). Teachers and student achievement in the Chicago public high schools. *Journal of Labor Economics* 25(1): 95–135; Chetty, R., John, N.F. and Jonah, E.R. (2013). *Measuring the Impacts of Teachers II: Teacher Value-Added and Student Outcomes in Adulthood*, Mimeo, Cambridge, MA, Harvard University; Hanushek, E.A. and Steven, G.R. (2012). The distribution of teacher quality and implications for policy. *Annual Review of Economics* 4: 131–157.
7 Hanushek, E.A. (2011, June). The economic value of higher teacher quality. *Economics of Education Review* 30(3): 466–479; Hanushek, E.A. et al. (2013, December). *Returns to Skills Around the World*, NBER Working Paper 19762, Cambridge, MA, National Bureau of Economic Research; Chetty, R. et al. (2014, September). Measuring the impacts of teachers II: Teacher value-added and the student outcomes in adulthood. *American Economic Review* 104(9): 2633–2679.
8 *Maisto et al. v. State of New York*, 51 N.Y.S.3d 800, 806 (Sup. Ct. 2016).
9 *Ibid*, 64 N.Y.S.3d 139 (App. Div. 2017).
10 *Ibid*, 149 N.Y.S.3d 599, 606–607 (discussion of expert witnesses) and 632–633 (discussion of causation) (App. Div. 2021).

7 The Case of New Mexico

David J. Armor and John R. Munich

Introduction

The New Mexico adequacy case begins with complaints filed against the State of New Mexico and its Public Education Department (PED) in 2014 by two groups of plaintiffs generally described as *Yazzie, et al. vs State of New Mexico, et al.* and *Martinez, et al. vs. State of New Mexico, et al.* The *Martinez* case was brought first by MALDEF, the Mexican American Legal Defense and Education Fund, on behalf of 17 parents of school-age children living throughout New Mexico. The *Yazzie* case was brought by the New Mexico Center for Law and Poverty on behalf of ten parents of school-age children and six school districts, including Santa Fe, Rio Rancho, and Gallup, among the largest school districts in New Mexico.[1]

These plaintiffs alleged that New Mexico and PED did not provide sufficient funding and resources for public schools in violation of the New Mexico state constitution, which provides for "free public schools sufficient for the education of . . . all the children of school age." More specifically, the complaints allege that the state does not provide sufficient funds and other resources so that children who are economically disadvantaged, or who have limited English proficiency (LEP), can attain proficiency levels comparable to non-disadvantaged students.

This chapter summarizes expert reports which evaluate two questions: (1) whether funding and school resources explain why children with economic and language disadvantages are less proficient than non-disadvantaged students, as assessed by statewide achievement testing, and (2) the extent to which additional funding and school resources can reduce achievement gaps between disadvantaged and non-disadvantaged students.[2] These evaluations rely primarily on data from New Mexico's extensive databases on student backgrounds, school resources, and student achievement test scores, although some reference is made to other data sources when appropriate.

Data and Methods

The data in this chapter come from files maintained by the New Mexico PED. These include math and reading achievement scores for students in Grades 3 to

8 and 11; student background data, such as race/ethnicity, free lunch status, and LEP; and a number of school and teacher characteristics, including per pupil expenditures, teacher salaries, teacher education, teacher experience, teaching credentials, pupil–teacher ratios, and teacher retention rates.

Achievement test data are available for approximately 750,000 students with math and reading scores for five school years starting in 2009–2010 and ending in 2013–2014. Table 7.1 shows summary statistics for student test scores, student background, and school resource characteristics for New Mexico students in Grades 3 to 8 during the 2013–2014 school year. The New Mexico public school population is predominantly from low-income families, with 72 percent of its students eligible for free/reduced lunch. Demographically, New Mexico public schools are majority Hispanic (62%), with the next largest group being non-Hispanic whites, which comprise about one-fourth of the student population. Another 10 percent are Native American, while black and Asian students comprise very small fractions of just 2 and 1 percent, respectively. Approximately 16 percent of Grades 3–8 students have limited

Table 7.1 New Mexico Average Student and School Characteristics.[a]

Characteristic	Mean or %	SD	Range
STUDENT BACKGROUND			
Math scores	37	12	0–80
Reading scores	40	11	0–80
% Free/red lunch	72%	45%	0–100%
% Asian	1%	11%	0–100%
% Black	2%	14%	0–100%
% Hispanic	62%	49%	0–100%
% Native American	10%	29%	0–100%
% White	24%	43%	0–100%
% Limited English	16%	37%	0–100%
% Disability	15%	35%	0–100%
SCHOOL/TEACHER RESOURCES			
Teacher experience	7	7.3	0–43
% Master's degree	39%	49	0–100%
Teacher salary	$44,248	8,472	$12,075–$81,304
% Teacher retention[b]	74%	13%	0–100%
% Level 2 credential[c]	52%	50%	0–100%
% Level 3 credential	29%	45%	0–100%
Pupils per teacher	15	2.6	0–27
Net per pupil expend.[c]	$7,420	$1,151	$5,130–$33,092

Notes
[a] These figures are based on approximately 150,000 public school students in Grades 3 to 8 in 2013–2014.
[b] Percentage of teachers remaining in the same school from the prior year.
[c] Level 2 is defined as a nine-year professional certificate and level 3 is a nine-year instructional leader.
[d] Same as operational; had a slightly higher correlation with achievement than total.

English skills (most likely due to being recent Hispanic immigrants), and another 15 percent have a disability qualifying them for special education services.

The average math and reading scores in 2014 were 37 and 40, respectively. Since proficiency was defined as a score of 40 or higher, in that year the average New Mexico elementary and middle school student was proficient or above in reading but not quite proficient in math.

The school and teacher resources available for this study include several measures of a teacher's professional training and background believed important for effectiveness and proficiency. These include years of experience, higher degrees, and licensure. Also available are pupils per teacher, which evaluates instructional effort, teacher salary, and net per pupil expenditures.[3] As of 2014, New Mexico teachers had an average of seven years of experience, and 39 percent had a master's or higher degree. Teacher average salary was $44,000 and just over 80 percent had a level 2 or 3 credential. The average pupils per teacher was 15, and the average teacher retention rate was 74 percent (about three-fourths of teachers in a school are in the same school the following year). Finally, the average operational expenditure per student is approximately $7,400.

The primary method used for estimating the effect of school resources on achievement in the New Mexico case is value-added regression (see Chapter 4), where test scores in one year are predicted as a function of test scores in the preceding year, along with student background and school resource variables in the current year. The regression gives estimates for the effect that a given factor has on test scores taking into account all of the other factors in the analysis. Before carrying out that analysis, we consider the "potential" effect of school resources by examining the source of achievement variation, and how much of that variation occurs between or within schools or school districts.

The Effects of School Resources on Achievement

There are several different ways to evaluate the potential effect of school resources on achievement. One way is called "partitioning" variation in test scores into two portions: a portion occurring within schools or districts and a portion lying between schools or districts. Since variations in test scores within a school or district are caused primarily by individual student differences, this method is useful for estimating the maximum potential effect of any school- or district-wide resource.

A second way is to compute correlations between achievement and various student background factors and school resource factors. Finally, the most accurate way to estimate school resource effects is to conduct a multiple regression analysis, which considers the relationship between student achievement and a given school resource, controlling for a student's background characteristics.

Estimating Potential Effect of School Resources: Within Versus Between Variation of Test Scores

Within and between analyses evaluate the potential effect of school and school district programs and policies on achievement by dividing the total variation of test scores into that portion occurring within schools or districts and that portion lying between schools or districts. Variation within a district cannot be affected by district-wide policies or resources such as expenditures, and variations within a school cannot be affected by school-wide programs or policies such as pupil–teacher ratio or a special program in that school. Since variations in test scores within a school or district are caused primarily by individual student differences, this method is useful for estimating the maximum potential effect of any school- or district-wide resource.

Figures 7.1 shows the percentage of variation in test scores that occurs between individual schools in the State of New Mexico. Only 11 percent of the variation in reading scores and about 14 percent of the variation in math occur between schools, suggesting that school-wide resources such as teacher characteristics (e.g., teacher experience or average salaries) can affect, at best, only about one-tenth of the variation in test scores. This suggests that about 90 percent of the variation in test scores is determined by variations among individual students, whether or not that variation is explained by measured student characteristics. At the school-district level, only about 5 percent of the variation in test scores lies between districts. This means, for example, that a

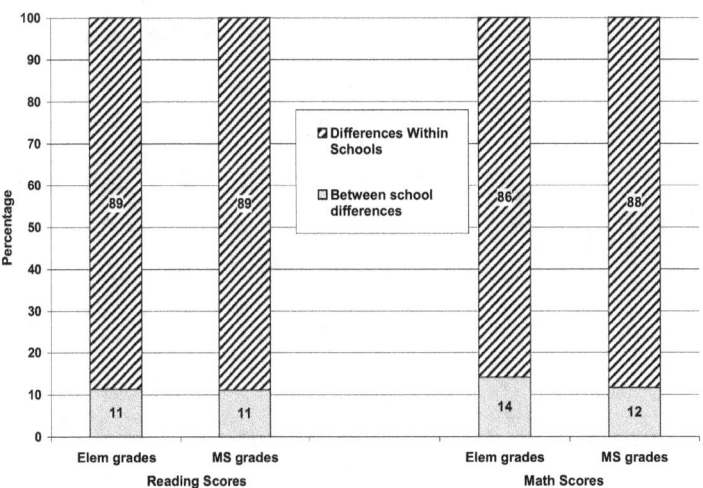

Figure 7.1 Variation in Test Scores Occurring Within Versus Between New Mexico Schools, 2014.

district-wide resource, such as per pupil expenditures, can impact, at best, only 5 percent of test score variation.

Correlation and Regression Analysis

The second method for assessing the potential effects of student, teacher, and school characteristics is to examine the simple correlation between a given student or school characteristic and test scores. Figures 7.2 and 7.3 show these correlations for Grades 3 to 5 math and reading scores, respectively, using New Mexico test scores between 2010 and 2014 (over 350,000 observations). Simple correlations range from −1 to +1, where +1 is a perfect positive association (as the characteristic goes higher, so does achievement), a −1 is perfect inverse relationship (as the characteristic goes higher, achievement goes lower), and 0 means no relationship in one direction or the other. A correlation of ±.1 or less is considered a very weak association, while a correlation of .5 or higher is considered fairly strong in social science research.

The patterns of correlations are quite similar for both math and reading scores, with all of the school and teacher resource characteristics having very small correlations. Of these, teacher retention has the strongest correlation, but that correlation is only .11 with elementary math scores and .09 with reading scores. All the remaining school/teacher resource correlations are less than .10. For math we have .08 for license level and salary, and .04 for

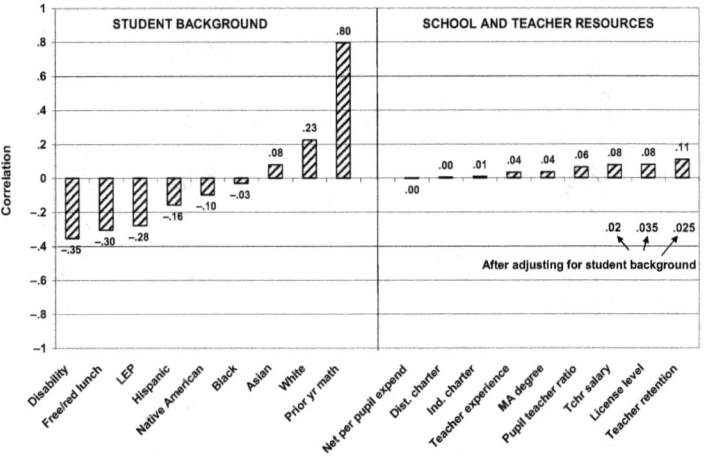

Figure 7.2 Correlations and Significant Regression Coefficients for New Mexico Grades 3–5 Math Scores.

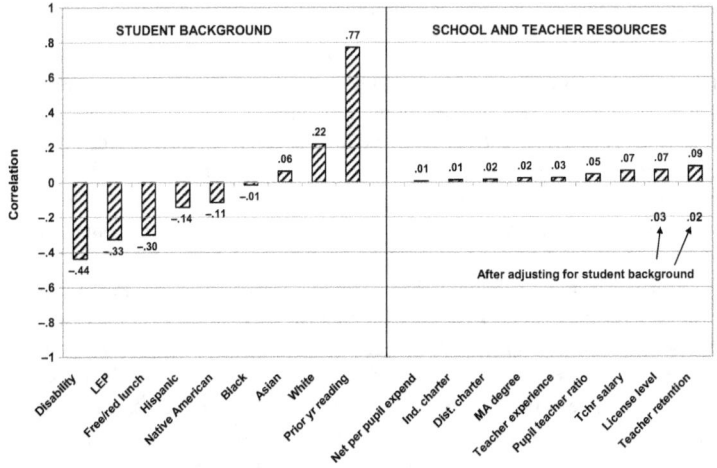

Figure 7.3 Correlations and Significant Regression Coefficients for New Mexico Grades 3–5 Reading Scores.

MA degree and years of experience (the .06 for pupil–teacher ratio is in the wrong direction). The reading correlations are approximately .01 smaller in each case. Per pupil expenditures have a 0 correlation for math and a very small correlation of .01 for reading.

In contrast, student background characteristics have much stronger correlations, particularly (for math) being white (+.23), LEP status (−.28), and free lunch (−.30). The highest correlation is observed for a student's prior year test score (.8 for math and .77 for reading), which clearly demonstrates that the best predictor of student achievement is that student's prior year score.

Also shown on Figures 7.2 and 7.3 are those regression coefficients for school and teacher resources that are statistically significant (at $p \leq .05$) after controlling for the student background characteristics. There are just three statistically significant coefficients for math, which are very small: approximately .03 for teacher retention and license level and .02 for teacher salary. There are only two for reading: .02 for teacher retention and .03 for license level.

It should be noted that these regression analyses were also carried out for middle school Grades 6 to 8, and in general the relationships were notably weaker. In fact, for math scores the only school resource to have a statistically significant effect for Grades 6 to 8 was teacher retention, and that standardized effect was only .02. Standardized effects for all the other teacher and school resources were .01 or less.

Estimated Effects of School and Student Characteristics Using SBA Test Results

The effects of school and student characteristics on achievement are estimated using the results of the multiple regression analysis, which allows estimation of a school or teacher characteristic holding all other characteristics constant, including the student's prior year test score. This approach estimates the contribution of a given school or teacher resource above and beyond the contribution of student demographic or socioeconomic background and prior year test score.

Tables 7.2 and 7.3 show the estimated effects of school and teacher resources on elementary SBA scores from 2010 to 2014 after taking a student's background into account. As discussed earlier, the only statistically significant resources for Grades 3–5 math are teacher's credential levels, teacher salary, and a school's retention rate for teachers. Per pupil expenditures, teacher experience, teacher education, and pupil–teacher ratio do not have statistically significant impacts on math scores, once student background is taken into account. For Grades 3–5 reading, only credentials and retention are statistically significant, and teacher salaries are not significant. For a given change in a characteristic, the estimated changes in actual test scores are shown in the third column, and "standardized" effects are shown in the fourth column.

Table 7.2 Estimated Effects of School/Student Characteristics on Grades 3–5 SBA Math Scores, 2010–2014[a]

Characteristic	Change or Comparison	Test score Changes	Standardized Effects[b]
TEACHER/SCHOOL			
Level 3 credential	vs. Level 1	0.9	.036
Level 2 credential	vs. Level 1	0.4	.019
Teacher retention	Plus 10%	0.2	.025
Teacher salary	Plus $10,000	0.2	.017
*STUDENT			
Asian student	vs. non-Hisp white	1.4	.012
Black student	vs. non-Hisp white	−1.4	−.016
Native American student	vs. non-Hisp white	−1.3	−.031
Hispanic student	vs. non-Hisp white	−0.8	−.032
Limited English	vs. non-LEP	−1.3	−.041
Free/reduced lunch	vs. not eligible	−1.5	−.055
Disability	vs. non-disabled	−2.9	−.085

Notes
[a] Per pupil expenditures, teacher experience, teacher with MA degree, pupils per teacher, and charters do not have statistically significant effects.
[b] The effect on math scores (in sd units) of a one standard deviation change in the characteristic.

Table 7.3 Estimated Effects of School/Student Characteristics on Grades 3–5 SBA Reading Scores, 2010–2014.[a]

Characteristic	Change or Comparison	Test score Changes	Standardized Effects[b]
TEACHER/SCHOOL			
Level 3 credential	vs. Level 1	0.7	.029
Level 2 credential	vs. Level 1	0.4	.017
Teacher retention	Plus 10%	0.2	.018
STUDENT BACKGROUND			
Asian student	vs. non-Hisp white	1.2	.012
Black student	vs. non-Hisp white	−1.0	−.012
Hispanic student	vs. non-Hisp white	−0.7	−.029
Native American student	vs. non-Hisp white	−1.3	−.035
Free/reduced lunch	vs. not eligible	−1.6	−.063
Limited English	vs. non-LEP	−2.0	−.072
Disability	vs. non-disabled	−3.8	−.124

Notes
[a] Per pupil expenditures, teacher experience, teacher with MA degree, pupils per teacher, and charters do not have statistically significant effects.
[b] The effect on math scores (in sd units) of a one standard deviation change in the characteristic.

Statistical significance is not a guarantee of educationally meaningful impact on student outcomes. Considering math scores first, where estimated resource effects are somewhat stronger, an increase in a school's teacher retention of 10 percentage points (e.g., from 65 to 75 percent) would be expected to increase SBA math scores by just .2 points, and the same is true for a teacher salary increase of $10,000. The potential effects of teachers with higher credentials are stronger, .4 points for a teacher with a level 2 credential versus one with a five-year standard credential, and .9 for a teacher with a level 3 credential. These potential effects are limited, however, because 80 percent of the teachers already hold level 2 and level 3 credentials (see Table 7.1).

Therefore, assuming that a $10,000 teacher salary increase was sufficient to raise teacher retention rates by 10 percentage points, and that all teachers were level 2 and level 3 (60 and 40 percent, respectively), our regression results estimate that math scores would be expected to rise by only about a half point overall.

For elementary reading scores, the estimated effects of school resources are even smaller. Teacher salary joins per pupil expenditures, experience, education, and pupil–teacher ratio in having no statistically significant effects on SBA reading scores. The effect of a level 3 credential is slightly smaller (.7), while the effects of a level 2 credential and teacher retention are the same as for math scores. *Thus the expected effect of having all level 2 and level 3 teachers plus an increase in retention rate of 10 percentage points would be less than a half point increase in elementary reading scores.*

In contrast, the estimated effects of student background factors are quite strong, even after controlling for prior year test score. All of the characteristics are statistically significant, and for math scores all but Hispanic status have estimated effects greater than 1 point. Hispanic status has an estimated effect of −.8 points compared to a non-Hispanic white student. These effects are additive, so the expected difference in math scores between a elementary white non-LEP student who is not on free lunch and a Hispanic LEP student who is eligible for free/reduced lunch would be about 3.5 points, assuming their prior year scores were the same and all of their school resources were the same (−.8 + −1.3 + −1.5 = −3.6). The estimated effects of student background factors for reading scores are similar, except—not surprisingly—the effect for LEP status is stronger,

The estimated effects of school resources for middle school students (Grades 6 to 8) are generally weaker than for the elementary grades, with one exception for reading scores. For math achievement, teacher retention rate is the only school resource that has a statistically significant relationship with math scores and the effect is slightly smaller. For reading achievement, retention rate and teacher credentials have effects similar to those for Grades 3–5, although the level 3 effect is smaller at 0.5. In addition, per pupil expenditures are statistically significant, although the effect is very small: a $1,000 increase in per pupil expenditure is associated with an increase of just one-tenth of a point. Even with the addition of an expenditure effect for middle school reading, increasing these resources for middle school students would have smaller estimated effects than for elementary students (less than one-half of a point).

Finally, to illustrate the very weak relationship between school expenditures and achievement, Figure 7.4 plots the relationship between operational school expenditures and math test scores for the 15 largest school districts in New Mexico, where the math scores are adjusted for student background. The districts have been sorted in order of adjusted math scores, with the lowest scoring districts on the left—Farmington and Carlsbad, whose average scores are about 35, and the highest scoring districts on the right, with Gadsden being highest with an average score of 43. Note that Carlsbad has the second-lowest adjusted math scores but the highest per student expenditures (about $8,100), while Gadsden has the highest adjusted math scores but spends only about $6,800 per student. The graph shows very clearly why there is a virtually no relationship between expenditures and background-adjusted achievement in New Mexico.

The expert report of Eric A. Hanushek also concluded that there was at best a very small relationship between additional spending and student achievement, as illustrated by Figure 7.5. The Hanushek report had similar exhibits showing very weak or no relationship between spending and achievement at various grade levels.

The Case of New Mexico 87

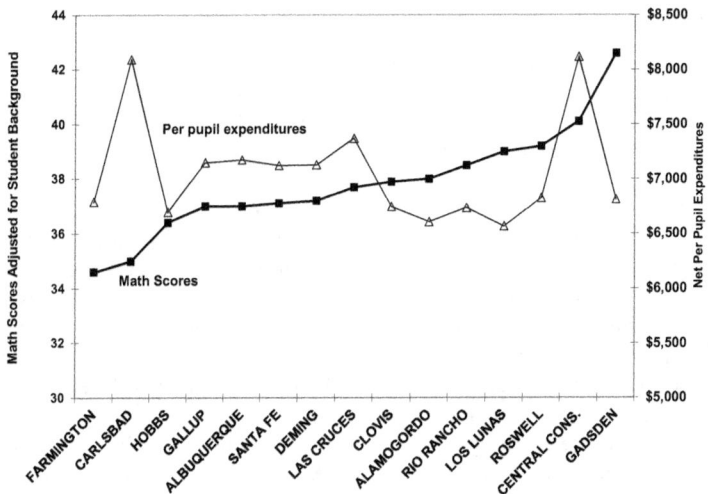

Figure 7.4 Math Scores Adjusted for Student Background vs. Per Pupil Expenditures for 15 Largest New Mexico Districts.

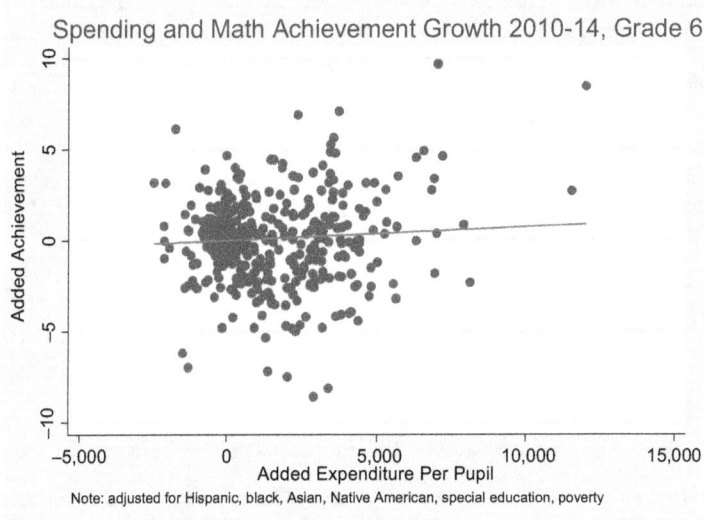

Figure 7.5 Relationship Between Spending and Math Achievement, All Districts.

Martinez–Yazzie **Court Decisions**

Following an eight-week hearing in the summer of 2018, the First Judicial District Court found that the State of New Mexico had violated student fundamental rights by failing to provide a sufficient public education, as requires by the New Mexico state constitution.

> It is not a sufficient answer to this systemic problem of poor outcomes by at-risk students to urge, as Defendants do, that the problems are caused by socio-economic factors not attributable to the school system. While the initial cause of the poor outcomes may not be the schools, steps can be taken by the educational system to overcome the adverse impacts of a student's background. As recognized by the legislature in Section 22–1–1.2, every child can learn and succeed. This conclusion is supported by the evidence.[4]

The evidence relied upon, mainly, was a report by plaintiffs' expert Jesse Rothstein. Rothstein testified about studies he and others have undertaken, showing that additional expenditures can raise student achievement. There is no indication that the Judge considered any of the analyses carried out by Armor and Hanushek, as illustrated here. Moreover, the State elected not to appeal the ruling.

In March 2019, the state passed a landmark budget, including an increase in the education budget by nearly $500 million. In October 2019, the *Yazzie* plaintiffs filed a motion for the court to direct the state to "take immediate and extraordinary steps to fulfill the mandates" outlined in Judge Singleton's original order, citing noncompliance. Claiming the state had not complied with the court's order, the *Martinez* plaintiffs filed a motion requesting further information from the education department.

In March 2020, the State moved to dismiss the lawsuit, claiming that the requirements for the courts injunction have been satisfied. Later, in March, all hearings were postponed due to the COVID-19 emergency. No new Court actions have taken place since that time.

Notes

1. *Yazzie v. State of New Mexico* (No. D-101-CV-2014-02224 N.M. Dist. Ct. 2014), consolidated with *Martinez v. State of New Mexico* (No. D-101-CV-2014-00793 N.M. Dist. Ct. 2014).
2. Unless otherwise noted, the empirical results in this chapter are drawn from the expert report of David J. Armor; some results are also drawn from the expert report of Eric A. Hanushek and will be noted as such.
3. They are also described as "operational" expenditures. Total per pupil expenditures was also available, but net expenditures had a stronger correlation with student achievement.
4. *Martinez v. State of New Mexico*, Westlaw 9489378 at 19 (slip op.) (N.M. Dist. Ct. July 20, 2018).

8 The Case of South Dakota

David J. Armor and John R. Munich

The South Dakota Case

The education adequacy lawsuit in South Dakota (*Davis v. South Dakota*) was initiated in 2006, when a group of families in three small school districts—Bonne Homme (Tyndall), Florence, and Garretson—sued the State of South Dakota for violating various sections of Article VIII of the South Dakota Constitution, which state:

> "The stability of a republican form of government depending on the morality and intelligence of the people, it shall be the duty of the Legislature to establish and maintain a general and uniform system of common schools throughout the state." (Section 1) and "The Legislature shall make such provision by general taxation and by authorizing the school corporations to levy such additional taxes as with the income from the permanent school fund shall secure a thorough and efficient system of common schools throughout the state." (Section 15)[1]

In its opinion on findings of fact and final decision, the trial court noted that this lawsuit was not an isolated case, considering that other adequacy lawsuits had been brought in other states. Most notably, the court cited the New York City adequacy case discussed in Chapter 6, *Campaign for Fiscal Equity v. State*, 719 N.Y.S.2d 475, 480 (N.Y. Sup. 2001). Stating that education has been recognized by courts as a "vital" feature of democratic societies, the Court also noted that this Court is not a "super-legislature," and that a statute cannot be declared unconstitutional "until it is proved beyond a reasonable doubt." The South Dakota Supreme Court affirmed the trial court's holding for the defendants on all counts. *Davis*, 804 N.W.2d 618 (S.D. 2011).

The Adequacy Lawsuit

During the discovery period, the plaintiffs and the State entered an agreement that a set of "focus districts" would be selected by plaintiffs and defendants for

DOI: 10.4324/9781003399117-8

the purpose of discovery and establishing evidence for the case. The plaintiffs selected 11 focus districts. In addition to the original plaintiff districts, they selected Aberdeen, Custer, Doland, Faith, Newell, Rapid City, Tulare, and Willow Lake. With the exception of Rapid City and Aberdeen, which were the second- and third-largest school districts in the State, the remaining plaintiff focus districts were much smaller with enrollments generally under 3,000 students.

The State defendants selected ten focus districts: Avon, Faulkton, Flandreau, Hamlin, McLaughlin, Miller, Sanborn Central, Sisseton, Shannon County, and White River. These were all small school districts with enrollments ranging from a few hundred to approximately 2,500 K–12 students. The Court noted that the focus district agreement was an agreement among the parties for the purposes of discovery, and the agreement was not approved (or required) by the Court. Later, but prior to the hearing, the plaintiffs dropped Aberdeen, Custer, Garretson, Newell, and Tulare. The State defendants, however, included those districts in their various assessments and analyses introduced into evidence, and in their proposed findings of fact, submitted to the court after the close of evidence.

Expert studies were carried out by David J. Armor and Eric A. Hanushek using South Dakota education data. The Sixth Judicial Circuit court cited, and agreed with, numerous conclusions offered by Armor and Hanushek based on these expert studies. For example, the Court summarizes conclusions from one of Armor's studies:

> Dr. Armor also conducted a rigorous statistical regression analysis. It demonstrated that, after controlling for (or taking into account) differences in South Dakota students' family and socioeconomic (SES) circumstances, nearly all of the same school resource measures (excepting teacher experience levels) had no statistically significant relationship with STEP outcomes.[2]

Dr. Hanushek also carried out independent analyses of the South Dakota data on relationship between achievement and school resources, and the Court summarized many of his expert opinions. For example:

> Dr. Hanushek also presented his own study of the Dakota STEP data which yielded results that were consistent with Dr. Armor's work—Dr. Hanushek found no statistically valid relationship between South Dakota student achievement and the level of resources in the schools (as measured by a number of different "inputs").[3]

Another conclusion cited by the Court was an analysis of the variation in test scores that lay within and between school districts. The Court said:

> Dr. Armor analyzed the variations in South Dakota students' test scores that existed within individual school districts, as opposed to between

the State's districts. What he found confirms his other work in this case—of all the variation in South Dakota test scores for the years and students he studied, Dr. Armor found that only about 10 percent of the differences in student test scores occurred between school districts while around 90 percent of the variations occurred within individual school districts. . . . The conclusion Dr. Armor drew from these results is that the significant resource and school policy differences that exist between South Dakota school districts are associated only slightly with variations in student outcomes, whereas the family and background differences that exist among children within districts (where the same district educational policies and level of resources apply to all children) are associated with around 90 percent of the variations in student test results.[4]

Data and Methods

Before discussing the Court's final conclusions, we will summarize several of Armor's expert analyses of the relationship between school resources and student achievement that laid the foundation for his expert opinions. Table 8.1 shows summary statistics for the data used in both Armor's and Hanushek's statistical analyses. Although some analyses were carried out using only the focus districts, the main statistical analyses carried out by defendants' experts utilized the full statewide dataset consisting of approximately 300,000 observations on 75,000 different students.

Per pupil expenditures were approximately $6,700 statewide, and teachers' salary averaged $34,000. Teachers had an average of 15 years of experience, and 24 percent had master's degree. Statewide, the number of teachers who were uncertified was less than 1 percent, although a very small number of school districts (approximately ten) had as many as 24 percent uncertified teachers. These were generally very small districts in rural areas. Finally, the average number of pupils per teacher was 14, with a maximum of 19.

Table 8.1 shows two types of test scores. Standardized scores have a mean of 100 and standard deviation of 10 for all grades. This version of the test scores is used in most analyses. The table also shows scale scores, which can be used to demonstrate growth in achievement over time. Scale scores are used for showing achievement growth in Figure 8.1.

Note that, in contrast to the states discussed in other adequacy cases in this volume, the South Dakota student population was predominantly White during the time of the study. In 2007, White students comprised 79 percent of the Grades 3 to 8 population, while Black and Hispanic students accounted for only 2 percentage points each. The largest minority student population in this state was Native American, with 16 percent of the Grades 3 to 8 student population in that year. Asian students comprised 1 percent of the South Dakota student population during this time period.

Table 8.1 Basic Statistics for South Dakota Data (Grades 3–8, 2003 to 2007).

Variable	N	Mean	SD	Minimum	Maximum
Math score (standardized)	279,924	98.7	9.2	46.9	144.3
Reading score (standardized)	279,460	98.3	8.5	57.4	137.2
Math scale scores	279,924	668	47	401	903
Reading scale scores	279,460	664	41	469	851
Per pupil expend.	297,909	$6,745	$1,751	$4,577	$27,947
Teacher salary	297,909	$34,371	$3,657	$22,500	$44,335
Teacher experience (years)	297,909	15.0	2.4	1	24
% MA degree	297,933	24.3	14.9	0	59.0
% Uncertified	297,909	0.7	1.6	0.0	24.2
Pupils per teacher	297,909	14.1	2.5	2.5	18.8
% Free lunch status	297,935	37%	48%	0%	100%
Title I	297,935	24%	43%	0%	100%
% Disability	297,935	15%	35%	0%	100%
% LEP status	297,935	4%	21%	0%	100%
% Native American	297,935	12%	33%	0%	100%
% Hispanic	297,935	2%	14%	0%	100%
% Black	297,935	2%	13%	0%	100%
% Asian	297,935	1%	10%	0%	100%
% White	297,935	83%	38%	0%	100%

Note: Number of individual students ≈76,000.

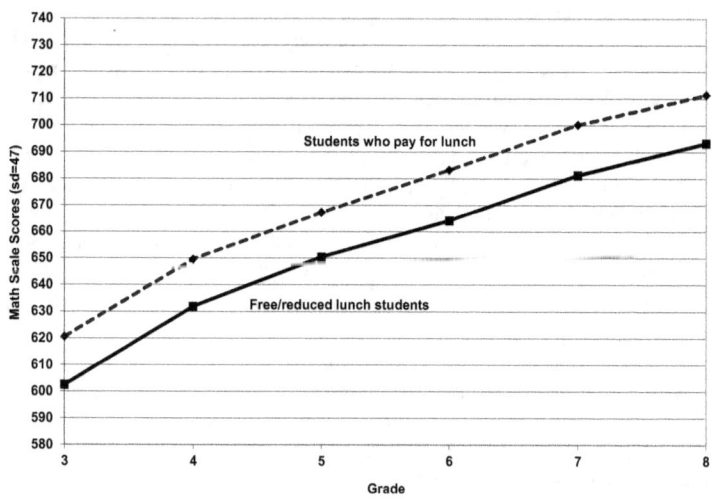

Figure 8.1 South Dakota Math Achievement Gains from Grades 3 to 8 by Poverty Status.

A number of the focus districts selected for the South Dakota case have higher percentages of Native American students. For example, among the plaintiffs' focus groups, Rapid City is 18 percent Native American. Among the defendant's focus groups, four are majority or predominantly Native American: Sisseton at 56 percent, White River at 78 percent, McLaughlin at 92 percent, and Shannon County at 92 percent.

It should also be noted that while a little under two-fifths of the South Dakota student population are at or below poverty (as indicated by free lunch status), many of the focus districts had much higher poverty levels: Faith, Willow Lake, Sanborn, and Sisseton students at approximately 60 percent poverty; while McLaughlin, Shannon, and White River students had poverty levels over 90 percent. These variations are crucial for understanding achievement test score patterns, given the strong relationship that exists between poverty and test scores.

The next two figures illustrate the importance of adjusting achievement test scores for socioeconomic factors before interpreting the potential effects of teacher characteristics and other school resources. Given the possibility that school resources such as teacher salaries, education, experience, and so forth are correlated with community economic characteristics—for example, more highly qualified teachers may seek out school districts with more middle-class families—it becomes necessary to control for student economic status before interpreting relationships between student achievement and teacher characteristics.

The relationship between student economic status and growth in math achievement is shown in Figure 8.1 using math scale scores. South Dakota students grow substantially in math as they progress from Grade 3 to Grade 8 and the subject matter becomes increasingly complex, going from integer arithmetic to fractions to algebra. The rate of growth slows somewhat over time, starting with annual growth of 30 points from Grades 3 to 4, a growth of 17–18 points per year for next three years, and then finally only about 11 points between Grades 7 and 8 as the limits of math knowledge is approached for the majority of students.

These results clearly demonstrate the challenge of overcoming poverty-induced achievement gaps, which start well before students enter kindergarten or Grade 1.[5] Note that the gains of low-income student are virtually identical to the gains of higher-income students, but because the starting gap is so large (about half of a standard deviation), it is very difficult for disadvantaged students to catch up. In effect, their rates of learning would have to be much higher than higher-income groups in order to catch up by eighth grade.

Because of these poverty-induced achievement gaps, it is necessary to adjust test scores for student background before estimating the strength of a given school resource on achievement. Figure 8.2 shows how the seventh-grade achievement gaps between White and Native American students changes after first adjusting for socioeconomic status and then adjusting for third-grade

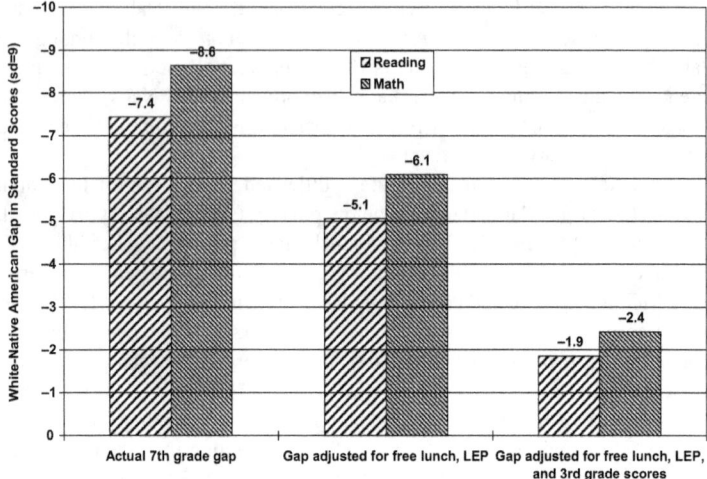

Figure 8.2 Explaining the Achievement Gap Between White and Native American Students.

achievement—which we assume to be similar to adjusting for a host of family background factors that explains the academic skills gap prior to starting school. The standardized math score gap of nearly 9 points—very close to one standard deviation—is reduced by a third, to 6 points, after controlling for free lunch and limited English proficiency (LEP) status. When seventh-grade scores are further adjusted for a student's third-grade scores, the gap is reduced to about 2.5 points. In other words, the Native American–White achievement gap for South Dakota seventh graders is reduced by nearly three-fourths after controlling for two student socioeconomic background characteristics and early achievement.

The Effects of School Resources on Achievement

The expert studies for the South Dakota case covered a variety of topics and utilized a variety of analytic methods and models to estimate the impact of school resources. The first method, which was emphasized in the trial judge's Findings of Fact, was the analysis of test score variation both within and between school districts. Between-district variation is most likely associated with differing district policies and practices, whereas within-district variation is more likely caused by differing compositions of student background characteristics.

The Case of South Dakota

This analysis demonstrates that about 90 percent of the variation in both reading and math achievement scores lies within districts, again demonstrating the importance of student background characteristics versus school resources. Between-district variation is slightly higher for math scores than reading scores, which suggests that school and teacher resources are somewhat more important for math scores and reading scores.

The most important results for Armor's expert study are shown in Figure 8.3 for math scores. This figure shows both simple correlations and standardized effects for school resources after controlling for student background. First, the right-most portion of the chart shows the simple correlations between math achievement and student background characteristics. These correlations are moderate in size, ranging between .2 and .3 in absolute value. The strongest correlation is −.31 between Title I status (a family poverty indicator) and math achievement, and close behind is having a disability with a correlation of −.28. The correlation for free lunch status is next at −.26, followed by Native American at −.22 and White at +.24. Interestingly, the correlations for Hispanic and Black, −.07 and −.08, respectively, are much lower than correlations observed in earlier chapters. For example, in the National Assessment of Educational Progress discussed in Chapter 5, the correlations for Hispanic and Black are −.25 and −.23, respectively. This no doubt reflects lower poverty rates for Hispanic and Black students in South Dakota. The correlation for LEP is −.17.

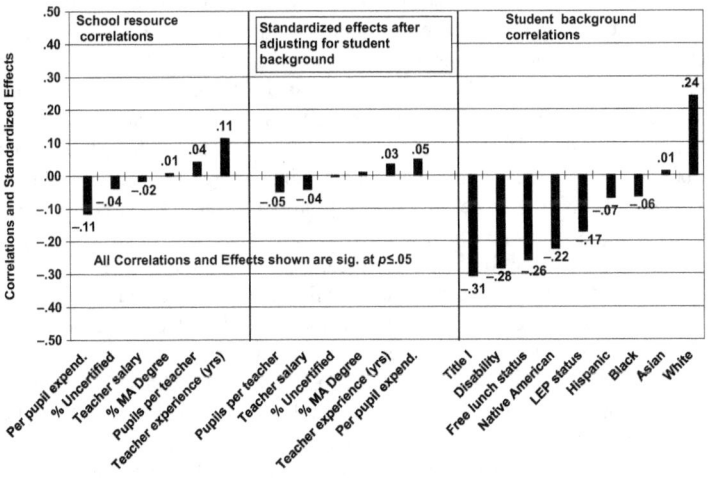

Figure 8.3 School Resource and Student Background Correlations with Math Scores; Middle Panel Shows School Resource Effects After Adjusting for Student Background (Grades 3–8, 2003 to 2007).

Most of these student background correlations are much stronger than the correlations between math achievement and school resources shown on the left-hand side of the figure. The strongest correlation observed for these school resources is .11, which is observed for teachers' years of experience. Per pupil expenditures also have a correlation of −.11, but it is in the wrong direction—it should be positive. The negative sign occurs most likely because of state and federal programs that allocate extra funds to districts with high-poverty levels; this produces an inverse relationship before controlling for student poverty levels. The remaining correlations are much smaller, with just −.04 for percentage uncertified teachers and .04 for pupil–teacher ratio (the latter of which is also in the wrong direction).

The middle panel of Figure 8.3 shows standardized effects for school resources after controlling for (taking account of) the student background factors shown on the right-hand side of the figure. The strongest school resource effects, after adjusting for student background, are −.05 for pupil–teacher ratio (the number of students per teacher) and +.05 for per pupil expenditures; both of these effect sizes now have the correct sign.[6] Teacher experience has a statistically significant standardized effect, but at .03 it is a fairly weak effect. Teacher salary is also statistically significant but it is in the wrong direction—it would be expected to have a positive relationship. The standardized effects for uncertified teachers and having an MA degree are near 0.

The analyses discussed up to this point have been based on the total elementary- and middle school population. In his expert testimony, Dr. Armor also presented analyses for the 21 focus districts. For each school resource, the focus districts were sorted from lowest to highest values on that resource, and then resources were plotted against math and reading proficiency scores, adjusted for student background. We will show the focus district results for per pupil expenditures, a school resource with one of the strongest standardized effects.

Figure 8.4 shows focus districts ordered from lowest to highest per capita expenditures, plotted against math and reading scores adjusted for student background. Visually, there is clearly very little relationship between expenditures and adjusted achievement scores.

It is clear from the foregoing statistical analyses of the South Dakota data, that the relationship between student achievement and student background characteristics are very strong, especially poverty indicators and racial/ethnic background. After taking these student characteristics into account using rigorous statistical techniques, the relationship between school resources and student achievement is quite weak. If spending was increased by $2,000 per student (at that time), and if the increased spending led to modest increases in teacher experience by two or three years and reductions in pupil–teacher ratio by two or three students, then we would expect math scores to raise by only 2 or 3 points. Such increases would only have a minor impact on the achievement gap between White and Native American students.

The Case of South Dakota 97

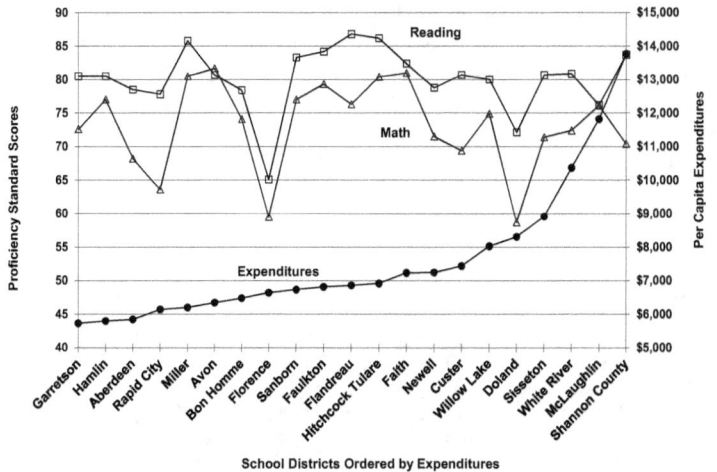

Figure 8.4 Per Pupil Expenditures and Achievement for Focus Districts Adjusted for Student Background (Grades 3–8 for All Years).

Final Disposition

After an extensive evidentiary hearing during which both plaintiffs and the State defendants presented their evidence, including both fact and expert witnesses, the trial court issued its final opinion:

> This action was commenced in 2006. In the years that followed, the Court has considered parties numerous motions and substantial briefing regarding the issues involved this case. A trial commenced on 2 September 2008. The last written closing was submitted to the Court on 30 January 2009. After consideration of over a month of live testimony, hundreds of exhibits including educational performance data, photographs, historical documents, and expert opinion, the many decisions from other states involving this issue, and arguments of counsel, this Court concludes that the current public school finance system does not violate the South Dakota Constitution or SDCL 6–15–1.

Following the trial court's decision summarized earlier, the plaintiffs appealed to the Supreme Court of South Dakota. After hearing arguments on both sides, the Supreme Court issued its final decision on August 31, 2011:

> The plaintiffs' evidence raises serious questions about whether the state aid formula is based on actual costs and whether local taxing procedures and

caps might have constitutional implications. The plaintiffs have also shown some groups of students are not achieving at desired levels and that some districts struggle to provide adequate facilities and qualified teachers. Even so, reasonable doubt exists that the statutory funding mechanisms or level of funding are unconstitutional. We are unable to conclude that the education funding system (as it existed at the time of trial) fails to correlate to actual costs or with adequate student achievement to the point of declaring the system unconstitutional. We affirm the trial court.[7]

Notes

1 *Davis v. State of South Dakota*, Sixth Judicial Circuit civ 06-244 Findings of Fact, Conclusions of Law, and Final Decision, December 2009.
2 *Davis v. State of South Dakota*, op cit., p. 85 (finding of fact #59).
3 *Davis v. State of South Dakota*, op cit., p. 87 (finding of fact #67).
4 *Davis v. State of South Dakota*, op cit., p. 88 (finding of fact #71).
5 See, for example, Armor, D.J. (2003). *Maximizing Intelligence*, New Brunswick, NJ, Transaction Publishers.
6 The coefficient for expenditures is obtained in a separate regression, by itself, because of collinearity with other school and teacher resources.
7 *Davis v. the State of South Dakota*, 804 N.W.2d 618 (S.D. 2011).

9 School Resource Effects in South Carolina

Bryan Michael Fores and David J. Armor

Introduction

The education adequacy lawsuits for North and South Carolina took place at different times, and under different circumstances, and have little in common except for the involvement of co-author Armor. Armor was an expert witness in the South Carolina case, which is where the data came from. He was not an expert in the North Carolina case, but rather one of his students obtained North Carolina data for a dissertation. Armor went on to analyze the North Carolina data for other projects, including an expert report for the *Swann et al. v. Charlotte-Mecklenburg* unitary status case and a study of school SES effects discussed in Chapter 11.

Further analyses of the South Carolina data were undertaken by Bryan Michael Fores for an undergraduate research program, and he is the principal author of the South Carolina chapter. Similarly, Anna Grace Garren conducted further analyses of the North Carolina data in connection with the same undergraduate research program, and she is principal author of the North Carolina chapter.

The South Carolina Adequacy Case

South Carolina's long history with education adequacy dates back to the 1990s, when a lawsuit was filed, *Abbeville County School District, et al. v. the State of South Carolina, et al.* We shall refer to that case as *Abbeville* for short. Today, the public school system of South Carolina enrolls roughly 770,000 pupils in kindergarten through Grade 12, according to 2017 student headcount records. There are 82 public school districts located throughout the state.

The South Carolina Department of Education report cards indicate that 43 percent of pupils in the state achieve or surpass reading levels, but only 37 percent satisfy math standards. Like other states in the South, South Carolina's poverty rate is 14 percent, which is comparable to poverty rates in Oklahoma (14 percent), Alabama (15 percent), and Arkansas (15 percent).

DOI: 10.4324/9781003399117-9

Given the correlation between poverty rates and school performance, South Carolina's relatively low proficiency rates in reading and math is not surprising.

One of the focal points in the dialogue over school funding in South Carolina is educational inequality in a region of the state termed the "Corridor of Shame." Dubbed after the title of a 2005 documentary exposing dilapidated school facilities and disparities in students' reading and writing levels, the Corridor of Shame comprises rural and economically depressed counties along Interstate 95.

The *Abbeville* case has been a centerpiece in the debate of educational reform in the state, making its way through the judicial system for over two decades. The primary legal question in *Abbeville* centered on whether the state had failed to fulfill its constitutional duty to provide all students with a "minimally adequate education." The *Abbeville* cases instigated a series of empirical studies from both parties into the relationship of school and teacher factors on South Carolina students' achievement.

In the first series of *Abbeville* trials, 40 poorer and mostly rural school districts across the State of South Carolina filed a declaratory judgment action in 1993 to challenge the State's school funding scheme.[1] Only eight of the school districts were later represented as trial plaintiffs in court. The principal grounds for dispute comes from an interpretation of the Education Clause in Article XI, Section 3 of the South Carolina Constitution, which stipulates that "[t]he General Assembly shall provide for the maintenance and support of a system of free public schools open to all children in the State." In 1996, a state court granted the State's motion to dismiss the case under the basis that the State funding scheme was not unconstitutional and that enforcing any remedial measures would undeniably encroach on legislative powers, thus violating the Separation of Powers Clause.

In an immediate appeal to the Supreme Court in 1996, plaintiffs instead alleged that the State failed to provide students with the bare minimum financing necessary to obtain an education. They argued that the wealth-sensitive formula of the Education Finance Act of 1977, which sets the statutory minimum funding based on district property values, disproportionately disadvantaged the State's poorest rural areas. The Supreme Court upheld the lower court's ruling but remanded the case to re-examine the education clause in the State Constitution.

In 2002, during the *Abbeville I Remand* trial, the attention shifted back to the issue of whether students in the plaintiff districts received a minimally acceptable education. Throughout the trial, discussions centered on the relationship between teacher characteristics and poverty on academic attainment. Defendant exhibits referenced Drs. Armor and Podgursky's analyses, which found that there was no evidence of a relationship between teacher characteristics and student achievement. Judge Thomas Cooper, who presided over the trial, stated that, despite their disparate methodologies, the plaintiffs reached the same conclusion regarding the absence of a strong positive association of teacher characteristics to academic achievement. The court later concluded that the state met its obligation to provide a minimally acceptable education, with the exception of early childhood. The decision was appealed by both the plaintiff and defendant.

In 2012, the Supreme Court heard the case's final oral arguments for *Abbeville II*. In 2014, the court ruled in favor of the plaintiff districts, in which the majority found that the State had "failed its duty to provide a minimally adequate education to children" as required under the State's constitution. However, the Court also added:

> We do not (nor could we legally) merely order the Defendants to disperse additional funding to the Plaintiff Districts. We believe that all parties could agree that—given that the Defendants have disproportionately funded poorer counties such as the Plaintiff Districts in the past with little noticeable impact on student achievement rates—money is not the answer.[2] The dissenting opinion of one Judge responded that the Court, in making the decision, had overstepped their boundaries to the Legislature in the Separation of Powers.

This complicated ruling prompted the two parties to seek a political resolution, rather than "through judicial oversight," in an attempt to address rural districts' financial inequities. The impact of this case led the State to pass a series of education reform bills, commission studies, and ultimately allocate $55.8 million in FY 2017–2018 to capital improvements for the original *Abbeville* plaintiff districts and districts with a high-poverty index.[3]

However, a few years later, in 2017, in a 3–2 ruling, South Carolina Supreme Court vacated its initial order in the *Abbeville II* lawsuit, marking a resounding halt in the decades-long case after citing the "measures they have taken to ensure students obtain the constitutionally necessary opportunity to receive an adequate education." In the court's majority opinion, Justice Kittredge stated that the Court's jurisdiction on state education had terminated on the basis of the violative separations of powers and judicial overreach.[4]

At the heart of the matter for the study, we will re-examine the influence of education spending on school and teacher resources, and the extent to which this effects academic achievement, especially for children in poverty. The next section will revisit some of the same themes using more recent data obtained after the 2002 study (through the 2005 school year) as well as statistical methods that were not available at the time of the original expert studies.

Data and Methods

Dr. Armor and Dr. Podgursky's 2002 study on the association between poverty, school resources, and achievement was based on more restricted data and simpler statistical methods than those available today. This chapter applies these more sophisticated statistical models in conjunction with updated data collected in the three years following the original study.

This section will analyze the effects of various student background characteristics, school resources, and school spending information to estimate their influence on academic achievement in South Carolina. Four cohorts of students enrolled from Grades 3 through 8 were evaluated during four school years from 2002–2003 to 2005–2006. Students can be evaluated in terms of their exposure to various school and teacher resources over these four school years.

Table 9.1 summarizes the various South Carolina student characteristics and school resources available for the statistical analyses. These characteristics and resources include student math and reading test scores, background data, including poverty status (via the free lunch program), a variety of school and teacher characteristics, and school expenditure information. The South Carolina dataset consists of a series of five cohorts of approximately 40,000–60,000 students, ranging between a total of 190,000 to 264,000 students at any given year. This student sample size is comparable to the approximately 353,000 pupils enrolled in Grades 3 through 8, based on South Carolina's 2021 enrollment headcounts.

It is worth emphasizing that the student's test scores were recorded over multiple years. By keeping their scores on file longitudinally, it becomes possible to track the progress of their academic achievement over time. In this case, the student's math and reading scores were derived from South Carolina's former Palmetto Achievement Challenge Test. It is the year-end assessment administered to South Carolina Grades 3 through 8 students until its successor, the Palmetto Assessment of State Standards, replaced it in 2009.

The student background variables available for the South Carolina dataset are rather restricted to basic demographic information, namely a student's race, gender, disability flag, and whether they participate in a free or reduced lunch program. In any given school year, males and females are almost evenly distributed by gender, at 51 and 49 percent, respectively. Around 55 percent of students are white. Black students, at 45 percent, comprise the second-largest racial group. Hispanic students make up a small percentage of the student body, at almost 3 percent. In measuring the impact of academic achievement, any student racial background variables are strictly interpreted in light of the socioeconomic disparities among the various groups. What will also operate as another variable related to socioeconomic status (SES) in later analyses is the free or reduced-price lunch variable—wherein nearly half of all students participate in the state's National School Lunch Program.

The South Carolina dataset also includes a broader set of school resources, such as physical classroom equipment, teacher credentials, and financial information from the various schools and districts. In particular, some variables pertaining to the classroom environment include the school's count of mobile classrooms, the percentage of classrooms missing in high-quality technology

Table 9.1 Summary Statistics for South Carolina data, Grades 3–8, 2003–2006.

Variable	Number	Mean	SD	Minimum	Maximum
Achievement Test Scores					
Reading scale score	866,283	100	10.0	59	141
Math scale score	873,932	100	10.0	61	133
Prior year reading score	697,383	100	10.0	55	141
Prior year math score	704,511	100	10.0	61	130
Student Background					
Disability flag	912,275	0.14	0.35	0	1
Male	912,265	0.51	0.50	0	1
White	912,219	0.55	0.50	0	1
Black	912,219	0.41	0.49	0	1
Hispanic	912,224	0.03	0.16	0	1
Other	912,219	0.02	0.13	0	1
Free lunch (%)	911,563	49	48	0	100
School Resources					
School; % Black	912,329	41	26.91	0	100
School % Hispanic	912,329	3	4.05	0	100
Repeated grade	912,332	0.04	0.19	0	1
School enrollment	907,764	680	276	20	1,925
Per Pupil Expenditures	893,902	6,018	1,153	2,173	18,690
Principal years	907,097	5.4	5.0	0	40
Number of mobile classrooms	869,071	8.0	15.8	0	100
Professional development dates	902,446	12.2	4.2	1.5	34.9
% Teacher with MA	905,994	51	11.4	0	100
Prime instruction time	899,087	89	2.4	76.3	99.4
Pupils per teacher	892,987	21	3.5	2.1	36.7
Teacher salary	905,935	41,170	2,692	28,739	54,938
Teacher attendance rate	899,150	95	2	84.8	100
% of returning teachers	866,760	85	7	45.2	100
% teachers with emergency license	707,360	5.2	6.4	0	55.6
Vacancies over nine weeks	707,023	0.8	2.7	0	44.4
Continuing contract teachers	727,468	82	11	0	100
% classes with no HQ tech	645,618	69	37	0	100
Number of teachers	906,999	46	17	2	156
School SES	912,321	0.00	0.46	−1.06	1.03

(which is greater than two-thirds at the time), and the school's pupil–teacher ratio (averaging 21 students per teacher).

One significant key metric that collectively represents school resources is the per pupil expenditure. Between 2003 and 2006, the average spending per student in Grades 3 through 8 was approximately $6,000, though this number does not entirely represent the unique circumstances of each district. For instance, Allendale County, one of the trial plaintiffs in the *Abbeville I* case, received over $10,000 from 2001 to 2003 after the State Superintendent of Education took over when the district consistently fell below state standards.[5]

Finally, South Carolina reports various teacher credentials and financial records in the dataset. These variables include the percentage of teachers with master's degree-level credentials, the number of days dedicated to professional development, and the percentage of teachers with emergency credentials. At the time, about 50 percent of teachers reported having a master's degree. School principals in South Carolina average 5.4 years of tenure. The schools also report salary information of teachers: the typical teacher in South Carolina between 2003 and 2006 earned an average of $41,170 annually.

We will use several statistical techniques to examine the relationship between student background, school resources, and academic achievement in South Carolina. The following section will compare the impact of South Carolina student test scores at the district and school level, perform a correlation analysis, and culminate with a discussion of various multiple regression models, namely a pooled cross-sectional design and a student fixed effects model.

Effects of Student Background and School Resources on Achievement

The Within- and Between-school and district variations, as applied in previous chapters, are the first of a series of statistical models. This section provides an overview of the impact of school- and district-level policies on students' test scores in South Carolina. In Figure 9.1, variations in test scores are partitioned into the fraction occurring *within* districts or schools and the fraction *between* them. In other words, this statistical analysis model indicates the extent to

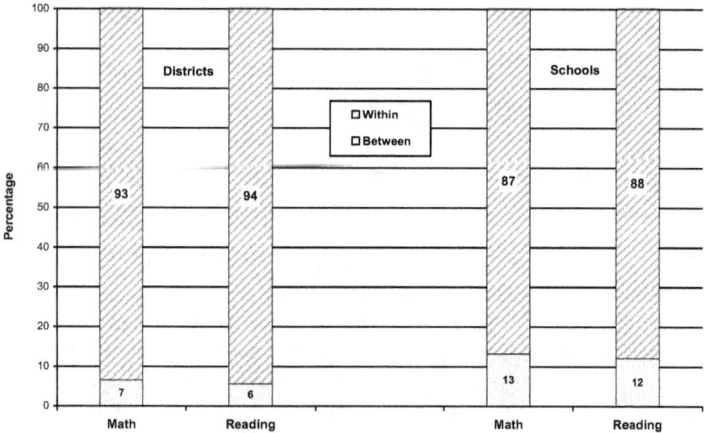

Figure 9.1 Variation in Test Scores Occurring Within and Between South Carolina Schools and Districts, 2005.

which institutional policies and programs are responsible for the change in test results or whether other factors are involved.

Observing South Carolina's policies at the district level, only 7 percent of the variation of math scores are explained by what occurs *between* districts. Results are also comparable to the variations in reading scores, wherein 6 percent are influenced at the district level. Here, policies instituted at the district level are thought to hold less influence in the variation of students' math and reading scores, given that changes at the district level are perhaps indirectly tailored to every student.

Notice how the influence of policies, while stronger, is still somewhat marginal at the school-level administration. The variation in math and reading scores represent only 13 and 12 percent *between* schools, respectively. However, at the school level, math and reading score variations are nearly twice that in district levels. Comparing South Carolina to other state school systems and testing mechanisms, test score variations are even lower than the other chapters that employ the same methodology at the school level (see Chapters 6 and 10).

There is a common theme in the relationship of upper-level district and school policies and what variation lies *within* them. Overall, most of the variation still lies within schools and districts, that is what school policies have not accounted for. Most of this variation, we argue, is caused by student socioeconomic differences, mostly arising from parental economic and education status.

Correlations Between Achievement, Student Background, and School Resources

Correlation analyses provide a preliminary assessment of potential student background and school resource influence on achievement. Figure 9.2 illustrates simple linear relationships between South Carolina students' math scores and the various student characteristics, school and teacher resources included in the presented dataset. Again, while the correlations in this model do not prove causation, the coefficients demonstrate an initial step toward understanding the relationship of students' backgrounds, school resources, and test scores.

Since the South Carolina dataset provides fewer data points for student background variables, it is still reasonable to infer that correlations between school/teacher resources and achievement are influenced, to some degree, by student background characteristics. Clearly, the range of coefficients generated from a student's background appears to be nearly double that of even the most influential school resources. For instance, a student enrolled in the free or reduced lunch program, which acts as a proxy for the student's household's poverty/socioeconomic conditions, has the strongest (negative) association with the student's math scores (−.38).

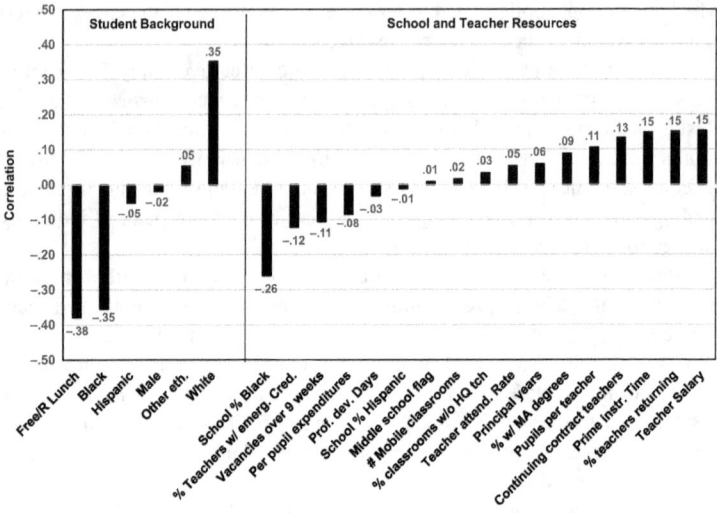

Figure 9.2 School Resource and Student Background Correlations for South Carolina Math Scores, 2003–2006.

Even some of the school and teacher variables with the strongest correlations, such as teacher pay, teacher retention rate, and prime instructional time (all at .15), have far smaller potential impacts on achievement than student poverty. Recognizing these relationships emphasizes the importance of socioeconomic disparities among individual student's factor in creating academic gaps and improving outcomes.

Note that one of the school resource factors is school percentage of Blacks, which is not a school resource per se—since it reflects a concentration of Black students—and has the strongest (negative) relationship with achievement, at −.24. The relationship between school composition and achievement is taken up in Chapter 11; it is explained there—using South Carolina data—that the correlation between a school-level variable and a student characteristic has elements of the ecological fallacy problem, so the true relationship may be considerably smaller (also see Figure 9.4 and the discussion of those results).

Correlations were also calculated for reading scores, and in general they were very similar in magnitude to the math correlations in Figure 9.2. Per pupil expenditures exhibit a weak and negative relationship (−.08). Other school resources, such as teachers' professional development days (−.03), the number of mobile classrooms (.02), and the percentage of classrooms without high-tech equipment (.03), also demonstrate fairly weak relationships.

Pooled Longitudinal Cross-Sectional Regression

Figure 9.3 illustrates a pooled longitudinal cross-sectional regression analysis of students' scores as a function of students' backgrounds and school resources in South Carolina. This model evaluates the relationship of resources to math test scores over time, controlling for student background. This model now shows coefficients for school resources, taking into account student background, so they reveal how much student background might have accounted for some part of the school resource effect.

Notice that the effects of poverty (e.g., free lunch status) and of being Black has been reduced somewhat (from −.38 to −.20 in the case of poverty), but the coefficients for all of the school resources have been reduced substantially, in many cases, to statistical insignificance. For example, pupil–teacher ratio—an indicator of instructional effort—has been reduced from a modest correlation of .11 to a standardized effect near 0. There are only three school resources that have more than marginal effects, which are prime instructional time (.13), teacher salary (.04), and teacher attendance rate (−.09).

The pooled longitudinal regression model for reading scores shows effects very similar to those observed for math scores, except the effects are slightly smaller. For example, the coefficient for prime instructional time has fallen to .11 and the coefficient for teacher attendance rate has been reduced to −.07. Another notable difference is that the coefficients for the student background variables are more pronounced, including the free/reduced lunch, racial, and

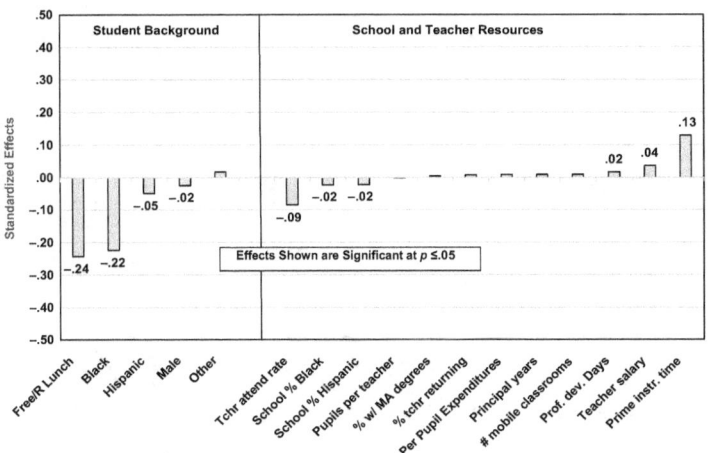

Figure 9.3 Standardized Effects for Longitudinal Regression, South Carolina Grades 3–8 Math, 2003–2006.

gender variables. While almost all student background variables are statistically significant, the same holds for only half of the school and teacher resources.

Student Fixed Effects

"Student Fixed Effects" models represent not only a method that controls for measured student background characteristics, as in the longitudinal regressions of the previous section, but also a model that includes the impact of "unmeasured" student background characteristics that are constant over time. In essence, student fixed effect models control for unmeasured student background characteristics such as basic student aptitudes, parent education, family wealth, and so forth.

Figure 9.4 shows results for the student fixed effect analysis for math scores. By controlling for unmeasured student characteristics, the standardized coefficients for school resources have been reduced to very small effects—none larger than .03. The .03 effect is for prime instructional time; the remaining coefficients for all school and teacher resources are .02 or less. We have also included a parallel analysis for free/reduced students only, to see if the results are constant across student socioeconomic levels. The analysis shows virtually no difference between the coefficients for all students and those for students in poverty.

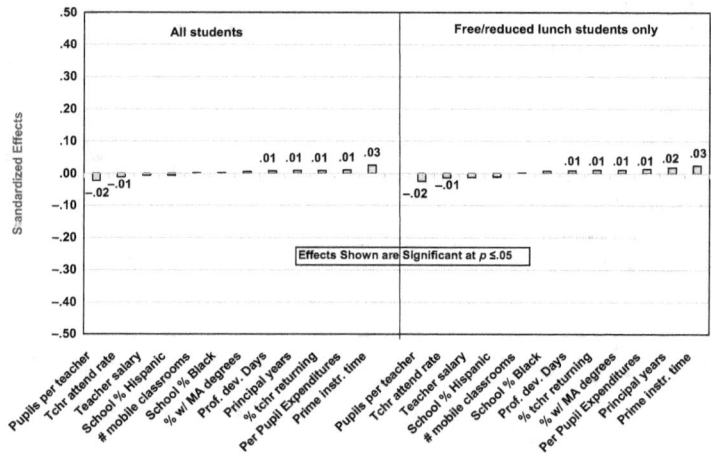

Figure 9.4 Standardized Effects for Student Fixed Effect Regression, South Carolina Grades 3–8 Math, 2003–2006.

Per pupil spending, which typically represents the level of school funding among schools in the state, while statistically significant, is very weak at .01. Among other school and teacher resources, teacher salaries at −.01 have no statistically significant effect on the total student population or the free/reduced lunch student subcategory.

A student fixed effect regression analysis was also carried out for reading scores. The coefficients are very similar to those for math scores, with the exception that no effect exceeds .02, and that effect is observed for prime instructional time. Another notable difference is that about half of the school and teacher resource measures fail to reach statistical significance. One anomaly is that teacher salaries have a negative effect on reading achievement, but at −.01 it is a very small effect.

Even though the coefficients are very small, there are a half dozen that have statistically significant effects. To illustrate the total effect of these resources, assuming that all were increased by substantial magnitudes, Table 9.2 shows the total cumulative effect of a hypothetical increase in school resources.

If South Carolina were to increase per pupil expenditures for students in Grades 3 to 8 by $3,000 (in unadjusted 2006 dollars), the original average expenditure would rise from approximately $6,000 to $9,000. As a result of increased funding, let us assume that instructional quality across the state raises average prime instruction time by 2 percent (from 89 percent), teacher retention by 5 percent (from 85 percent), average principal tenure by five years (from 5.4 years), professional development days by five (from 12 days), and decreases the pupil–teacher ratio down to 17 students (from 20 students). The predicted gain from this chain of substantial improvements would increase students' average math scores by only 1 point. While the adjustments are, of course, theoretical, they illustrate the enormity of the challenge to improve student achievement by increasing traditional school resources, including expenditures, class size, and teacher retention.

Table 9.2 Effect of Increasing School Resources on Math Scores in South Carolina.

School Resource	Change	Effect on Math Scores
Per Pupil expenditures	+$3,000	0.36
Prime instruction time	+2%	0.22
Pupils/teacher	−3	0.20
Retention	+5%	0.07
Principal years	+5	0.05
Professional development	+5 Days	0.10
Total change		**Gain of 1.0**

Notes

1 *Abbeville County School District et al. v. State of South Carolina* (2005). 93-CP-31-0169, https://nces.ed.gov/edfin/pdf/lawsuits/Abbeville_v_sc.pdf
2 *Abbeville County School District et al. v. State of South Carolina* (2014). 410 S.C. 619, 767 S.E. 2d 157, https://casetext.com/case/abbeville-cnty-sch-dist-v-state-5
3 See https://ed.sc.gov/data/reports/finance/cfo-reports/other-finance-reports/abbeville-equity-district-reports/abbeville-equity-district-comprehensive-reports/abbeville-comprehensive-report-2018/; www.scstatehouse.gov/reports/DeptofEducation/Abbeville%20Capital%20Improvement%20%20Report%202017%20Final.pdf
4 *Abbeville County School District et al. v. State of South Carolina* (2017). 410 S.C. 619, 767 S.E. 2d.
5 *Abbeville County School District et al. v. State of South Carolina* (2005). 93-CP-31-0169, https://nces.ed.gov/edfin/pdf/lawsuits/Abbeville_v_sc.pdf

10 School Resource Effects in North Carolina

Anna Grace Garren and David J. Armor

Introduction

Although North Carolina does have an adequacy lawsuit, none of the authors of this book had a role in the lawsuit, either as an attorney or expert witness. Rather, North Carolina was included in this treatise because co-author Armor and his students had carried out various education research studies using North Carolina data.[1] The extensive achievement, student background, and school resource data available from these other education policy studies made it possible to investigate education adequacy issues using the same data.

The North Carolina Adequacy Case

Leandro v. the State of North Carolina case, henceforth the *Leandro* case, was first filed in 1994. Nearly 30 years later, the case is still not resolved because the courts have not yet found North Carolina to be in compliance with the state constitution's mandate to provide each child with an adequate education. In 2020, the court ordered the plaintiff and defendant to develop a long-term plan to bring the state up to compliance, but at the time writing the state has yet to fully comply with this order.

When the *Leandro* case was filed, the plaintiffs were parents, students, and school boards in Hoke, Halifax, Robeson, Vance, and Cumberland counties, some of North Carolina's poorest school districts.[2] The North Carolina Supreme Court pushed the case to trial in 1997,[3] and in 1999, a trial was conducted to examine education in Hoke County only (John Locke Foundation, 2022). In 2002, the court's decision emerged, finding a violation of the state constitution's mandate for a sound, basic education. The court ordered the state to implement the following: certified teachers, competent principals, and necessary resources.[4]

This decision was appealed by the state, and in 2004 the North Carolina Supreme Court affirmed their earlier decision. However, they ruled that the mandates could only be applied to Hoke County because that was the only school district examined at trial.[5] Therefore, separate hearings would be needed

DOI: 10.4324/9781003399117-10

for other counties. However, no such hearings have occurred. Over time, remediations evolved to include all of North Carolina, not just Hoke County.

In 2016, defendants and plaintiffs sought mutually agreed upon consent orders, which ultimately mandated North Carolina to fund programs for better education, though funding would require the legislature's approval, who was not a defendant in the lawsuit. In 2018, the plaintiffs and the North Carolina Department of Justice asked the trial court to have an independent group study the adequacy of North Carolina schools and provide recommendations for remediation. WestEd was chosen to be the independent party that would provide recommendations for all counties in North Carolina, not just Hoke County.

WestEd recommended the following:[6]

- Each school be staffed with a trained and competent teachers and principals
  - Recruitment
  - Competitive pay
  - Ongoing professional development

- Provision of resources necessary for equal access to a basic, sound education
  - Finance system providing adequate funding, especially to at-risk students
  - Assessment and accountability system for student performance
  - Assistance for low-performing schools and districts
  - Early childhood education
  - High school to higher education and workforce expectations and opportunities

In 2020, the court ordered the State to make a plan to implement the recommendations.[7] In 2021, the Department of Justice presented the "Comprehensive Remedial Plan" to trial court. It included 146 actions to be taken across the state, even though the trial was limited to Hoke County. The plan would require legislative approval for implementation. The court ordered the state to implement the $5.4 billion plan by 2028.[8]

In 2021, both parties asked the trial court to mandate that $1.7 billion was transferred out of the State treasury, which would require action on the part of the State Controller and Treasurer, neither of whom were parties in this lawsuit. This would be illegal as only the General Assembly has the power to make appropriations; however, the judge directed this transfer anyway, asking the State Controller to treat it as an appropriation.[9] The State Controller appealed this, and the Court of Appeals agreed. Due to public backlash, the North Carolina Supreme Court reviewed the Court of Appeals' decision, ultimately sending the case back to the trial court to determine whether they could mandate the $1.7 billion transfer, this time with a different trial judge. The next year, the new trial judge ruled that the transfer could not be enforced and that the increase in the allocation for education in the state budget provided a portion of the necessary funds.[10] In 2022, the North Carolina Supreme Court ruled that the North Carolina legislature must fund years two and three of the Comprehensive Remedial Plan.[11]

This chapter addresses the potential and likely effects of additional resources by examining the relationship between academic achievement and various school and teacher resources, including expenditures, controlling for student background. We will analyze data obtained after the second *Leandro* decision, in addition to using some statistical techniques that were not available at that time.

Data and Methods

Table 10.1 shows basic statistics for the North Carolina data available for Grades 3 to 8 and from 2003 to 2005. Note that test scores were available

Table 10.1 Summary Statistics for North Carolina data, Grades 3–8, 2003–2005.

Variable	Observations	Mean	Std. dev.	Minimum	Maximum
Achievement					
Math score	1,773,676	264	11	221	307
Reading score	1,762,491	257	10	216	290
Prior year math	885,953	262	10	227	307
Prior year reading	883,052	256	10	216	287
Student Background					
Parent education (years)	1,764,949	13.4	2.1	10	18
Limited English proficiency (LEP)	1,773,617	0.03	0.18	0	1
Free/reduced lunch	1,773,609	0.82	0.94	0	2
Disability	1,772,906	0.13	0.33	0	1
Black	1,773,670	0.30	0.46	0	1
Hispanic	1,773,670	0.06	0.24	0	1
Asian	1,773,670	0.02	0.14	0	1
White	1,773,670	0.58	0.49	0	1
School Resources					
Teacher certification	1,764,319	84.2	11.3	0	100
Teacher <3 years exp	1,738,925	24.2	10.7	0	69
% teachers MA+	1,738,925	25.0	9.1	0	86
Teacher turnover	1,716,963	20.2	9.6	0	100
Students/instruct. comp	1,766,108	4.0	3.8	0.13	377
Number of books	1,755,812	18.4	10.8	0	271.7
% provisional teacher	1,764,319	5.2	4.2	0	50
% highly qualified teacher	1,772,783	82.4	14.6	0	100
Class size	1,766,027	21.6	2.9	10	42.33333
% National board cert	1,566,223	3.5	3.2	0	33
Current instr PPE	1,732,156	4333	392	3570	8791

for approximately 1.7 million observations, although since students could be assessed up to three times during this time period, there are approximately 600,000 different students in this analysis.

Given the availability of up to three years of data for each student, it was possible to run several types of regression models, including repeated measures and student fixed effect models. Those models and results will be discussed in subsequent sections.

Relation Between Academic Achievement and School Resources

Within Versus Between School Variation

We first examine the variation of achievement scores within schools/districts versus the variation between schools/districts. This variation, shown in Figure 10.1, indicates the extent to which policies at the school or district level could be responsible for achievement variation in schools or school districts. Variation between districts reflects effects of specific district policies, as well as variation due to schools and to individual student characteristics. Variation between schools most likely reflects either school resources or practices, while a large portion of within-school variation will be due to the background characteristics of individual students.

At the district level, only 3 percent of the variation in both math and reading scores are explained by the factors between districts, with a considerable

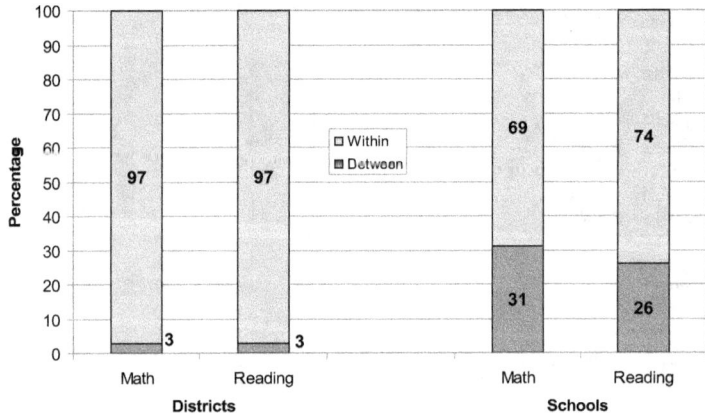

Figure 10.1 Variation in Test Scores Occurring Within Versus Between North Carolina Schools and Districts, 2005.

97 percent explained by the factors within districts. This indicates that policies implemented at the district level are less influential than student background characteristics.

At the school level, 31 and 26 percent of the variation in math and reading scores are explained by the factors between schools, with 69–74 percent of the variation within schools. This suggests that policies and programs implemented at the school level have a greater impact on achievement than policies at the district level. Nonetheless, this suggests that a lot of the variation in test scores is due to student background characteristics.

Correlations Between Achievement, Student Background, and School Resources

Figure 10.2 summarizes simple linear relationships, or correlations, between math scores and student characteristics, school resources, and teacher resources. The correlations do not establish causation but suggest the potential effects of student background versus school and teacher characteristics on academic achievement. The large correlations between achievement and student background variables strongly suggest, at the very least, that some—and possibly a large portion—of the school resource and teacher correlations are caused by the student social, demographic, and economic characteristics.

Note that most of the student background characteristics have larger correlations with achievement than the strongest school resources and teacher characteristics. The largest correlation between math scores and a school resource

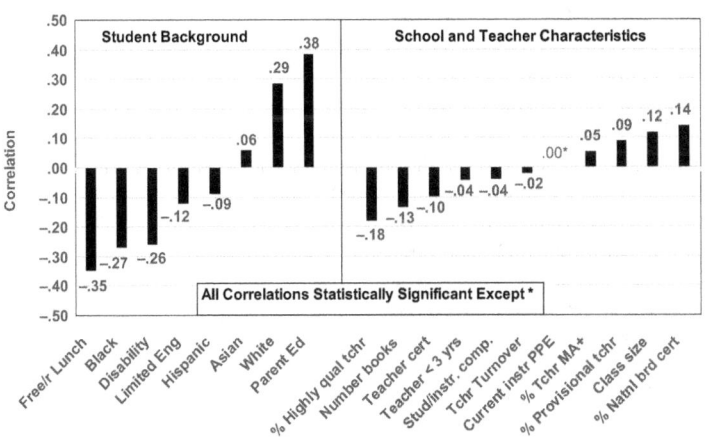

Figure 10.2 School Resource and Student Background Correlations for North Carolina Math Scores, 2003–2006.

characteristic is the percentage of highly qualified teachers, which is .18. That correlation is smaller than the correlations for student race (Black and White), poverty status, and parent education which are −.27, .29, −.35, and −.37, respectively (Figure 10.2). A similar set of comparisons exists for reading scores, with correlations of −.25, .29, −.36, and −.38, respectively (figure not shown).

The correlations for the remaining school and teacher resources are smaller than .15, which reflects fairly weak relationships. For math, we see a correlation of .14 for national board-certified teachers, −.13 for a number of books in the library (wrong sign), and .12 for class size. The class size correlation is also the wrong sign; it should be negative if smaller class sizes improve achievement. The only other correlation with absolute size in double digits is −.10 for teacher certification. This correlation also has the wrong sign, at least if we believe that more certified teachers should, in theory, improve achievement.

These resource effects with the wrong sign can arise if school districts have policies to improve achievement by increasing certain resources in schools with low performance levels. If those additional resources do not raise achievement—which we contend is often the case—then the result of the additional resources for low-performing schools will be a negative relationship.

Finally, there is only school resource with a correlation which is not statistically significant, and that is the correlation for current expenditures for instructional purposes. The correlation between math achievement and expenditures is 0. This correlation is expected to be positive, but again the lack of a relationship can be caused by scenarios where more financial support is provided for lower-performing schools. If those funds do not raise achievement, the net effect is a null relationship, or even a negative correlation. This possibility will be tested by the regression analyses that follow.

Pooled Longitudinal Cross-Sectional Model

The results shown in Figure 10.3 are from what is called a "pooled longitudinal cross-sectional regression" analysis. This model shows the relationship between school resources and achievement over time, removing the effects of the measured student background variables and also year. While this is still a regular linear regression model, it takes advantage of the over-time data by pooling estimates for differing school years, thereby averaging out possible year-to-year variations in relationships. Thus, these coefficients reflect average relationships between test scores and school resources after removing the effect of the measured student background characteristics.

These regression results reveal the very large impact that student background has on the school resource relationships. After controlling for student background, we now see that half of the school and teacher resource variables no longer have statistically significant relationships: class size, years of

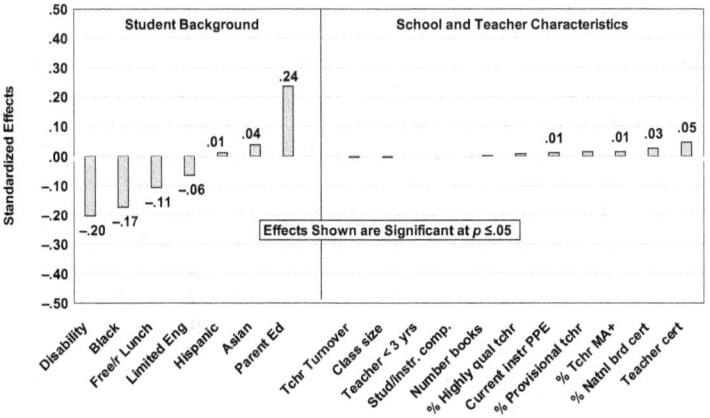

Figure 10.3 Standardized Effects for Longitudinal Regression, North Carolina Math Scores, 2003–2005.

teaching experience, instructional computers, and a number of books in the library. The remaining school resource characteristics are statistically significant but the coefficients are all quite small, being less than or equal to .05. The .05 effect occurs for teacher certification, while National Board Certification adds an additional effect of .03. The only other school resources that have statistically significant effects (in the expected direction) is percentage of teachers with master's degree or higher and current per pupil expenditures for instruction, but these last two resources have very small effects of just .01.

Meanwhile, the coefficients for student characteristics have been reduced by much smaller magnitudes—again reflecting that student background has much stronger effects with achievement than school resources. The strongest relationships occur for disability, being black, free lunch status, and parent's level of education.

The magnitude and direction of the regression coefficients are generally consistent across reading and math scores, but there are some differences. For example, teacher certification has no relationship with reading scores. National board certification is weaker at .01 (but still statistically significant), while provisional certification is stronger at .02. Having an MA degree is the same for both reading and math at .01. Finally, while instructional expenditures is a +.01 for math scores, it is −.01 for reading scores (both are statistically significant). This may be due to the fact that schools with lower reading scores are getting more funding for special remedial services; we are not suggesting that more funding causes lower reading scores. At any rate, regardless of sign, an effect of .01 is very small, whether it is positive or negative.

Student Fixed Effects

The final analysis which examines the relationship between school resources and achievement is a "student fixed effect" analysis. This is a statistical model that evaluates the effect of school resources after controlling for all student background variables, whether measured or unmeasured. When all of a student's background is controlled for, both measured and unmeasured, the impact of school and teacher characteristics and resources become even weaker—so that very few of the school resources reach statistical significance.

Figure 10.4 show the standardized effects of school resources after controlling for all student background factors, both measured and unmeasured, in North Carolina. It also shows the same analyses for students in poverty, in case students in poverty have a differing pattern of school resource effects than students not in poverty.

When accounting for all of a student's background, North Carolina school resources have very little effect on achievement outcomes. Only a few of the effect estimates reach statistical significance, and those significant effects are no larger than .02. For math, the results for all students show a significant effect of .02 for national board-certified teachers, and a negative effect of −.01 for class size. The other two significant effects, provisional license and per pupil expenditures, the coefficients are in the wrong direction. For students in poverty, the coefficient for national board-certified teachers is even smaller at .01.

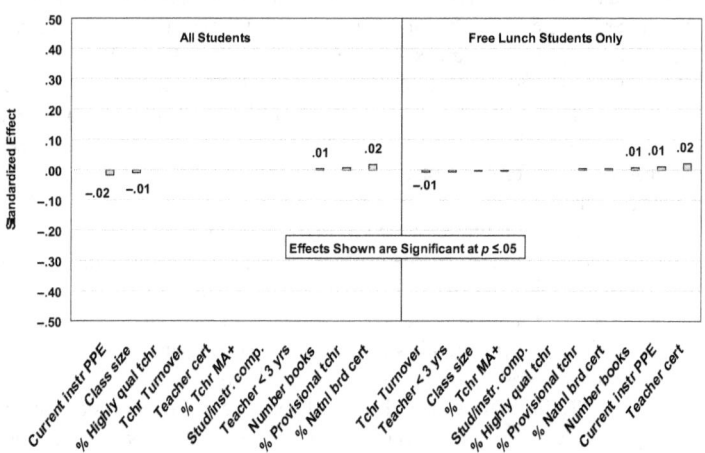

Figure 10.4 Standardized Effects for Student Fixed Effects Regression, North Carolina Grades 3–8 Math, 2003–2005.

The results for per pupil expenditures is interesting, showing one of the few times we have seen a reversal between a school resource effect for the full sample and that same resource for the poverty subsample. For the full sample, expenditures has a negative effect of −.02 and a positive effect of +.01 for the poverty subgroup. This could be a concrete illustration of a policy that allocates more funds to schools with high proportions of poverty-level students, and those schools show a positive relationship between spending and test scores.

For reading, the results are even weaker. For all students only four resource coefficients are statistically significant, and only two reach −.01 (expenditures and class size) and they are in the wrong direction. For students in poverty one significant coefficients is .01 (provisional certification) and one other is −.02 (class size). So virtually no significant amount of the relationship is due to school resources.

Conclusion

The results of North Carolina are nearly identical to those in South Carolina, despite the fact that each study measured different aspects of school resources. Basically, student socioeconomic and demographic backgrounds have very large impact on achievement, while school and teacher characteristics have very weak or nonexistent relationships with both reading and math achievement scores.

Note

1 Armor was an expert witness in the *Charlottesville-Mecklenburg* unitary status case in 1998; see also Watkins, S.J. (2006). *The Effect of Charter School Attendance on Raising Academic Achievement and Closing the Minority-White Achievement Gap*, PhD Dissertation, George Mason University; Armor, D.J. and Duck, S. (2007, September). *The Effect of Black Peers on Black Test Scores*, Education Working Paper Archives, University of Arkansas.
2 *Leandro v. North Carolina*, 343 N.C. 512 (1996)
3 *Leandro v. North Carolina*, 346 N.C. 336 (1997)
4 *Hoke County Board of Education v. State of North Carolina*, 358 N.C. 605 (2004)
5 *Ibid.*
6 WestEd, Learning Policy Institute, & Friday Institute for Educational Innovation at North Carolina State University (2019). *Sound Basic Education for All: An Action Plan for North Carolina*, San Francisco, CA, WestEd.
7 *Consent Order on Leandro Remedial Action Plan for Fiscal Year 2021*, 95-CVS-1158 (September 11, 2020)
8 *Comprehensive Remedial Plan*, 95-CVS-1158 (June 2021)
9 *November 2021 Order*, 95-CVS-1158 (November 10, 2021)
10 *April 2022 Order*, 95-CVS-1158 (April 26, 2022)
11 *Hoke County Board of Education v. State of North Carolina*, 2022-NCSC-108 (November 4, 2022)

References

Leandro v. State of North Carolina Explained. (2022, August 15). John Locke Foundation. www.johnlocke.org/leandro-case-explained/

Leandro—Public Schools First NC. (2022, November). Retrieved November 14, 2022, from www.publicschoolsfirstnc.org/know-the-issues/sound-basic-education-leandro/

11 School Resource Effects Using International Assessments (PISA)

Sonia Sousa and E.J. Park

Introduction

International comparisons of academic achievement were greatly enhanced by the introduction of the Program for International Student Assessment (PISA) in the 2000s by the Organization for Economic Co-operation and Development (OECD). PISA assesses academic achievement of 15-year-old students from over 60 countries, including all OECD countries, in reading, math, and science. It also assesses a variety of student background characteristics, along with measures of various types of school resources, including teacher characteristics, classroom measures, and broader school organizational features (OECD, 2012).

PISA tests, as well as the accompanying student and school questionnaires, are designed to allow comparisons across countries, so they are likely to capture information different from that captured by assessments designed to collect information only of US students, such as the National Assessment of Educational Progress (NAEP) data assessed in Chapter 5. It is, therefore, relevant to devote this chapter to assessing whether the magnitude of school resource effects on US students' academic achievement (as discussed in Chapters 5 to 9) also holds when US school and student characteristics are measured by a set of internationally comparable variables. The PISA survey also allows us to devote the last part of this chapter to investigate the magnitude of school resource effects in large developed countries on par with the United States: Japan, South Korea, United Kingdom, Germany, France, Italy, Spain, Canada, and Australia.[1]

The PISA student questionnaire collects information on student demographic characteristics, such as gender, primary language at home, and kindergarten attendance. It also collects items to measure family socioeconomic status (SES). These include parents' occupation, parents' education, family structure, and household possessions (including computers, cars, and books). Compared to the SES factors assessed in the NAEP assessments, PISA survey falls short in accounting for child poverty (proxied in US students by the proportion of students receiving free and reduced lunches) and for unmeasured family background characteristics such as wealth and family income, proxied in US studies by race and ethnicity variables. A few additional family variables specific to certain countries are available but often with restriction—for example, for the United States, ethnicity variables are not publicly available.

PISA's school questionnaire collects a considerable range of information about school and teacher characteristics, some of which differ from that measured in US-specific assessments (Chapter 5).[2] A major feature of the PISA survey is that it allows us to account for school institutional factors, some of which are unavailable in the US-specific assessments. School institutional factors measured in the PISA survey include sources of school financing (whether public or private), proportion of girls in the school, ability-based grouping of students within school, accountability procedures, admissions selectivity based on past academic records, parents' pressure on school academic standards, and size of the school community.

The PISA survey also allows us to account for a slightly different set of teacher and classroom resources than the US-specific assessments (see Chapter 5). Both measure class size and hours for math/science instruction students have per week. PISA survey adds other school characteristics such as school size, student–teacher ratio, and instructional resources, such as school computers linked to the web, instructional computers per student, school material's quality, and teacher shortage. Finally, the PISA survey offers somewhat fewer items about teacher characteristics than US-specific assessments. The PISA survey allows us to account for the proportion of certified teachers and the proportion of math teachers with a master's degree. In addition to these, the US-specific assessments also account for tenure, experience, types of certification, and teacher race/ethnicity (possibly proxies for the effectiveness of teaching students with similar race/ethnicity backgrounds), which are unavailable in the PISA survey.

Brief Literature Review

International achievement data allow for examination of relative importance of family and school factors on achievement across countries with different characteristics. Using 1994–1995 Trends in International Mathematics and Science Study (TIMSS) data, Baker et al. (2002) finds that family SES effects are stronger than school resources effects regardless of a country's economic development. This finding is broadly supported by studies using PISA data up to 2009 (Nonoyama-Tarumi, 2005; Nonoyama-Tarumi & Willms, 2010; Sousa et al., 2012).

When considering a more extensive set of school factors, research suggests that the way family SES and school resources factors interact depend on school institutional factors. Fuchs and Woessman (2007), using PISA 2000 data, and Woessman et al. (2009), using 2003 PISA data, conclude that both

School Resource Effects Using International Assessments (PISA) 123

family SES and school institutional factors have strong effects on student achievement. They also find that the effects of school resources are mixed. A handful of cross-national studies corroborate this finding. Xia (2009) compares the United States with 20 developed economies of different sizes and finds that factors such as learning structure and parental involvement plays an important role at explaining achievement gaps between the United States and the other 20 developed economies, after controlling for family SES and school resources. Comparing Canada, United States, and Finland, Beese and Liang (2010) concludes that the differences in the structure of the education systems affect the international rankings. Sousa et al. (2012) uses a comprehensive set of measures of both family SES and school factors from PISA 2006 and 2009 to compare math and science achievement in the United States vis-à-vis nine large OECD countries on par with the United States. It finds that while family SES has a strong effect on country-specific students' achievement, it does not significantly explain the US achievement gap with other comparable countries. School programmatic and institutional factors contribute more to the US achievement gap than family SES. Similarly, comparing United States and South Korea, Park (2013) finds that relative importance of school-level institutional factors on student achievement depends on the country context, though in both countries the school factors play a lesser important role compared to the family factors.

Descriptive Statistics

In the interest of comparability with the US-specific assessment explored in Chapter 5, this chapter analyzes the latest PISA survey focused on math, which was conducted in 2012. Focusing on academic achievement in math, as opposed to reading or science, has the additional benefit of being less dependent upon cross-country cultural differences that may be more likely to affect measures of reading and language arts.

Table 11.1 shows descriptive statistics for math achievement, as well as student and school characteristics captured in the PISA 2012 survey, which will be analyzed in this chapter. Student's math score is the average of the five plausible values that PISA estimates for each student.[3] Just under 5,000 US 15-year-old students participated in the PISA 2012 survey. The background of the students sampled is broadly comparable to that in US-specific assessments (see Chapter 5). The sample contained 50–50 male–female, 86 percent use English as their first language at home, and 78 percent live in a two-parent family. Students average 1.7 years of pre-kindergarten and kindergarten attendance. Parental educational level averages 13.7 years, which is nearly two years above high school graduation.

About 90 percent of the students attend public schools; just over half attend schools located in towns; nearly 40 percent attend city schools and only about

Table 11.1 Descriptive Statistics for 2012 PISA 15-Year-Old Students, US Sample.

Variable	Number	Mean	SD	Minimum	Maximum
Math Score	4,978	482	87	211	765
Student background					
Male	4,978	0.51	0.50	0	1
English as primary language at home (vs. other)	4,866	0.86	0.34	0	1
Kindergarten attendance (years)	4,914	1.73	0.48	0	2
Two-parents family	4,466	0.78	0.41	0	1
Highest parental occupational status (scale)	4,708	55	21	11	89
Highest parental educational level (years)	4,869	14	2.6	3	16
Index of home possessions	4,938	0.21	1.11	−4.2	3.8
No. of books at home	4,889	2.87	1.42	1	6
No. of cars at home	4,855	3.26	0.79	1	4
No. of computers at home	4,865	3.01	0.92	1	4
School institutional factors					
Public school (vs. private)	4,978	0.90	0.30	0	1
Size of the school community—village (<3,000)	4,894	0.10	0.29	0	1
Town (3,000–100,000 people)	4,894	0.51	0.50	0	1
City (over 100,000 people)	4,894	0.39	0.49	0	1
Parents' pressure on academic standards (0–2 scale)	4,698	1.20	0.71	0	2
Proportion of girls	4,894	0.48	0.11	0	1
Academic selectivity (vs. no selectivity)	4,762	0.57	0.50	0	1
Students' ability grouping within schools (vs. no grouping))	4,763	0.80	0.40	0	1
Accountability—achievement data posted publicly (vs. not posted)	4,721	0.91	0.29	0	1
School resources					
Proportion of certified teachers	4,607	0.95	0.13	0	1
Math teachers with master's degree	4,416	0.66	0.37	0	1
Teachers' shortage (scale)	4,821	−0.39	0.94	−1.1	3.6
Student–teacher ratio	4,698	17	10	0.9	118
Hours spent learning math or science	3,101	4.26	2.11	0	30
Class size	4,823	26	5.35	13	43
School size	4,769	1375	853	69	4,219
Instructional computers per student	4,564	0.97	0.74	0.1	5.0
Proportion of school computer linked to the internet	4,424	0.94	0.19	0.2	1
School materials' quality (scale)	4,821	0.36	1.08	−2.0	2.0

10 percent attend village schools. School population is fairly split at 48–52 female–male. About 57 percent of students are admitted to schools based on their past academic performance, 80 percent are grouped at school by their abilities, and 91 percent see their academic performance being accountable to the public.

Regarding school resources, where PISA and US-specific assessments overlap, the two samples show similar characteristics. In the PISA 2012 survey, about 95 percent of US teachers are certified and 66 percent have a master's degree, but the average school reports some degree of teacher shortage. The number of students per teacher averages 17 students and students receive an average of 4.3 hours of math or science instruction per week. Students attend classes of a size averaging 26 students and schools averaging 1,375 students. The average number of instructional computers per student is approximately one, and about 94 percent of school computers are linked to the internet. The average school indicates limited if any shortage or inadequacy of educational resources (lab equipment, library materials, textbooks, or computer and software for instruction).

Consistent with Chapter 5, this chapter presents three types of analyses to show the relationship between US students' academic achievement and student or school characteristics: (1) between versus within school variation in test scores; (2) simple correlations; and (3) standardized effects of each characteristic after removing the effect of all other measured characteristics using cross-sectional regression analysis, for the United States and also for other comparable OECD countries.

Between Versus Within School Analysis—United States

The between versus within analysis partitions the variation of student achievement scores into two components: (1 between schools score variation and (2) within schools score variation. The between school variation reflects the effects of all school-wide programs, policies, and resources that can vary from school to school. The within school variation, for the most part, reflects the effects of individual student and family characteristics that vary from student to student within the same school.

Consistent with US-specific assessment in Chapter 5, PISA survey also reveals that within-school variation accounts for the dominant share of US students' achievement differences. Within school variation, which measures student and family background effects, accounts for about three-quarters of US students' achievement differences in both math and science. This result suggests that increasing school resources such as teacher quality or class sizes and/or changing school program and institutional factors such as academic selectivity can only go so far as improving US students' academic achievement. This is because school factors overall are responsible for only about one-quarter of the variation of math and science test scores.

The advantage of this straightforward analysis is twofold. First, both individual student variation and school variation can be estimated without having explicit measures of student or school factors. Therefore, this analysis captures both measurable and unmeasurable student background characteristics, as well as school resource, program, and institutional factors. Second, this analysis makes little if any assumptions about direction of causation and model specification. The disadvantage of this analysis is that it does not allow us to answer the question of which of the individual student and school factors contribute more significantly to explain academic achievement differences. Both the correlation analysis and the regression analysis that follow attempt to respond this question, although with the caveats that (1) the results are limited to measurable factors and (2) contingent upon making assumptions about causation and modeling specification.

Correlation Analysis—United States

Figure 11.1 shows the simple correlations between US students' academic achievement, as measured by math test scores, and each of the school and student characteristics available from the PISA 2012 survey. Consistent with the results of US-specific assessments (Chapter 5), correlations with student characteristics are about twice as strong as compared to the school resource factors. Among student characteristics, the strongest correlations are with (proxies for) family economic background, parental occupation,

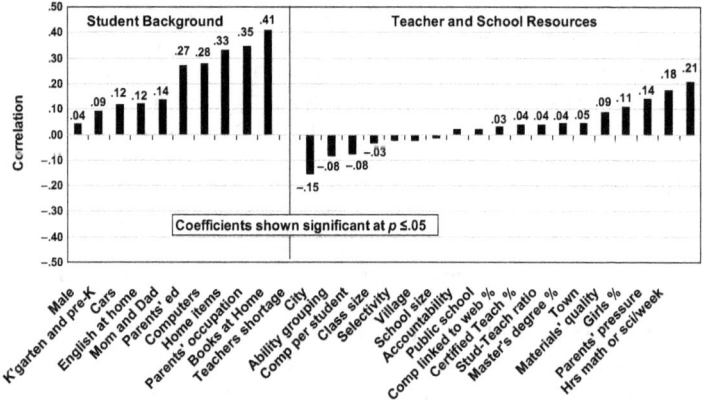

Figure 11.1 School Resource and Student Background Correlations for 2012 PISA USA, Age 15.

and parental education, all substantially correlated with academic achievement.[4] The strongest correlation is with books at home +.41), most likely a proxy for parents' intellectual ability and interest, followed by an index of home possessions, a proxy for family income (+.33), parents' occupational status (+.35), having computers at home which is a possible proxy for economic or educational background (+.28), and finally parents' education (+.27).

In contrast, the strongest correlations for school resources are only half this magnitude. For example, weekly hours of math or science instruction has the strongest correlation (+.21), followed by parents' pressure on school academic standards (+.18), teacher shortages, (−.15), and proportion of girls in the school population (+.14).

The correlation for quality of instruction materials (+.11) is not very strong before controlling for other factors. Regarding teacher quality factors, the correlations are weak for teachers with a master's degree (+.05) and for certified teachers (+.04). Correlations with computer school resources are even weaker at or below .04. Correlations for class size and school size are statistically indistinguishable from zero, even before controlling for student background.

Finally, the correlations for accountability procedures, ability grouping, and academic selectivity, all aspects of school institutional factors, are statistically indistinguishable from zero before any controls.

Standardized Effects—United States

Figure 11.2 shows the standardized effect of each characteristic on US math scores obtained from cross-sectional regression analysis. Standardized effects are measured in standard deviations, which ensure comparability across characteristics (originally expressed in different metrics), in the same way correlations are comparable across characteristics. Unlike correlations, standardized effects measure the effect of the characteristic in question after removing the effect of all other measured characteristics. They represent the effect, in standard deviations of the dependent variable, of a standard deviation change in the independent variable, controlling for all other measured independent variables.

Consistently with the results of US-specific assessments, most of the school resource characteristics are either very small or statistically not significant after controlling for student background characteristics.[5]

Unlike the correlations shown in Figure 11.2, there are only five school resource characteristics that are significantly different from zero, everything else being equal: hours of math or science instruction, teacher shortage, instructional computers per student, proportion of girls, and parental pressure on school academic standards. The strongest effect is the hours of math or science instruction per week with an effect of 0.16 SDs.

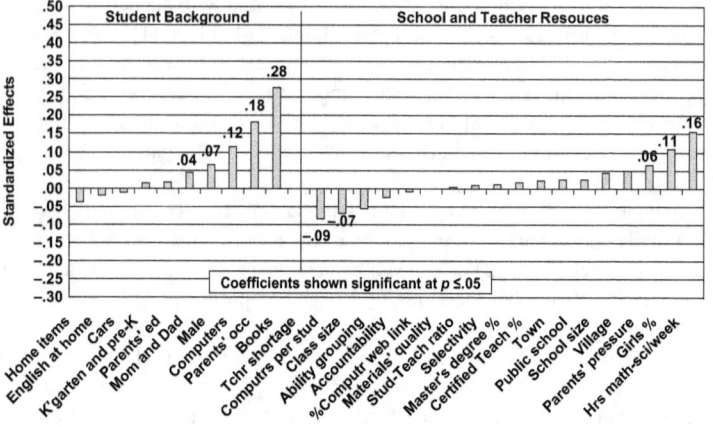

Figure 11.2 Standardized Effects for School Resource and Student Background, 2012 PISA USA, Age 15.

Given that the SD of math or science instruction is about 2 hours per week and the SD for math achievement is 87 (see Table 11.1), assuming a causal relationship and holding everything else constant, an increase of 2 hours of math or science instruction per week would lead to an increase of only 14 math score points (.16 × 87) per US student, on average. This is an increase of only about 3 percentage points over the PISA mean math score. Similarly, a reduction of teacher shortage by about 1 SD would lead to an increase of about 7 math score points per US student, on average (less than 2 percent of the mean score). The second-largest effect is the proportion of girls in the school population (+.11 SD). This is somewhat counterintuitive, since boys have significantly higher math scores. One possible explanation could be that a higher percentage of girls have an overall positive effect due to an improved behavioral climate.

The results also suggest that increasing the number of instructional computers per student would be detrimental for math scores, which is certainly not the intended effect. This may be a result of having more computers in special classes with a high rate of students with learning disabilities of some type. Finally, increasing parents' pressure on school academic standard also appears to be beneficial for student math scores (effect size +.06 SD), after controlling for student background and other measured school and teacher factors.

The remaining school resources and school institutional factors are statistically indistinguishable from zero, keeping everything else unchanged. These include class size, school size, student–teacher ratio, quality of instructional materials, and school computers linked to web. School institutional factors such as students' ability grouping within schools, accountability procedures, and academic selectivity are also statistically indistinguishable from zero, holding everything else constant. The teacher education/training factors are also statistically indistinguishable from zero, after controlling for students' background and other measured school factors.

The conclusion we draw here from the results in Figure 11.2 have three main limitations. The first limitation derives from the cross-sectional nature of the PISA data, which limits our ability to establish a clear cause-and-effect relationship between school factors and academic achievement. With cross-sectional data, we cannot control for student's prior academic achievement history and this limits our ability to establish the extent to which school factors cause achievement disparities or whether they are designed as compensatory responses to low academic achievement. The second limitation is that the results in Figure 11.2 are for the whole US sample, including students of all income levels and race/ethnic backgrounds. It is possible that the effect of school and teacher factors differs by income and racial/ethnic subgroups, but we cannot test this with PISA data due to lack of measures for student poverty and race/ethnicity. However, the analysis of US NAEP scores in Chapter 5 shows that there are no important differences among these different categories of students.

The third limitation of the results in Figure 11.2 is whether the small effects of teacher and school factors, once students' background is accounted for, also hold when investigating the school factor effects in large developed countries on par with the United States. We can address this issue by conducting comparative analysis for the United States and the OECD comparable countries, which is the focus of the next subsection.

International Comparisons

We also conducted a similar analysis of math achievement for the United States and the nine large developed countries on par with the United States: Japan, South Korea, United Kingdom, Germany, France, Italy, Spain, Canada, and Australia. Since standardized effects are measured in SDs, this makes the magnitude of the effects comparable across characteristics.[6]

When we broaden the sample to include both US students and students from the other large developed countries comparable to the United States, the teacher and school effects continue to be very small, after controlling for student background and country-specific fixed effects. However, although small, most of the school and teacher effects are now statistically significant, keeping everything else unchanged, because the sample size is much larger (about 130,000 students compared to the US sample size of about 5,000).[7]

The strongest effect is again hours of math or science instruction per week (+.12 SD). It is followed by school size (+.09 SD) and parents' pressure on academic achievement (+.08 SD), keeping everything else constant. In contrast to the results for the United States only, school resources such as quality of instructional materials, class size, and instructional computer linked to web have a significant though small effect, all around +.03 SD, and teacher shortage (−.02 SD), holding everything else constant. Teacher factors also have significant but small effects (+.02 SD). In addition to parents' pressure on academic achievement already mentioned (+.08 SD), various other institutional factors are also statistically significant, though small, such as accountability and selectivity (+.03 SD), as well as students' ability grouping, which has a rather counterintuitive inverse effect (−.05 SD).

The results of this analysis have some limitations. They share two of the limitations discussed for the case of the US data in Figure 11.2 These are: (1) the inability to establish a clear cause-and-effect relationship between school factors and academic achievement due to the cross-sectional nature of PISA data; and (2) the incapacity to draw conclusions on the impact of teacher and school effects for specific demographics, namely for low income and for different race/ethnic groups, due to lack of data.

A third limitation of these results is specific to cross-country samples. Cross-cultural differences may cause a characteristic to take on somewhat different meanings in different countries. This in turn may affect the findings we draw, affect the significance of some effects, or cause unexpected negative effects. For example, cultural factors can cause variations in student motivation and parental emphasis on schooling. Finally, there are other school factors that PISA does not measure, which may be relevant for explaining academic achievement in an international context. Examples include length of school year, length of school day, curriculum, and how time and resources are used.

Notes

1 PISA survey also collects student-assessed class environment variables (namely, disciplinary climate and teacher–student relations). Many researchers have often emphasized these factors when explaining academic achievement. We do not include these factors in this research as their relationship with academic achievement is likely to be influenced by student characteristics such as their attitude toward achievement.
2 PISA utilizes school-based surveys, based on a stratified and clustered sampling design. See OECD (2009), for details on sampling design. Probability weights are used to account for the sampling design.
3 See OECD (2009) for more details about how PISA calculates plausible scores for each student.
4 A strong correlation can either be negative (−), indicating an inverse relationship, or positive (+), indicating a synchronous relationship.
5 The estimation method is full information maximum likelihood (FIML), which corrects for missing values. As a result, the standardized effects are based on the full sample size of $N = 4,978$ students. The standard errors are robust and clustered by school.
6 The estimation method is FIML, which corrects for missing values. As a result, the standardized effects are based on the full sample size of $N = 131,046$ students. The standard errors are robust and clustered by school. The country-specific effects are modelled as fixed effects.

7 The between versus within analysis confirms the small effect of school factors below that found for US students only. The between school score variation accounts for less than one-tenth of the students' math and science achievement differences across the ten OECD countries, which compares to one-quarter of the US students.

References

Baker, D.P., Goesling, B., & Letendre, G.K. (2002). Socioeconomic status, school quality, and national economic development: A cross-national analysis of the "Heyneman-Loxley effect" on mathematics and science achievement. *Comparative Education Review* 46: 291–312.

Beese, J., & Liang, X. (2010). Do resources matter? PISA science achievement comparisons between students in the United States, Canada and Finland. *Improving Schools* 13(3): 266–279.

Fuchs, T., & Woessman, L. (2007). What accounts for international differences in student performance? A re-examination using PISA data. *Empirical Economics* 32: 433–464.

Nonoyama-Tarumi, Y. (2005). *A Cross-National, Multi-Level Study of Family Background and School Resource Effects on Student Achievement*, Doctoral Dissertation, Columbia University, New York.

Nonoyama-Tarumi, Y., & Willms, J.D. (2010). The relative and absolute risks of disadvantaged family background and low levels of school resources on student literacy. *Economics of Education Review* 29: 214–224.

OECD. (2012). *PISA 2012 Results in Focus: What 15-Year-Olds Know and What They Can Do With What They Know* (Paris: OECD Publisher).

Park, E.J. (2013). *Explaining Achievement Disparities between the United States and South Korea*, Doctoral Dissertation, George Mason University, Arlington, VA.

Sousa, S., Park, E.J., & Armor, D.J. (2012). Comparing effects of family and school factors on cross-national academic achievement using the 2009 and 2006 PISA surveys. *Journal of Comparative Policy Analysis: Research and Practice* 14(5): 449–468.

Woessman, L. et al. (2009). *School Accountability, Autonomy and Choice Around the World* (Cheltenham, UK: Edward Elgar).

Xia, N. (2009). *Family Factors and Student Outcomes*, Doctoral Dissertation, Pardee RAND Graduate School, Santa Monica, CA.

12 The Impact of School Composition

Aron Malatinszky and David J. Armor

Introduction

Social science researchers and policymakers alike have long held interest in the effects of school composition—the distribution of a student's in-school peers along dimensions such as race, sex, socioeconomic status, or ability—on achievement. In principle, a relationship between school composition (in any dimension) and achievement could yield a crucial policy tool for improving educational outcomes. Indeed, the types of classmates to which students are exposed constitute a certain school resource as well: one that districts can adjust by intentionally redistributing students across schools.

In particular, school socioeconomic composition, or school SES, has been subject to considerable attention in education research in the past half century, having received substantial emphasis in the original analyses of the Coleman Report and in integration efforts throughout the last half of the twentieth century. The Coleman Report itself detected a powerful correlation between school SES and a variety of outcomes, concluding that "the social composition of the student body is more highly related to achievement, independently of the student's own social background, than is any school factor" (Coleman, 1966, p. 325). A later re-analysis of the Coleman data by Marshal Smith found that the relationship was due to a coding error, which Coleman himself acknowledged (Smith, 1972).

While this statistical relationship constituted a striking feature of the American educational landscape in and of itself, the degree to which the correlation translates to a true causal effect of school SES on achievement has been debated in academic circles since the original release of the Coleman Report. A potential selection issue is immediately apparent: would a student with primarily low-SES classmates truly perform better in a higher-SES school, or does the correlation merely capture the tendency of higher-achieving students, who may well outperform other students regardless of their school composition, to attend higher-SES schools?

In the decades since, both the social context, in which schools operate, and the tools that social scientists have developed to assess composition effects

DOI: 10.4324/9781003399117-12

have evolved significantly. This chapter provides an overview of the academic literature on measuring the effects of school SES on achievement, particularly highlighting a handful of studies in the past decade that have focused on overcoming the potential selection issue.

Fifty Years After Coleman: A Review of the Literature

The literature on school SES effects was long characterized by a series of cross-sectional studies, including the Coleman Report, finding a positive relationship between SES aggregated at the classroom, grade, or school level and student achievement. One of the key findings of the Coleman Report was the strong relationship between fellow-student background characteristics, aggregated at the grade level for each school, and individual achievement, controlling for individual student characteristics.

Several studies on school SES effects following the Coleman Report confirmed the strong statistical relationship between aggregate SES and individual achievement, though by the 1970s, a growing concern over whether these findings were driven by true effects or selection had emerged (Alexander et al., 1979). As early as 1971, St. John and Lewis showed that the relationship between school SES and achievement appears to diminish when controlling for prior reading achievement (1971). Controls for prior achievement and the longitudinal analysis of achievement growth became increasingly commonplace in the school effectiveness literature by the 1980s (Hoffer et al., 1985).

The transition to analyzing achievement growth helped alleviate some of the concerns over the potential selection issue. Intuitively, controlling for baseline levels of achievement should shift focus away from the variation in students' outcomes due to differences in initial ability that might otherwise be falsely attributed to the schools they attend. Nonetheless, this merely transforms the issue into one of selection on unobservable characteristics that relate to achievement growth, rather than achievement levels. Moreover, only some confounding unobservable characteristics could be related to prior achievement at all.

Into the twenty-first century, studies on school SES effects have placed emphasis on tackling the potential selection issue through increasingly sophisticated statistical methods. Rumberger and Palardy (2005) find a positive effect of school SES on test score growth across four subjects with nationally representative data on high school students using hierarchical linear modeling, an approach developed to separate the effects of individual-level characteristics from those of group-level characteristics. In an alternative direction, by calculating students' probabilities of attending schools with given levels of aggregate SES using observable individual, parent, and peer characteristics and using them as regression weights in a propensity score matching approach, Crosnoe (2009) concludes that low-income students experience diminished math and science test score growth and increased psychosocial problems when attending higher-SES schools.

While both of these studies introduce an extensive array of controls, they nevertheless rely on different methods of controlling for observable features without eliminating the threat of selection on unobservable confounds. More recent approaches to studying school composition effects have turned to statistical techniques that are expressly designed for dealing with unobservable confounds, such as fixed effects and instrumental variable regression methods.

In a particularly compelling study using a student fixed effects approach, which was discussed in Chapter 4, with longitudinal administrative data from North Carolina, Lauen and Gaddis (2013) find negligible effects of classroom poverty levels on test scores. Moreover, the authors find that their estimates are significantly smaller than what they would find using a cross-sectional or growth model approach.

In 2018, we made a novel contribution to the school SES literature ourselves, along with Dr. Gary Marks of the University of Melbourne, extending the fixed effects approach used by Lauen and Gaddis (2013) to an unprecedented three-state longitudinal sample with more than three million student-year observations. The following section presents some brief motivation for our study's approach, leveraging the depth and structure of the longitudinal sample used in our study, and a summary of our study's results.

Armor et al. (2018)

To motivate the use of fixed effects analysis in measuring the impact of school SES on student achievement, we begin with an illustrative approach. First, consider any given student in our three-state sample—say, a low-income white third-grader in a low-SES school in Arkansas. We know the student's math achievement score, as it is an observable outcome. In identifying the effects of school SES, however, we're interested in comparing this observable outcome to one we do not see in the data: the math achievement score that the exact same low-income white third-grader in Arkansas would have gotten had they attended a high-SES school. By definition, this conceptual comparison score, called a *counterfactual* outcome, can never be observed.

Before considering how one can circumvent this fundamental issue in drawing causal inferences, consider the relationships we see in the data without any sophisticated statistical analysis. Figure 12.1 shows math achievement scores for four cohorts of low-income students as they progress from third to eighth grade in Arkansas. For this graph, low-income students are divided into four groups: white students in low-SES schools, white students in high-SES schools, black students in low-SES schools, and black students in high-SES schools. Standardized achievement scores are calibrated to show growth over the six-year period.

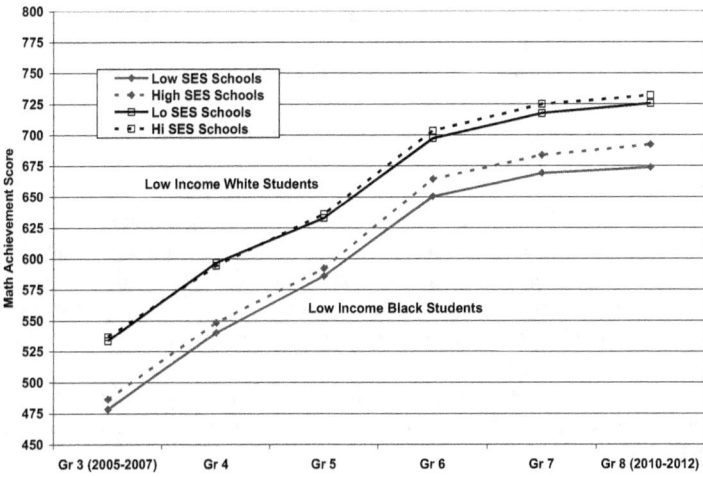

Figure 12.1 Math Scores for Low-Income Students by Race and School SES, Arkansas.

The first, and perhaps most important, observation in Figure 12.1 is the comparison of mean achievement scores for low-income students between low- and high-SES schools. The mean math achievement growth over six years among low-income black students in low-SES schools is 195 points, compared to a growth of low-income black students in high-SES schools of 206 points. Since the standard deviation here is approximately 100 points, the achievement growth difference of 9 points is relatively small: around 2 percent of the baseline level. The same is true for low-income white students: low-income white students in low-SES schools gain 192 points, compared to 195 points for low-income white students in high-SES schools.

Moreover, there is very little change in the black–white achievement gap over this six-year period; all four groups show quite substantial increases in achievement but not at very different rates. In low-SES schools, for example, the black–white achievement gap among low-income students is a striking 55 points in third grade, and still 50 points in eighth grade: a 10 percent reduction over six years.

This illustration of the data doesn't necessarily lend itself to any causal inferences; Figure 12.1 merely compares growth across averages. While it presents an interesting comparison in trajectories of the average low-income white third-grader in a low-SES school and the average low-income white third-grader in a high-SES school, the latter set of outcomes can only approximate the counterfactual outcomes we are interested in. This may well be an apples-to-oranges comparison if the students attending low-SES schools fundamentally differ from the students attending high-SES schools in ways that can affect achievement growth. In other words, this simple analysis is subject to the same potential selection issue discussed in the previous section.

Suppose, however, that any fundamental differences between observably identical students attending low-SES and high-SES schools, insofar as they affect test scores, are fixed at baseline. That is, the impact of any unobservable student characteristic related both to school SES and achievement outcomes remains unchanged throughout the sample period. This is the key assumption in fixed effects analysis. Given this assumption, fixed effects analysis solves the problem of unobserved student characteristics by entering an independent indicator variable for each student in the regression equation, thus controlling for any fixed features that are specific to each student.

When test scores are available for individual students across three or more years, as they are in most statewide achievement databases, modern statistical software packages can be used to estimate student fixed effect models when there are large numbers of observations (e.g., in the millions, like in our three-state sample). Although fixed effect models are not new, the ability to estimate high-dimensional multiway fixed effect models in statewide achievement databases—with hundreds of thousands of students, thousands of schools, and dozens of years and grade levels all representing individual sources of unobserved heterogeneity—is still a relatively recent development.

The advantage of student fixed effect models is that they control for both measured and unmeasured time-invariant student background attributes that can contribute to student achievement. When estimating the effect of school SES on academic achievement, a student fixed effects regression will not only control for the measured student characteristics of race and poverty, but it will also control for the unmeasured student characteristics of parent education, baseline family wealth, and any other stable family characteristic that influences achievement and that is not explicitly included in the regression equation.

The key specification in our own 2018 study is a fixed effects regression analysis. We analyze individual achievement test scores in Arkansas, North Carolina, and South Carolina for students in Grades 3 to 8 over periods of four to eight years. School SES is measured by the percentage of low-income students in a given school in a particular year and grade. The study concludes that school SES effects nearly vanish after controlling for student and grade-by-year fixed effects.

Similar to Lauen and Gaddis (2013), we relate our results to estimates obtained using pooled cross-sectional and growth models. Similar to the series of cross-sectional analyses supporting the original findings on school SES effects in the Coleman Report, the pooled cross-sectional analyses show strong standardized effects for individual student SES, ranging from .22 in Arkansas to .32 in North Carolina in math and from .23 in Arkansas to .33 in North Carolina in reading, and moderate effects for school SES, ranging from .12 in Arkansas to .16 in South Carolina.

In contrast, however, the student fixed effects analyses produce coefficients for student SES and school SES that are zero or very close to zero. To reiterate, in concurrence with Lauen and Gaddis (2013), the student fixed effect models show, in all three statewide databases, that there is virtually no relationship between the socioeconomic composition of schools and the academic achievement of students once measured and unmeasured fixed student background are controlled for.

While our study's findings are broadly consistent with those of previous observational studies with similar empirical methodologies, the study itself is not without limitations. It is compelling to see that school SES effects diminish as more controls are added, but it is still possible that time-variant confounders—any unobserved factors affecting both school SES and achievement in a manner that varies with respect to time—bias the results. Since time-variant confounders, by definition, are not fixed over time, they are not controlled for in the fixed effects framework.

A more testable concern over the results of the study emerged in the years after its publication. Sciffer et al. (2020) raise the issue of potentially insufficient within-variance for estimating a fixed effects model. Fixed effects regression eliminates any stable differences between individuals from the analysis, thus relying on only the portion of variance in treatments and outcomes that occurs within individuals over time. When treatments don't change over time at all, within-variance is zero and fixed effects estimation is not possible. When treatments change only in trivial amounts over time, fixed effects estimation is noisy and results may be unreliable. The concern voiced by Sciffer et al. (2020) was that school SES may fall under the latter case if grade-level peer composition in schools varies little from year to year.

In Malatinszky and Armor (2021), we respond to this concern with a series of diagnostic tests whose results suggest that school SES varies over time more than one might think. Figure 12.2 considers the proportion of grade-level peers classified as low income for each student-year observation in our Arkansas sample, taking the difference between the highest proportion and the lowest proportion each student experiences in his or her observed educational career and plotting the distribution of differences across students.

The median difference in the distribution shown in Figure 12.2 is a sizeable 9 percentage points; under this measure, over 90,000 Arkansas students experience changes in school SES of almost 20 percentage points or more. Accordingly, introducing student fixed effects to the regression analysis in our 2018 study doesn't significantly increase the standard errors of our effect estimates, even when students who move between schools (whether for structural or non-structural reasons) and grade-repeaters are omitted from the analysis sample.

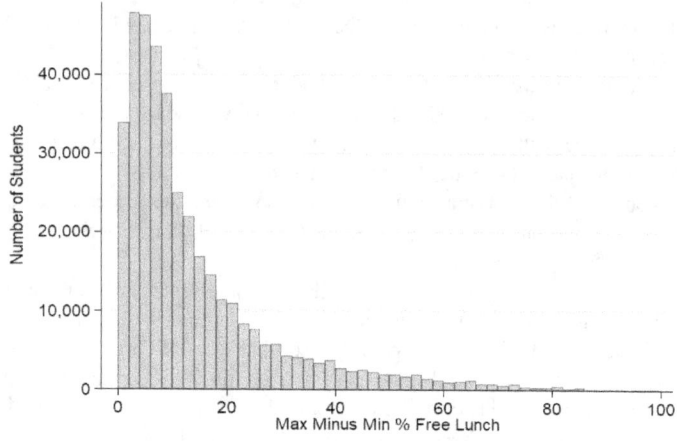

Figure 12.2 The Distribution of Within-Student Ranges for Low-Income Status.

As a result, the concern over insufficient within-variance for estimating fixed effect models does not appear to be a substantive issue.

Subsequent Developments in the Literature

In the years since the publication of the article, there has been continued research and interest in the use of longitudinal and quasi-experimental models in studying the effects of school composition in the social sciences.

Recent econometric advances in the literature on the economics of education have facilitated the measurement of school value-added by leveraging the random variation in school assignment induced by tiebreakers in the school choice algorithms implemented in several urban school districts. In these school choice settings, applicants to public schools submit ranked lists of preferences for school programs, and schools determine admission priorities for each student based on school- or district-specific rules. To select between equally prioritized students, schools use tiebreakers, which are typically randomly drawn lottery numbers or cutoffs in admissions criteria. Given a student's submitted preferences, granted priorities, and exposure to admissions cutoffs, Abdulkadiroğlu et al. (2017) and Abdulkadiroğlu et al. (2022) derive propensity scores capturing the student's probability of admission to each school. Controlling for these propensity scores, offers of admission are functions of exogenous tiebreakers and thus conditionally random, yielding viable instruments for school attendance to use in an instrumental variables regression framework.

Using this novel statistical technology, Angrist et al. (forthcoming) find that causal value-added measured under this framework is uncorrelated with school racial composition in the New York City and Denver public school systems, suggesting that the observable correlation between achievement growth and school racial composition largely reflects the selection of students into schools, rather than a causal link.

In another application, Angrist et al. (2022) investigate the statistical tendency of students in New York City and Boston public schools who choose to attend schools outside of their neighborhoods (i.e., students who are "bused" in the modern context) to achieve higher standardized test scores and college-going rates than those who attend neighborhood schools. The authors find that this phenomenon reflects the selection of students into schools as well; using a similar instrumental variables regression framework yields precise null effects of non-neighborhood school attendance on achievement and college attendance, in spite of marked integrative effects.

Elsewhere in the social sciences, researchers are actively developing and applying longitudinal methods for uncovering school composition effects. Using a lagged score value-added model with nationally representative data from the Early Childhood Longitudinal Study, kindergarten class of 2010–2011, Dumont and Ready (2020) find no effect of school SES on achievement, but a negative effect of school minority composition on achievement growth.

Borrowing a methodology developed in the public health literature, Carbonaro et al. (2023) use longitudinal data from North Carolina with a structural nested mean model using regression with residuals to estimate the longer-term, cumulative effects of school SES. Though they find statistically significant negative effects of cumulative exposure to school poverty throughout Grades 4 to 8 on eighth-grade student achievement, the effects are quite small—particularly when assessed relative to typical variation in eighth-grade test scores.

In summary, the literature on school compositional effects is still as active and contentious as it was when our own contribution was published in 2018. In spite of this persistency, the literature has exhibited significant evolution, with several new studies abandoning the cross-sectional approaches of earlier work in favor of more modern quasi-experimental and longitudinal methods. The findings of Angrist et al., in particular, are consistent with our findings of very small or no effect of school SES.

References

Abdulkadiroğlu, A., Angrist, J.D., Narita, Y., & Pathak, P.A. (2017). Research design meets market design: Using centralized assignment for impact evaluation. *Econometrica* 85(5): 1373–1432.

Abdulkadiroğlu, A., Angrist, J.D., Narita, Y., & Pathak, P.A. (2022). Breaking ties: Regression discontinuity design meets market design. *Econometrica* 90(1): 117–151.

Alexander, K.L., Fennessey, J., McDill, E.L., & D'Amico, R.J. (1979). School SES influences-composition or context? *Sociology of Education* 52(4): 222–237.

Angrist, J., Gray-Lobe, G., Idoux, C.M., & Pathak, P.A. (2022). *Still Worth the Trip? School Busing Effects in Boston and New York (No. w30308)* (Cambridge, MA: National Bureau of Economic Research).

Angrist, J., Hull, P., Pathak, P.A., & Walters, C.R. (Forthcoming). Race and the mismeasure of school quality. *American Economic Review: Insights*.

Armor, D.J., Marks, G.N., & Malatinszky, A. (2018). The impact of school SES on student achievement: Evidence from US statewide achievement data. *Educational Evaluation and Policy Analysis* 40(4): 613–630.

Carbonaro, W., Lauen, D.L., & Levy, B.L. (2023). Does cumulative exposure to high-poverty schools widen test-score inequality? *Sociology of Education* 96(2): 81–103. https://doi.org/10.1177/00380407221147889

Coleman, J.S. (1966). *Equality of Educational Opportunity* (Washington, DC: U. S. Department of Health, Education, and Welfare).

Crosnoe, R. (2009). Low-income students and the socioeconomic composition of public high schools. *American Sociological Review* 74(5): 709–730.

Dumont, H., & Ready, D.D. (2020). Do schools reduce or exacerbate inequality? How the associations between student achievement and achievement growth influence our understanding of the role of schooling. *American Educational Research Journal* 57(2): 728–774.

Hoffer, T., Greeley, A.M., & Coleman, J.S. (1985). Achievement growth in public and catholic schools. *Sociology of Education* 58(2): 74–97.

Lauen, D.L., & Gaddis, S.M. (2013). Exposure to classroom poverty and test score achievement: Contextual effects or selection? *American Journal of Sociology* 118(4): 943–979.

Malatinszky, A., & Armor, D.J. (2021). Comment on MG Sciffer, LB Perry, & AM McConney, "critiques of socio-economic school compositional effects: Are they valid?". *British Journal of Sociology of Education* 42(5–6): 609–615.

Rumberger, R.W., & Palardy, G.J. (2005). Does segregation still matter? The impact of student composition on academic achievement in high school. *Teachers College Record* 107(9): 1999–2045.

Sciffer, M.G., Perry, L.B., & McConney, A. (2020). Critiques of socio-economic school compositional effects: Are they valid? *British Journal of Sociology of Education* 41(4): 462–475.

Smith, M.S. (1972). *Equality of Educational Opportunity: The Basic Findings Reconsidered*, Cambridge, MA., Center for Educational Policy Research, Harvard Graduate School of Education.

St. John, N.H., & Lewis, R. (1971). The influence of school racial context on academic achievement. *Social Problems* 19(1): 68–79.

13 What Works If Conventional Resources Do Not?

David J. Armor and Anna Grace Garren

Introduction

Earlier chapters in this book have examined numerous research and data sources to test the effects of school resources on K–12 academic achievement as measured by standardized testing. The evidence in these earlier chapters is overwhelming that conventional resources—expenditures, class sizes, teacher qualifications and experience, and principal qualifications—have, at best, very small impacts on achievement. These impacts appear to be on the order of .05 or less in the metric of standardized effects. This chapter aims to expand this inquiry by investigating special programs or policies that appear to have larger impacts on academic achievement than conventional resources, particularly for students from disadvantaged backgrounds.

Three bodies of research are investigated. The first is a 2017 meta-analysis by Jens Dietrichson and his colleagues, which identifies certain interventions that appear to be more effective than conventional resources for low-income students. The second source is a series of programs and studies by Roland Fryer and colleagues in Harlem charter schools, and whose results were exported to several large high-poverty districts. The third source is teacher effectiveness as measured by the so-called value-added methods. All three of these sources appear to produce standardized effects over .20, which is substantially higher than conventional resources.

The Dietrichson et al. Meta-Analysis

The discussion in this section is based on the research paper, "Academic Interventions for Elementary and Middle School Students with Low Socioeconomic Status: A Systematic Review and Meta-Analysis," by Jens Dietrichson et al.[1] This meta-analysis synthesizes the results from a large number of studies that aim to raise achievement scores of students from lower-socioeconomic families.

All selected studies were required to utilize either randomized controlled trials (RCTs) or quasi-experimental designs. The review broke down the

Table 13.1 Number of Studies, Weighted Average ES, Confidence Intervals, I^2, and τ^2.

Intervention Component	k	Average ESs	95% CI	I^2	τ^2
Incentives	8	0.01	[−0.02, 0.04]	59.9	0
After-school programs	3	0.02	[−0.06, 0.11]	36.9	0
Summer programs	8	0.03	[−0.06, 0.12]	47.7	0.01
Coaching students	11	0.04	[−0.14, 0.22]	60.4	0.03
Psychological interventions	7	0.05	[−0.16, 0.26]	73.3	0.05
Personnel development	8	0.07	[−0.05, 0.18]	97.2	0.02
Increased resources	2	0.08	[0.01, 0.15]	0.0	0
Computer-assist. instruction	9	0.11	[−0.01, 0.22]	69.5	0.02
Content changes	9	0.15	[0.03, 0.28]	76.6	0.02
Coaching personnel	10	0.16	[0.04, 0.28]	94.2	0.03
Cooperative learning	10	0.22	[0.10, 0.34]	74.1	0.02
Small-group instruction	4	0.24	[0.00, 0.48]	86.1	0.05
Feedback and monitoring	5	0.32	[0.18, 0.47]	70.1	0.02
Tutoring	36	0.36	[0.26, 0.45]	65.3	0.05

Source: This table is adapted from Table 3 in the Dietrichson article.

different studies according to the type of intervention, and 14 different types were identified. Table 13.1 is adapted from a table in the study, and it shows the number of estimates for each type of intervention (k), the average standardized ES, and the 95% confidence levels. A graph showing the average ESs, arranged from smallest to largest, is shown in Figure 13.1. It is clear that the largest average ESs are observed for the interventions of cooperative learning (ES=.22), small-group instruction (ES=.24), feedback and monitoring (ES=.32), and one-on-one tutoring (ES=.36).

We wanted to choose one of these high-impact interventions to conduct a more in-depth review of case studies to examine whether there might be any special conditions that might be inflating ESs. For several reasons, we selected tutoring for a more intensive review. First, it has by far the largest effect, being a third higher than small-group instruction. Second, it is based on the largest number of independent studies—36—which is more than three times as many studies as coaching which has the second largest. Finally, it is less likely to require substantial specialized knowledge and skills to implement compared to other techniques such as cooperative learning. Note that the second- and third-highest effects, small-group instruction, and feedback/monitoring are based on only four or five studies, respectively.

In our initial examination, we noted that some of the ESs were very large for individual subtests in many of the 36 tutoring studies, often exceeding 1.0. Some of these subtests involved very basic skills, such as letter recognition or counting, which might not be good predictors for the type of skills assessed in standardized reading and math achievement tests used in higher grades.

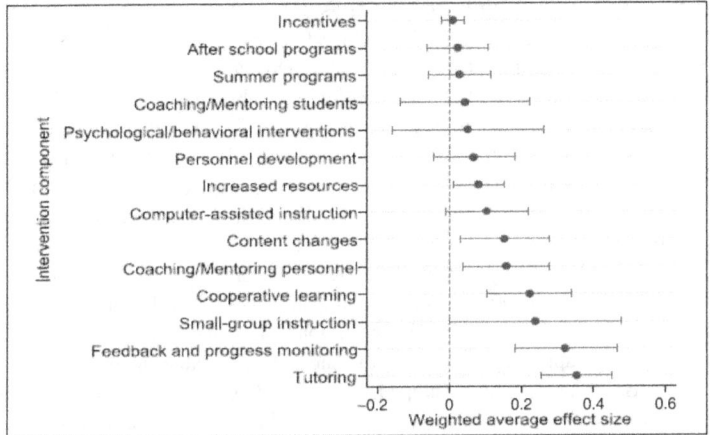

Figure 13.1 Average Effect Size on Achievement for Alternative Interventions.
Source: Copy of Figure 5 in Dietrichson et al. article.

That is, they might not be valid predictors of reading or math achievement. To remedy this concern, we re-did the meta-analysis for the tutoring intervention excluding ESs where the test used to evaluate tutoring effectiveness had a criterion validity coefficient less than or equal to .8.

Each study used in the meta-analysis was reviewed to determine the method of evaluation, usually a pencil-paper standardized test. We then researched each test's predictive or concurrent validity coefficient. We found validity coefficients for 85 percent of the 299 ESs. When more than one coefficient was provided, these values were averaged. If no coefficient was found, it was not included in our meta-analysis. The following tests met our inclusion criteria, and therefore studies that used these tests to evaluate the effectiveness of their tutoring interventions were included in our meta-analysis:

1. Slosson Oral Reading Test
2. Woodcock Johnson Diagnostic Reading Battery Test (WJ-DRB)
3. Dynamic Indicators of Basic Early Literacy Skills (DIBELS)
4. National Assessment of Educational Progress (NAEP)
5. Test of Written Spelling (TWS)
6. Test of Word Reading Efficiency (TOWRE)
7. Woodcock Reading Mastery Test (WRMT)
8. Group Reading Assessment and Diagnostic Evaluation (GRADE)
9. Woodcock Johnson III (WJ-III)
10. Northwest Achievement Level Test (NALT)

We calculated the distribution of ESs as we removed studies that had validity below the threshold for that distribution. Generally speaking, as the validity threshold increases, the mean ES decreases. This confirmed our concern that the inclusion of studies with lower validity—usually tests of simple skills like letter recognition—tended to raise the average ES. For the final weighted average ES of tutoring on achievement, we excluded all ESs whose studies had validity coefficients lower than 0.8. This refinement excludes 53 percent of the ESs from the original study, and 44 percent of the ESs for which we found validity coefficients.

Figure 13.2 is a box plot that compares the ES distribution before and after excluding studies according to the validity threshold. The lower part of the figure is a box plot of the original distribution of ESs, while the upper figure is the result after applying the validity threshold of .80. Rather than the original average ES of .36, the new average is .29 for studies with validity coefficients ≥ .80. Note that this refinement substantially reduces the number of outliers—those with ESs over 1.0—from 12 to 5.

We argue that this refinement is a better estimate for the effect of tutoring on achievement, since it is based on studies with adequate validity for predicting future achievement. Since the estimated mean is still affected by some very high outliers, the median ES of .24 may be a more reasonable estimate

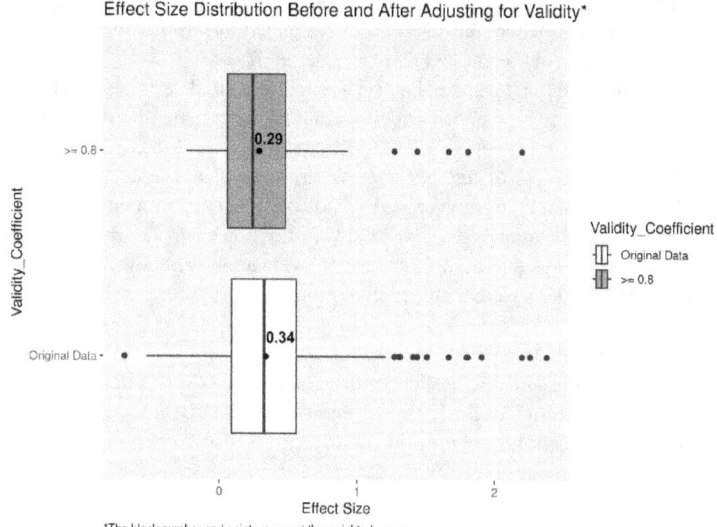

Figure 13.2 Tutoring Effect Sizes Before/After Adjusting for Validity.

Note: Median ES After = .24.

for the tutoring effects. This reduces the final ES by about one-third from the original value of .34. Despite this refinement, the tutoring effect is still higher than all but one of the other interventions—feedback and monitoring, and of course we have not evaluated the validity of other studies. If the other interventions were subjected to the same validity standards, their values may drop as well.

The Roland Fryer Studies

The second major focus of this chapter comes from a series of studies by Roland Fryer and his colleagues from the Education Innovation Laboratory in the Department of Economics at Harvard University. The research was initiated in a series of studies on the charter school program in Harlem, New York, including "Are High-Quality Schools Enough to Increase Achievement Among the Poor?" and "Getting Beneath the Veil of Effective Schools."[2]

That body of research found that several types of school policies and resources had very strong effects on raising student achievement among high-poverty students, a majority of whom were Black, but other types of resources did not. Data on demographics and outcomes were provided by the NYC Department of Education, but other data were gathered by the Fryer team through surveys of principals, teachers, and students, in addition to lesson plans and observations.

Consistent with the research review in Chapter 2 as well as the seven independent studies presented in Chapters 5 through 11, the Fryer team found that the following school resources either were uncorrelated with student achievement or had very weak relationships:

- Class size
- Per pupil expenditures
- Teacher certification credentials
- Teacher with master's or higher degrees

In contrast, they found the following inputs to explain nearly half of the variation in student achievement:

- Frequent teacher feedback
- Data-guided instruction
- High-dosage tutoring (especially one on one)
- Increased instructional time (including tutoring)
- A "culture" of high expectations on the part of teachers and administrators

In order to test the exportability of these "best practices," Fryer's team was offered an opportunity to implement these practices in the Houston public school system using an RCT (randomized experimental) design. The 16 lowest-performing elementary schools, predominantly low-income Hispanic students, were divided randomly into treatment and control groups. In a supplemental quasi-experimental design, they added all remaining elementary schools into the control group. In subsequent refinements, they also added low-performing middle and high schools to the experiment. The elementary schools were two-thirds Hispanic, one-fourth Black, 95 percent economically disadvantaged, and approximately half had limited English proficiency.

The Fryer team implemented five interventions, growing out of their experience evaluating successful charter schools in Harlem: extended learning time, human capital, high-dosage tutoring, data-driven instruction, and a culture of high expectations. Here's their method of implementation in the treatment schools:

- *Extended learning time*: In elementary schools, the school year was extended by 35 days, Saturday classes were encouraged, and non-instructional activity was reduced. In secondary schools, the school year was extended by ten days, Saturday classes were encouraged, and the school day was extended by one hour Monday through Thursday.
- *Human capital*: School leadership and teachers were replaced based on supervisor evaluations, interviews, peer rating index, and value-added data. In addition, staff were provided feedback ten times more than the control setting.
- *High-dosage tutoring*: Fourth, sixth, and ninth graders were provided with additional tutoring. Fourth graders were tutored by being pulled out of class. Sixth and Ninth graders were tutored via an extra class period. The non-tutored secondary grades who were behind received an extra online class.
- *Data-driven instruction*: Preliminary testing that reflected state standards were administered to the students, and the results were used for one-on-one meetings between teachers and students to set performance goals.
- *Culture of high expectations*: Schools and students signed "contracts" similar to those used in many charter schools; also, components of this category include group work, less non-instructional activity, stricter rules, data tracking, goals posted, and less uniform infractions.

The results of the Houston experiment for elementary schools are summarized in Table 13.2. Standardized effects for math are approximately .25 for elementary students (significant at $p \leq .01$). Effects for reading are not statistically significant. Effects for middle and high school students (not shown) were slightly less at .20 (significant at $p \leq .01$).

Similar results were found for a parallel experiment carried out by the Fryer team in the Denver public schools. In both of these experiments, high-dosage tutoring comprised an important component of the effect, thereby

Table 13.2 Summary of Houston Elementary Treatment Effects for Fryer Study.

	2011	2012	2013	Pooled
Math		**.23**	**.26**	**.25**
(SE's)	—	(0.085)	(0.095)	(0.082)
N		39,464	36,010	75,474
Reading		.09	.11	.10
(SEs)	—	−0.055	−0.061	−0.052
N		39,464	36,010	75,474
Years of treatment		0.931	1.791	1.335

Note: Standardized effects in bold are significant at $p < .05$. (SE's in are Standard Errors, not standardized effects).

adding further support for the Dietrichson meta-analysis findings about the effectiveness of tutoring. Moreover, in a separate analysis, the Houston intervention had statistically significant effects for Hispanic students but not Black students, consistent with the findings of the Schueler meta-analysis of turnaround interventions discussed in Chapter 2. Indeed, the Fryer experiments for Houston and Denver were among the studies included in the Schueler meta-analysis.

We note that the ESs of the Houston Experiment (for math) are about the same size as the ESs found in the revised estimate for tutoring. It raises the important question of whether interventions that just use intensive tutoring services for low-performing students, plus monitoring to track them, might generate the same gains without the major costs and disruption caused by the school reorganization intervention.

Teacher Value-Added Assessment

Among teacher characteristics, teacher value-added scores are the only characteristic based on student performance. Basically, value-added scores are calculated by taking the average performance of a teacher's students (in a given year) on standardized tests, adjusted for various student background characteristics know to affect performance. Then that value-added score is used as a teacher characteristic for predicting the performance of a new group of students during the next and subsequent school years.

There has been a major debate in the education research literature on the degree to which value-added scores predict achievement. Some education economists, such as Hanushek and Chetty, believe not only that value-added scores are valid predictors, but that they also do a better job predicting student performance than more traditional credential-based measures.[3] Other education economists, such as Rothstein, are critical of value-added scores, particularly for predicting longer-term student outcomes.[4] The primary criticism of Rothstein is that teacher switching is correlated with student achievement, creating some ambiguity in the causal assumption that teacher value-added measures can predict student achievement without bias. It should be noted that Fryer, in the studies cited earlier, finds teacher value-added assessments to be useful predictors for student achievement.

It is not possible, here, to settle some of the methodological issues concerning the use of teacher value-added scores for predicting longer-term student outcomes. However, it is possible to show some evidence about the short-term effects of teacher value-added scores on student achievement as compared to the more traditional teacher credentials such as education, experience, certification, and so forth using data from a mid-atlantic state.

Figure 13.3 shows the simple correlations between math scores and student background factors, conventional school and teacher resources, and teacher value-added scores for all students in Grades 3 to 8. Test scores were available from 2008 to 2015. The correlations for student background characteristics and conventional resources are very similar to the correlations shown in other chapters. The strongest student background correlation is −.27 for the poverty indicator of free and reduced lunch, while racial background is close behind with Black at −.23 and white at .21. Asian and English as second language are next at .08 and −.06, respectively.

Traditional teacher credentials have relatively small correlations with math scores. The strongest is teacher retention at .07 and next is .05 for those with

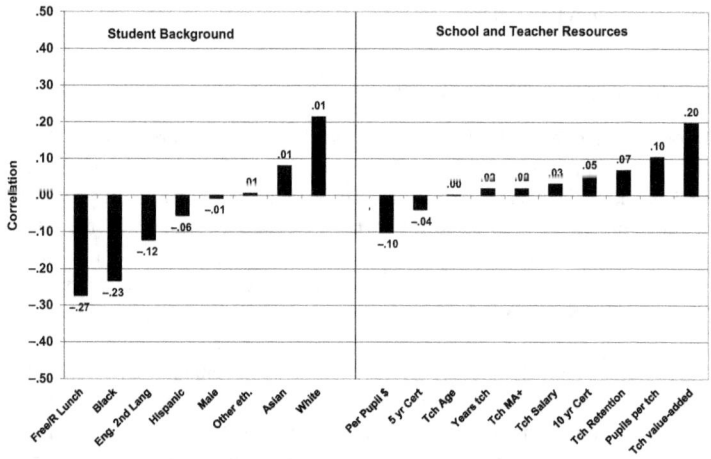

Figure 13.3 Student Background and School Resource Correlations with Math Scores, 2008–2015.

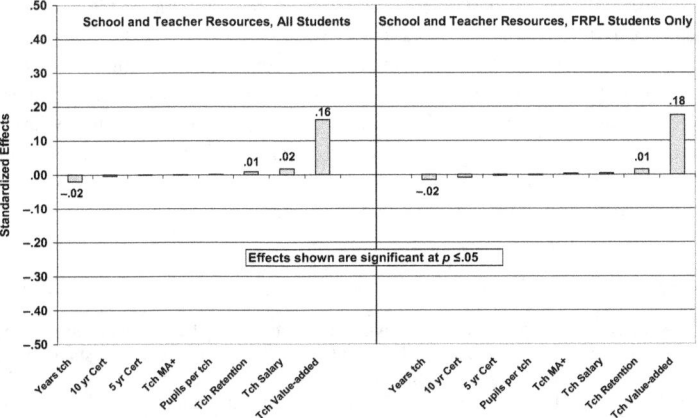

Figure 13.4 Standardized Effects of School Resource on Math Scores, 2008–2015.

ten-year credentials. Teachers with MA degree and years of teaching have quite small correlations of .02. Pupils per teacher (a surrogate for class size) and expenditures have correlations of .10 and −.10, respectively, but these are in the wrong direction—no doubt reflecting a common practice of giving more expenditures to school districts with higher poverty rates—so they can have smaller classes.

Clearly, the correlation of .21 between student math scores and teacher value-added scores is stronger than any correlation observed in this book between a conventional school resource and achievement. This is the only teacher characteristic that has a correlation approaching the strength of student background characteristics such as race.

Figure 13.4 shows the standardized effects of school resources on math achievement after controlling for student background. Two analyses are shown, one for all students and one for free/reduced lunch students only. This procedure tests for the possibility that school resources have a different relationship for low-income students than higher-income students. In this case, we see very little difference in the two analyses for conventional resources, with the possible exception of teacher value-added scores.[5]

After controlling for student background—and excepting teacher value-added scores—there is virtually no relationship between math achievement and other school resources. The strongest conventional school resource is for teacher salary, but the standardized effect is only .02; teacher retention has dropped to just .01. In contrast, the coefficient for teacher value-added scores remains very strong at .16 for all students and actually increases to .18 for low-income students. After controlling for student background characteristics and students' prior achievement, the effect of teacher value-added scores is nearly as large as the effect of students' race.

These data support the policy conclusion of education economists Hanushek, Rivkin, and Chetty that selecting teachers on value-added scores can have dramatic, positive effects on achievement. This result is also consistent with the work of Fryer and colleagues that recruiting and retaining teachers according to their value-added profiles, and placing them in low-income schools, could make significant progress in closing achievement gaps.

Notes

1 Dietrichson, J., Bøg, M., Filges, T. and Jørgensen, A.K. (2017). Academic interventions for elementary and middle school students with low socioeconomic status: A systematic review and meta-analysis. *Review of Educational Research* 87(2): 243–282.
2 Dobbie, W. and Fryer, R.G., Jr. (2011). Are high-quality schools enough to increase achievement among the poor? Evidence from the Harlem children's zone. *American Economic Journal: Applied Economics* 3: 58–187; Dobbie, W. and Fryer, R.G. (2013). Getting beneath the veil of effective schools: Evidence from New York city. *American Economic Journal: Applied Economics* 5: 28–60.
3 Hanushek, E. and Rivkin, S.G. (2012). The distribution of teacher quality and implications for policy. *Annual Review of Economics* 4: 131–157; Chetty, R., Friedman, J. and Rocko, J. (2014). Measuring the impact of teachers I & II. *American Economic Review* 104(9): 2633–2679.
4 Rothstein, J. (2017). *Revisiting the Impacts of Teachers*, IRLE Working Paper No. 101–117, University of California, Berkeley.
5 Note that per capita expenditures are not shown in the figure; that resource is run separately due to collinearity between expenditures and all of the school and teacher resource variables (especially teacher salary). The coefficient for per capita expenditures is −0.03 for all students and −0.02 for poverty students.

14 Summary and Conclusions

David J. Armor

Toward the end of Chapter 1 of this monograph, we noted that "[d]espite the availability of more extensive achievement data and the more sophisticated statistical techniques used in this book, our findings . . . are not that dissimilar to Coleman's." It is remarkable that, despite the severe limitations of the data and methods available to the Coleman team—and to those who reassessed the original data, such as contributors to the 1972 volume edited by Professors Mosteller and Moynihan[1]—their original conclusions are supported, almost without exception, after nearly 60 years.

Whether we examine national achievement testing from the National Assessment of Education Progress (NAEP), international testing by the Program for International Student Assessment (PISA), statewide achievement testing in five states across the nation, or the numerous achievement studies in the research literature, and despite using or reviewing the most sophisticated statistical techniques available, we have shown that

- After controlling for student background, variations in per capita expenditures explain only very small portions of the variation in achievement test scores;
- The types of school resources that most directly influence the level of expenditures—class size, teacher experience and education, teacher certification, and teacher salaries—have very small relationships with student test scores after taking student background into account;
- A very high portion of the variation in test scores is explained by student and family background factors including parental education and income, student race and ethnicity (themselves surrogates for many unmeasured family characteristics), and limited English proficiency; and
- Students of all socioeconomic backgrounds show substantial amounts of learning, but achievement gaps that exist at the beginning of schooling tend to be propagated throughout the school years, showing that schooling has an effect but those effects tend to be uniform across groups of students.

These conclusions do not mean that student achievement (as determined by standardized testing) is not measuring something meaningful or that test scores are unrelated to what students are actually learning. Indeed, in Chapters 1 and 2 we saw that the National Assessment of Education Progress (NAEP) test scores clearly changed over the 30-year time span between 1990 and 2023, and those changes are undoubtedly related to important changes in national and local education policies.

First, national achievement test scores clearly improved between 1990 and 2013, quite dramatically in some grades. These achievement gains are most likely due to national education policy changes that focused on K–12 academic achievement levels, including the Improving Americas School Act of 1994 and the No Child Left Behind (NCLB) Act in 2000. This legislation led to widespread mandatory achievement testing in all public K–12 school systems and to major changes in school accountability requirements. While the primary goal of these legislative initiatives was to reduce the achievement gap between lower- and higher-income families, and especially the Black–White achievement gap, in fact achievement gains were substantial for all groups until 2013.

Second, there is little doubt that what caused the extreme and unprecedented drop in mathematics achievement scores between 2019 and 2022. Because of the COVID-19 crisis, in-class schooling was shut down or severely curtailed in nearly every part of the nation, a massive reduction of face-to-face instruction on a scale not seen in modern history. We interpret these declines of 7 points in eighth-grade math as accountability losses, because lack of in-class instruction removes the basic accountability function of our K–12 education system: in-class, in-person schooling, where teachers can monitor the learning process on a daily basis. The reading losses of three points are less dramatic, perhaps indicating that reading proficiency is less dependent on student–teacher interactions.

Ironically, that very shut down enables us to interpret another trend in the national NAEP data discussed in Chapters 1 and 2, which is the decline in NAEP scores between 2013 and 2019. Although some education economists have linked these to the 2008 recession, a better explanation is termination of the Annual Yearly Progress requirements when ESSA replaced NCLB in 2015. Most states that had recession-induced school funding had restored that funding by 2016, yet test scores for most states continued to fall (or leveled off) until 2019.

More explicit tests of school expenditure effects are found in the meta-analysis of Chapter 2 and the five adequacy case studies in Chapters 6 through 10, which find standardized effects of .03, .2, .02, .05, .01, and 0, respectively. Considering that the average effect size in the meta-analysis is about 0.02, we can say that all of the studies and data assessed in this book support a conclusion that the effect of school expenditures is not zero, but it is quite small. As such, the evidence is overwhelming that simply raising school expenditures, without regard to how that money is spent, is likely to have very small impacts on raising student test scores or closing achievement gaps.

Not surprisingly, and in fact by way of explanation, this study has reviewed numerous evaluations for most of the conventional school resources that money can buy—smaller class sizes (or lower pupil–teacher ratios), more teachers with MA or higher degrees, more certified teachers, teachers with more experience, higher teacher salaries, and greater teacher retention rates.[2] We have estimates from the meta-analyses discussed in Chapter 2, the analysis of the NAEP eighth-grade math scores, five case studies from adequacy lawsuits, and the analysis of PISA data for USA's 15-year-olds.

Table 14.1 is a summary of the standardized effects for most of the conventional school resources discussed in this book (other than expenditures). The first row shows the median values from the meta-analyses discussed in Chapter 2; the second row shows effect sizes from the NAEP eighth-grade math analysis in Chapter 5; the next five rows are results from the case studies discussed in Chapters 6 through 10; and the last row shows results from Chapter 11, which estimated effect sizes from the PISA data for the US students. Not all resources are assessed in every study, but the New York and New Mexico case studies are the most complete.

Of course, we would not expect all estimated effects to be the same or even close. Nevertheless, the variation in the sizes of these standardized effects, across very different data sources using diverse methodologies, is quite limited. Indeed, the agreement among these studies is quite remarkable, and variations are generally small with one or two exceptions.

Teachers having a master's degree (or higher) shows the greatest agreement, with nine standardized effect sizes ranging from −.02 to +.02. There is less agreement for teacher experience, with only one study—the national NAEP analysis in Chapter 5—agreeing with the meta-analysis effect size of .05. Likewise, teacher certification shows two case studies, New Mexico and North Carolina, with effect sizes the same or very close to the meta-analysis.

Table 14.1 Summary of Estimated School Resource Effects (Standardized).

Source	Teacher Master's +	Teacher Experience	Teacher Certification	Teacher Retention	Teacher Salary	Class Size/PTR
Meta-analyses	.00	.05	.05	.00	–	–
NAEP USA	.02	.05	.02	–	–	−.01
New York	−.02	.00	.00	.01	.03	−.02
New Mexico[a]	−.01	.00	.04	−.01	.02	.00
South Dakota	.01	.03	.00	–	−.04	−.05
South Carolina	.01	–	.03	.01	−.01	−.02
North Carolina	.01	.00	.05	.00	–	.00
PISA[b]	.02	–	.02	.09	–	−.06

Notes: [a]Grades 3–5 used due to slightly larger effects than Grades 6–8.
[b]Teacher retention is defined as no teacher shortage.

Somewhat surprisingly, teacher retention shows the smallest effect size with the exception of the PISA study, although the PISA measure is quite different from the other case studies. In the PISA data, we have a variable named "shortage of qualified teachers." That may well indicate a more serious staffing problem than the rate at which teachers fail to return to their same school in the subsequent school year.

Teacher salary shows the most variation of any of these conventional school resources, with effect sizes ranging from .03 in New York to −.04 in South Dakota. Finally, we see more agreement for the effect of class size or pupil–teacher ratios. Effect sizes range from 0 in New Mexico and North Carolina to the negative effects of −.05 in South Dakota and −.06 in the PISA data. However, the average for all of these effect sizes is only .01. This variation in class size effects mirrors the variation in the research literature, such as the modest positive effects of class size reductions found for the Tennessee Star experiment compared to the negative effects found for smaller class size policies implemented by the California class size reduction initiative.

Needless to say, we have been only partially successful in convincing all adequacy case Judges that more money—even a lot more money—is unlikely to increase achievement or close achievement gaps between low-income minority students and higher-income White students. In the five adequacy cases discussed in this book, we were successful making those arguments in South Dakota and South Carolina but unsuccessful in New York and New Mexico. Our failure in New York is especially distressing, given the aftermath of the education adequacy "wars" in that state.

After a recession-induced pause in K–12 school spending between 2011 and 2013, New York State increased per pupil school spending from about $22,000 in 2013 to nearly $26,000 in 2019 (in constant 2021 dollars). At least some of these increases were justified in terms of the needs of economically disadvantaged students. But did these sizeable spending increases have an impact on academic achievement and/or achievement gaps? Figure 14.1 shows, most emphatically, that they did not. In fact, after many years of improvement, both Black and Hispanic achievement plunged following the 2014–2015 school year.

New York's eighth-grade NAEP math achievement levels for Black students fell from its high of 264 in 2015 to 258 in 2019—*a loss of 6 points* prior to the COVID-19 crisis. During the COVID-19 shutdown, eighth-grade math dropped another 7 points to 251 in 2022. The pre-COVID-19 loss took Black eighth-grade math achievement back to 2007 levels, and then the COVID-19-related losses reduced it *literally* to where it stood in the year 2000! The New York State Black–White achievement gap, which was 40 points in 1996, was reduced to 26 points by 2015—a reduction of about one-third. Then, after NCLB Act was replaced by ESSA, the New York achievement gap widened back to 34 points in 2019 despite these massive spending increases, and the gap widened another point to 35 in 2022. The Black–White gap now stands at a full

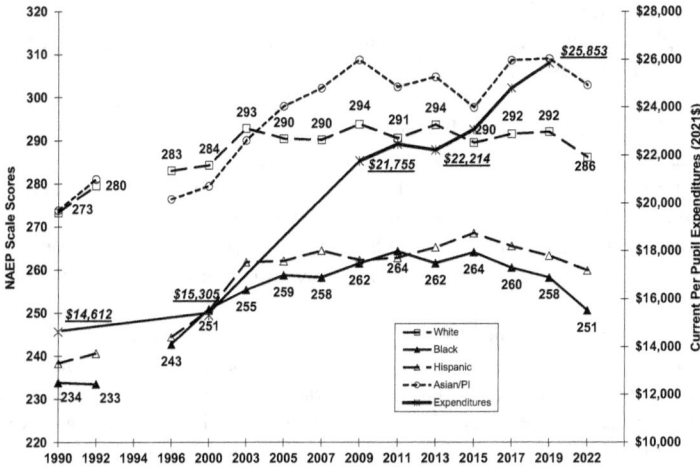

Figure 14.1 NAEP Eighth-Grade Math Scores by Race/Ethnicity and Per Capita Expenditures for New York State.

standard deviation, which takes it back to where it was in the early 2000s. New York's increased expenditures clearly did not fulfill the plaintiffs' claims, which were memorialized by the highest Court in the state.

There may be at least a partial antidote to this rather discouraging picture of money's failure to fix the achievement gap. The promising practices described in Chapter 13, plus several of the reforms from school turnaround interventions discussed in Chapter 2, offer possible pathways for improving academic achievement for disadvantaged students. These practices include one-on-one tutoring and replacing less effective with more effective teachers using value-added methods. It is quite possible that some of these practices can be implemented without major new expenditures. For example, tutoring of children in the lower grades could use college students as tutors.

The key to the success of future interventions is to monitor and target individuals or groups who are achieving below the standards for that grade level and then devise tutoring programs that address the specific skill deficiencies in question. These should be implemented as early as possible starting in kindergarten and continuing through the elementary grades. Targeting those in need, and focusing on tutoring those students as they progress through elementary school, is the most cost-effective way to reduce the achievement gap.

In addition, national- and state-level policymakers should consider reinstating some of the accountability policies of the NCLB program, which appears to have been effective in raising achievement between the early 1990s and 2015 when it was abandoned. If this policy is further targeted on those schools with high proportions of disadvantaged children, we might be able to resume the achievement gains observed during those years and, ultimately, further reduce achievement gaps with a cost-effective education policy.

Finally, according to all of the evidence reviewed in this book, the *least* effective way to improve achievement may be court interventions in response to adequacy lawsuits. The problem with these cases is they are focused almost entirely on money and not on what reforms or programs are most likely to improve achievement for low-achieving groups. This is precisely the wrong focus, because according to the studies reviewed here, more money—and the conventional resources that more money buys—are not going to fix the problem of low achievement.

Courts are accustomed to a theory of causation that usually requires a *yes* or *no* answer—or guilty versus not guilty—not a statistical likelihood that a certain policy or program will have an average effect of a certain size. When a Court accepts the testimony of an expert who looks at Figure 2.3 and says "yes, more money will improve achievement," the Court does not ask the logical follow-up questions, which are "how much money?" and "what should it be spent on?" and "how much improvement will that money produce?" Those questions should be examined, debated, and eventually decided by a more deliberative body, hopefully with input from experts who can interpret this evidence and recommend policies most likely to improve achievement for those needing it most.

Notes

1 Mosteller, F. and Moynihan, D.P., eds. (1972). *On the Equality of Educational Opportunity*, New York, Random House.
2 Technically, teacher retention itself is not strictly a resource, but we assume it is influenced by resources such as salary, smaller class sizes, and other types of improved working conditions.

Index

Note: Page numbers in *italics* indicate a figure and page numbers in **bold** indicate a table on the corresponding page.

Abbeville County School District, et al. v. the State of South Carolina 99–100
Abbeville I case 103
Abbeville I Remand trial 100–101
Abbott districts, failure 35
Abbott v. State of New Jersey 35
academic achievement: school SES, effect (estimation) 136
academic achievement, school resources (relationship) 4; New York 67–70; North Carolina 114–119
accountability 130; policies 14
achievement: academic achievement, school resources (relationship) 67–70; eighth-grade math achievement (New York State) *73*; growth, school effectiveness 133; New York State achievement/adequacy 63; outcomes 118; prediction, value-added scores (usage) 147–148; school resources, effect 80–88; school resources, effect (South Dakota) 94–96; school SES, causal effect 132; student achievement, teacher principal behaviors (effect) *23*; student background/school resources, correlations (New York) 68, 70; student background/school resources, correlations (North Carolina) 115–116; student background/school resources, correlations (South Carolina) 105–106; student background/school resources, effects (South Carolina) 104–109; white students/Native American students (South Dakota), achievement gap (explanation) *94*
achievement gaps 155; closing 38; narrowing 13–14
adequacy: allegations 33; litigation 33–40; plaintiffs, impact 37
adequacy cases: New Mexico 78; New York 63; North Carolina 111; South Carolina 99; South Dakota 89
adequacy lawsuits: foundations 33–34; occurrence 5
adequate yearly progress (AYP): benchmarks, minimum (requirement) 13; goals, ending (impact) 14
alternative interventions, achievement (average effect size) *143*
American Recovery and Reinvestment Act 23
Armor, David J. 5; expert study 90, 95; expert study/opinions, data/methods 64–67; expert testimony 96

Index

Baker v. Carr 33
Basic Educational Data System, usage 65
between analysis/within analysis: contrast 44–45; hypothetical results *45*
between-district variation 94–95
between school analysis/within school analysis, contrast (United States) 125–126
between-schools score variation 44, 67–68, 81, 90–91, 104, 114, 125
Black scores, increase 16
Black students, NAEP eighth-grade math scores *74*
Black–White achievement gap: 2013 NAEP 59; affected 16; Arkansas 135; current 16; goal 152; improvement 27; New Jersey 74; New York 154; trends 2
Black–White differences, averaging 16–17

California class size reduction initiative 154
Campaign for Fiscal Equity (CFE) v. State 89
Campaign for Fiscal Equity (CFE) v. State of New York 35–36, 63, 76
capital expenditures 11
causal inference 14
causal relationship: assumption 59; gold standard 18
causation: absence (indication), zero correlation (impact) 47; issue 37; question 38–39
cause-and-effect relationship 60
Civil Rights Act of 1964, passage 3
class size 10, 11, 17–18, 39, 48, 56, 60, 70, 75, 109, 116, 122, 145, 151, 154
Coenen meta-analysis 21
Coleman data, re-analysis 132
Coleman, James S. 1–4
Coleman Report (1966) 1, 3–8, 16, 27; Armor et al. 134–138; cross-sectional designs, usage 44; education policies, research methods (changes) 42; findings 4; literature developments 138–139; literature review 133–139; school SES effects 136–137; study 39
Coleman thesis 5
college-going/college-persistence rates 328
Committee for Educational Rights v. Edgar 34
Common Core curriculum, implementation 38
Comprehensive Remedial Plan 113
confidence intervals **142**
controlled experiments (gold standard) 42
conventional resources, limitations 141
cooperative learning, intervention 142
correlation analysis 44, 45–47; United States 126–127; usage 56–58
correlations: calculation 106; computation 67–68, 80; patterns 82–83
counterfactual outcome 134
COVID-19 crisis (2020) 1–2, 152
cross-cultural differences, impact 130
cross-sectional data 48–49, 61
cross-sectional designs: inclusion 10; usage 44
cross-sectional effects 60
cross-sectional models 51–52
cross-sectional regression 49; analysis 127
culture of high expectations 146

data-driven instruction, usage 146
data-guided instruction, usage 145
Davis v. South Dakota 89
descriptive statistics: NAEP eighth-grade math sample **57**; PISA 15-year-old students **124**; school resource effects 123, 125; usage 56
desegregation cases 30
Dietrichson, Jens (meta-analysis) 141–145

disadvantaged students, non-disadvantaged students (school spending differences) *17*
district-wide policies/resources 81
Does Money Matter? (Brookings Institution) 11
double-blind random designs 42
Dynamic Indicators of Basic Early Literacy Skills (DIBELS) 143

Early Childhood Longitudinal Study 139
education: economics, econometric advances 138; fundamental right 32; policies, research methods (change) 42; production functions 50; shock/awe 1; study approach/data/methods 42
education adequacy: cases, landscape 34–35; law, state 30; lawsuits, foundations 33–34; litigation 33–40; litigation, theories/proof 36–40
Education Finance Act of 1977, formula 100
effect sizes, skewed distribution 16
eighth-grade math achievement (New York State) *73*
eighth-grade math scores: National Assessment of Educational Progress (NAEP), relationship *2, 3, 58*; school resource effects *61*
eighth-grade NAEP math achievement (New York State) 154–155
English (language), usage 123
"Equality of Educational Opportunity" (Coleman) 1
equality of educational opportunity survey (EEOS) 3
equalizing payments 32–33
equity claims 33
equity lawsuits 30
error term, inputs (presence) 53
Every Student Succeeds Act (ESSA) 154–155; program, adoption 14
exogenous tiebreakers, functions 138

expectancy effects: experiments 42; phenomenon 14
explanatory studies, gold standard 6
explanatory variables, coefficients 53
extended learning time, usage 146

feedback, basis 142
focus districts, South Dakota case 89–90, 93, 96–97
Foundation Aid Formula: disbursement reduction 64; enactment 76
free lunch program, usage 102
free lunch versus paid lunch students (contrast) 16, 55–56, 61, 65, 79, 86, 102, 117
Fryer, Roland 141, 145–147
funding systems, reformation 32–33

general education production function, notation 51
Ginsburg, Alan 25
government, republican form (stability) 89
Greene, Jay P. 15
Group Reading Assessment and Diagnostic Evaluation (GRADE) 143

Hanushek, Eric A. 11, 86; debate 10; expert study 72–76, 90
Hedges, Larry 11; debate 10
high-dimensional multiway fixed effect models, estimation (ability) 136
high-dosage tutoring 145, 146
high expectations, culture 146
high-impact interventions 142
High Need Rural (SES/demographic category) 65
High Need Urban/Suburban (SES/demographic category) 65
high school graduation rates 24, 38
high-SES schools, student grouping/scores 134–135

Hoke County, mandates (application) 112
Houston Elementary treatment effects, summary (Fryer study) **147**
Houston Experiment 147
human capital, examination 146
human learning, processes 38–39

Improving Americas School Act of 1994 152
inadequacy, proving 36
instructional computers per student, number 125
instructional time, increase 145
instruction materials, quality (correlation) 127
integrative effects 139
intervention component **142**

Jackson, C. Kirabo 12; studies 15
judicial questions 30

Kentucky Constitution, education clause (satisfaction) 34

Large City (SES/demographic category) 65
Leandro v. the State of North Carolina 111, 113
learning time, extension 146
Levittown U.S.F.D. v. Nyquist 34
Liddell v. Board of Educ. 31
limited English proficiency (LEP) 56–57, 78, 83, 86, 94, 113
Limited English Proficient (LEP), student classification 56, 58
longitudinal administrative data 134
longitudinal data: availability 47; pooling 52; student fixed effect models 49, 53–54; value-added models 49, 52–53
longitudinal databases, creation 9
low-achieving groups, achievement (improvement) 156
lower-achievement schools, turnover (negative effects) 22

low-income status, within-student ranges (distribution) *138*
low-income students: math scores (race/school SES basis) *135*; test scores, increase 60–61
Low Need(s) (SES/demographic category) 65, 70
low-SES schools, student grouping/scores 134–135

Mackevicius studies 15
Maisto v. State of New York 64
Marks, Gary 134
Martinez, et al. vs. State of New Mexico, et al. 78; court decision 88
math achievement: 27, 56, 73, 86, 116, 123, 134, 142, 154; gains (South Dakota), grades 3–8 (poverty status basis) *92*; gap 2; spending, relationship *87*
math instruction, standard deviation 128
math scores: adjustment *87*; longitudinal regression, standardized effects (North Carolina) *117*; school resources increase, effect (South Carolina) **109**; school resources/student background correlations (South Carolina) *106*; school resource, standardized effects *149*; school resource/student background correlations (North Carolina) *115*; school resource/student background correlations (South Dakota) *95*; SIG Program, effect *25*; student background/school resource correlations *148*; student fixed effect analysis, results 108, *108*
mental wellness 34–35
Missouri v. Jenkins 31
money, importance 36
monitoring, basis 142
multiple regression: analyses 44, 47–49, 68, 70; model 53
Munich, John R. 5

Index 161

National Assessment of Educational Progress (NAEP) 143; eighth-grade math sample, descriptive statistics (usage) **57**; eighth-grade math, school resources/student background (standardized effects) *59*; eighth-grade math scores, basis *155*; fourth-grade math test 74; Hispanic/Black correlations 95; mathematics achievement scores 12; math scores, per pupil expenditures *13*; NCES sponsorship 12; scores, analysis 129; tests, usage 10; usage 55; US Department of Education oversight 44; US national achievement data, generation 5–6

National Assessment of Educational Progress (NAEP) data 152; analysis 6–7; assessment 121; usage 60

National Assessment of Educational Progress (NAEP) eighth-grade math scores: per pupil expenditures *3*; race/ethnicity basis *2*; school resource *58*; student background correlations *58*

Nation's Report Card 1

neighborhood schools, attendance 139

New Jersey, inflation-adjusted current expenditures per pupila 73–74

New Mexico: average operational expenditure per student 80; correlation, usage 82–83; districts, spending/math achievement (relationship) *87*; districts, student background/per pupil expenditures contrast (math scores adjustment) *87*; grades 3–5 math scores, correlations/regression coefficients *82, 83*; grades 3–5 math scores, school/student characteristics (effects estimation) **84**; grades 3–5 reading scores, correlations/regression coefficients **85**; local property tax, elimination/reduction 32–33; within New Mexico schools/between New Mexico schools, test scores (variation) *81*; Public Education Department (PED) 78–79; regression analysis 82–83; school resources, potential effect (estimation) 81–82; school/student characteristics (effects estimation), SBA test results (usage) 84–88; student rights violations 88; test scores, within variation/between variation (contrast) 81–82

New Mexico adequacy case 78; achievement, school resources (effect) 80–88; data/methods 78–80; outcomes, systemic problem 88

New Mexico average student/school characteristics **79**

New York: academic achievement, school resources (relationship) 67–70; court decisions 76–77; grades, student/school characteristics **66**

New York adequacy: case, Hanushek report (adaptation) 72–76; lawsuit, *Maisto v. State of New York* 64

New York State: achievement/adequacy 63; adjusted spending *73*; Education Department databases, maintenance 65; eighth-grade math achievement *73*; legislature, school funding 72–73; NAEP eighth-grade math scores *155*; between New York State schools, within schools (test scores variation) 69; students, enrollment 65

New York State grades 3–5 math: school resources/student background, standardized effects *71*; scores, school resource/student background correlations *69*

162 *Index*

No Child Left Behind (NCLB) 55; expiration 1–2; program, accountability policies 155–156
No Child Left Behind (NCLB) Act 152; ending, impact 14; implementation 9; passage 13, 55; replacement 154–155; termination 2
No Child Left Behind (NCLB) law: adoption 43; operation 23
non-disadvantaged students, disadvantaged students (school spending differences) *17*
non-school factors, impact 36–37
North Carolina: academic achievement, school resources (relationship) 114–119; achievement, student background/ school resources (correlations) 115–116; adequacy case 111–113; Comprehensive Remedial Plan 113; data, grades 3–8 (summary statistics) **113**; data/ methods 113–114; education (equal access), resources provision (necessity) 112; math scores, longitudinal regression (standardized effects) *117*; math scores, school resource/student background (correlations) *115*; within North Carolina schools/ districts, between North Carolina schools/districts (variation) *114*; pooled longitudinal cross-sectional model 116–117; within school/ between school variation 114–115; school resource effects 111; school staffing, WestEd recommendation 112; student fixed effects 118–119; transfer enforcement, trial court disagreement 112–113
Northwest Achievement Level Test (NALT) 143

objective credentials, quality relevance 19
Oklahoma Education Association v. State 34

one-on-one tutoring 142
one-unit increase, impact 50
operational expenditures 11
opposing claims, impact 36–37
Organization for Economic Co-operation and Development (OECD) 7; countries, math/ science achievement, comparison 123; PISA introduction 121

paid lunch students, free lunch students (contrast) *61*
Palmetto Achievement Challenge Test 102
Palmetto Assessment of State Standards 102
partitioning variation 80
pencil-paper standardized test, usage 143
people, morality/intelligence (effect) 89
per capita expenditures 21; academic achievement gains *15*
per pupil expenditures: South Dakota 91; student background adjustment (grades 3–8 for all years) *97*; student background, contrast (math scores adjustment) *87*
physical wellness 34–35
pooled longitudinal cross-sectional data *49*, *52*
pooled longitudinal cross-sectional model (North Carolina) 116–117
pooled longitudinal cross sectional regression: analysis (North Carolina) 116; South Carolina 107–108
pooled longitudinal regression model 107–108
poverty: effects 107; status 116
poverty-induced achievement gaps 93–94
poverty-level students, low-income students (comparison) 60
powers, separation 34
principal position, importance 22
professional development 19

Program for International
Assessment (PISA) 7; 15-year-
old students, descriptive statistics
124; analysis 47; correlation
analysis (USA) 126–127;
descriptive statistics 123, 125;
international comparisons
129–130; OECD introduction
121; between school analysis,
within school analysis (contrast)
125–126; standardized effects
(USA) 127–129; studies,
data generation 5–6; United
States, school resource/student
background correlations *126*;
usage 44, 121
property values, stability 32
public K-12 monetary school
expenditures, classroom size
(relationships) 11
public school: appropriations, claim
36; student attendance 123, 125
pupil-teacher ratio 81, 96, 103, 107;
impact 85

quasi-experimental designs, usage
15, 42, 141

race SES, basis *135*
randomized controlled trials
(RCTs) 14; designs 10, 14, 43;
experiments/quasi-experimental
designs, impossibility 61; usage 6,
42, 141, 145
reading scores: correlations,
calculation 106; pooled
longitudinal regression model
107–108
regression: coefficients, grades 3–5
math scores *82*; cross-sectional
regression 49; equation, usage
54; multiple regression analyses
47–49; multiple regression
model 53; North Carolina math
scores, longitudinal regression
(standardized effects) *117*; pooled
longitudinal cross-sectional

regression (South Carolina)
107–108; running 70
regression analyses: New Mexico
82–83; statistical regression
analysis 90
regression models: description 50;
value-added regression models
70–72
Robinson v. Cahill 30
Rodriguez v. San Antonio 31–32
Roland Fryer studies 145–147;
Houston Elementary treatment
effects, summary **147**
Rose v. Council for Better Education
34–35
Rothstein, Jesse 88

*San Antonio Independent School
District v. Rodriguez, supra* 33
SBA math scores, school/student
characteristics (effects
estimation) **84**
SBA reading scores, school/student
characteristics (effects
estimation) **85**
SBA test results, usage 84–88
school characteristics: effects
estimation (grades 3–5 SBA math
scores) **84**; effects estimation
(grades 3–5 SBA reading
scores) **85**; effects estimation,
SBA test results (usage) 84–88;
hypothetical standardized effects
48; test scores, hypothetical
correlations 46
school expenditures 11–17;
disadvantaged students, non-
disadvantaged students (school
spending differences) *17*; effects
152; effects, research literature
14–16; national data 12–14; per
capita expenditures, academic
achievement gains *15*; spending
gaps, race/poverty analysis 16–17
School Improvement Grant (SIG)
Program, effect 24, *25*, 26
school reorganization: effects,
intervention features basis *26*;

effects, school demographics basis 26; studies 23–27
school resource effects: descriptive statistics, usage 123, 125; estimation, method 80; literature review 122–123; North Carolina 111; Program for International Assessment (PISA) usage 121; South Carolina 104–109
school resource research: between analysis, within analysis (contrast) 44–45; approach 11; correlation analysis 45–47; cross-sectional data 48–49; longitudinal data, student fixed effect models 49, 53–54; longitudinal data, value-added models 49, 52–53; multiple regression analyses 47–49; pooled longitudinal cross-sectional data 49, 52; state 9; study approach 42, 43–44
school resources 6; academic achievement, relationship 67–70; achievement/student background, correlation (New York) 68, 70; achievement/student background, correlation (North Carolina) 115–116; achievement/student background, correlation (South Carolina) 105–106; characteristics, study availability 67; contribution 84; correlations 115–116, 127; effects, estimation 86, **153**; factors 106; increase, effect (estimation) 71, measures 45; NAEP eighth-grade math scores 58; PISA/US-specific assessments, overlap 125; potential effect, estimation 81–82; standardized effects 59, 96, 149; student achievement, causal link (establishment) 63; student background correlations (New York State grades 3–5 math scores) 69; student background correlations (PISA USA) 126; student background correlations (South Dakota) 95; student background, standardized effects (PISA USA) 128; types 151
school resources, effect(s): NAEP, usage 55; New Mexico 80–88; South Dakota 94–96
schools: composition, impact 132; inputs, student achievement (relationship) 63; institutional factors 128–129; management practices 22; programs, concept 6; reform, methods 24; SES, variance 137; socioeconomic composition 132; variation, within variation (contrast) 68
school SES: basis 135; causal effect 132; correlation 132; effects, estimation 136; effects, studies 133–134
Schueler meta-analysis 25
science instruction, standard deviation 128
selectivity 130
Serrano II (court decision) 32
Slosson Oral Reading Test 143
small-group instruction, intervention 142
Smith, Marshal 132
Smith, Marshall S. 25
socioeconomic backgrounds 151
socioeconomic status (SES) 4; characteristics, measurement (absence) 66; circumstances, differences 90; family SES, measurement 121–122; integration 56; measure 70; school SES, impact (measurement) 134; student SES 55; variable 102
South Carolina: achievement, student background/school resources (correlations) 105–106; achievement, student background/school resources (effects) 104–109; adequacy case 99–101; data/methods 101–104; dataset, inputs 102–103; data, summary statistics **103**; defendants,

Index 165

funding proportion (problem) 101; Department of Education reports cards, indications 99–100; grades 3–8 math, student fixed effect regression (standardized effects) *108*; math scores, school resources increase (effect) **109**; math scores, school resource/ student background (correlations) *106*; pooled longitudinal cross-sectional regression 107–108; school resource effects 99; school resource factors 106; within South Carolina schools/districts, between South Carolina schools/ districts (test scores variation) *104*; student fixed effects 108–109; student socioeconomic differences 105; student test scores, school-level/district-level policies (impact) 104–105

South Dakota: achievement, school resources (effect) 94–96; Constitution, violation (absence) 97; data, statistics **92**; education data, Armor/Hanushek expert studies 90; expert studies 94; focus districts (per pupil expenditures/achievements), student background adjustment (grades 3–8 for all years) *97*; math achievement gains, grades 3–8 (poverty status basis) *92*; statistical regression analysis 90; STEP outcomes 90; student economic status, math achievement growth (relationship) 93; student population, poverty level 93; student test scores, variation 90–91; white students/ Native American students, achievement gap (explanation) *94*

South Dakota adequacy: case 89; data/methods 91–94; lawsuit 89–91; state aid formula, basis (questions) 97–98; trial, commencement 97

South Dakota Codified Laws (SDCL) 6-15-1, violation (absence) 97

spending gaps, race/poverty analysis 16–17

standardized effects: estimates, providing 48–49; evaluations 20–21; measurement, standard deviations (usage) 129; metric 141; school resource/student background (PISA USA) *128*; United States 127–129; usage 58–60, *59*

state court equity lawsuits 31–33

state-for-state comparisons, difficulty 38

state governments, defense assembly 5

state-level standardized test scores 39

state-mandated standardized tests 38

State of New York, student enrollment 64

state revenues, reduction 64

state-specific student data 390

statistical analyses (South Dakota) 96

statistical insignificance 107

statistical regression analysis 90

statistical significance 85

STEP outcomes, relationship 90

student achievement: improvement, potential 17; rates, effect 101; school inputs, relationship 63; school resources, causal link (establishment) 63; teacher principal behaviors, effect *23*

student background: achievement/ school resources, correlations (New York) 68, 70; achievement/ school resources, correlations (North Carolina) 115–116; achievement/school resources, correlations (South Carolina) 105–106; adjustment, grades 3–8 for all years (South Dakota) *97*; characteristics, control 80; characteristics, correlations 115–116; controls 151;

correlations (NAEP eighth-grade math scores) *58*; effects (South Carolina) 104–109; factors, effects (estimation) 86; per pupil expenditures, contrast (math scores adjustment) *87*; school resource correlations (South Dakota) *95*; school resource correlations, New York State grades 3–5 math scores *69*; standardized effects *59*
student background/school resource correlations (math scores) *148*
student characteristics 44; coefficients 117; effects estimation (grades 3–5 SBA math scores) **84**; effects estimation (grades 3–5 SBA reading scores) **85**; effects estimation, SBA test results (usage) 84–88; hypothetical standardized effects *48*; test scores, hypothetical correlation *46*
student fixed effects: analysis (math scores) 108, *108*, 118; model 49; North Carolina 118–119; regression, standardized effects (North Carolina) *118*
Student Fixed Effects models, representation 108–109
Student Information Repository System, usage 65
students: ability grouping 130; academic achievement (assessment), standardized tests (usage) 65–66; academic skills, contribution 55; Black students, NAEP eighth-grade math scores *74*; demographic characteristics 55; economic status, math achievement growth (relationship) 93; fixed effect models 49, 53–54; fixed effect regression, standardized effects (South Carolina grades 3–8 math) *108*; growth component, incorporation 38; lifetime incomes, class size/teacher effectiveness (effect) *75*; Limited English Proficient (LEP) classification 56, 58; New Mexico average student/school characteristics **79**; poverty levels, control 96; poverty-level students, low-income students (comparison) 60; prior-year achievement, addition 52; public school attendance 123, 125; SES effects 136–137; socioeconomic status (SES) 55; variables 52
student test scores: teacher certification effects *21*; teacher education effects *20*; variation (South Dakota) 90–091
subgroups, analysis 60–61
subject-matter knowledge 19
subject-matter tests, goal 22
super-legislature 89
Swann et al. v. Charlotte-Mecklenburg 99

teachers: behaviors, effect *23*; certification credentials 145; certification effects *21*; characteristics 11, 18–23, 122; correlations 115; credentials, correlations 148–149; education effects *20*; education evaluations 19; effectiveness *75*, 75–76; effects, meta-analyses 19; efficacy 19; experience 81; feedback 145; income, analysis 75; leadership characteristics 22–23; primary agents, role 18; principal characteristics 22–23; quality indicators 58; resource, contribution 84; resource, correlations 116; retention rates, increase 153; role, importance 74–75; salaries (South Dakota) 91; salaries, average 81; salaries, variation 154; salary, impact (absence) 72; turnover 19, 22, 70; value-added assessment 147–150; value-added measures 148; value-added scores 149
Tennessee Star experiment 10
Tennessee Star study 18

Test of Word Reading Efficiency (TOWRE) 143
Test of Written Spelling (TWS) 143
test scores: between analysis/within analysis, contrast *45*; partitioning variation 80; between school variation, within school variation (contrast) 44; student/school characteristics, hypothetical correlations *46*; variation 81–82, 151; variation (within schools/ New York State schools, contrast) *69*; within variation, between variation (contrast) 81–82
time-invariant student characteristics, control 49
time-invariant student factors 54
Tocqueville, Alexis de 30
total expenditures, division 12
Trends in International Mathematics and Science Study (TIMSS) data, usage 122
turnaround effects/efforts 25, 27
tutoring: effect sizes, validity (adjustment) *144*; high-dosage tutoring 145, 146

United States: assessments, results 127; correlation analysis 126–127; math/science achievement, comparison 123; between school analysis/ within school analysis, contrast 125–126; standardized effects 127–129; students, achievement differences 125–126
unqualified teachers, NYC school employment 36

validity coefficients, determination 143
value-added analysis 74–75
value-added assessment (teachers) 21, 147–150; goals 22
value-added methods 141

value-added models 49, 52–53; assumption 53
value-added regression: models, usage 70–72; usage 49
value-added score, usage 147–148

wealth classifications, impact 32
weighted average ES **142**
white students/Native American students (South Dakota), achievement gap (explanation) *94*
within New Mexico schools/between New Mexico schools, test scores (variation) *81*
within New York schools/between New York State schools, test scores (variation) *69*
within North Carolina schools/ districts, between North Carolina schools/districts (variation) *114*
within school/between school, variation (North Carolina) 114–115
within schools score variation 125
within-school variation: impacts 114; usage 45
within South Carolina schools/ districts, between South Carolina schools/districts (test scores variation) *104*
within-student ranges, distribution *138*
within-variance, insufficiency 137
within variation, school variation (contrast) 68
Woodcock Johnson Diagnostic Reading Battery Test (WJ-DRB) 143
Woodcock Johnson III (WJ-III) 143
Woodcock Reading Mastery Test (WRMT) 143

Yazzie, et al. vs State of New Mexico, et al. 78; court decision 88

zero conditional, presence 51

For Product Safety Concerns and Information please contact our EU
representative GPSR@taylorandfrancis.com
Taylor & Francis Verlag GmbH, Kaufingerstraße 24, 80331 München, Germany

www.ingramcontent.com/pod-product-compliance
Lightning Source LLC
Chambersburg PA
CBHW051746230426
43670CB00012B/2177